When Dana Was
THE SUN

Dana in His Famous Corner Office.

(*From Henry Wolf's Engraving of a Painting by Corwin Knapp Linson.*)

When Dana Was
THE SUN

A Story of Personal Journalism

By

CHARLES J. ROSEBAULT

ILLUSTRATED

GREENWOOD PRESS, PUBLISHERS
WESTPORT, CONNECTICUT

Originally published in 1931
by Robert M. McBride & Company, New York

First Greenwood Reprinting 1970

Library of Congress Catalogue Card Number 73-100201

SBN 8371-4009-9

Printed in the United States of America

To memories of stirring days and gallant nights, of fine companions and the mutual ambition to make good when

Dana was THE SUN

Contents

CHAPTER   PAGE

I. DANA, THE LAUGHING PHILOSOPHER, AND HIS *Sun* THAT SHONE FOR ALL.............. 3

II. A TYPE THAT CANNOT BE KEPT DOWN—DAYS AT BUFFALO, CAMBRIDGE, SCITUATE...... 7

III. AN EXPERIMENT IN COMMUNISM—HAWTHORNE—THE MECCA OF CELEBRITIES.... 16

IV. ON THE VERGE OF DEEPER RADICALISM WHEN FATE INTERVENES—MARRIAGE—THE BEGINNING OF A NEW ADVENTURE—A SUBEDITOR OF THE *New York Tribune*....... 24

V. ASSOCIATION WITH HORACE GREELEY—NEW YORK AT THE CLOSE OF THE 'FORTIES—EUROPE LURES DANA ABROAD........... 29

VI. IN THE BLOOD-RUNNING STREETS OF PARIS—LOUIS NAPOLEON—WITH THE REBELS OF BERLIN 38

VII. BACK TO GREELEY—BADGERING POOR HORACE —THE EDUCATION OF AN EDITOR........ 46

VIII. SLAVERY AND SECESSION TAKE FIRST PLACE IN NEWSPAPER DISCUSSION—GREELEY DISCHARGES DANA...................... 55

IX. CONTACTS WITH STANTON—A REPORTER FOR THE UNITED STATES GOVERNMENT, ASSIGNED TO "COVER" GENERAL GRANT........... 64

X. THE CAMPAIGN BEFORE VICKSBURG—DANA COMPILES A PORTRAIT GALLERY—WRITES HIS LITTLE GIRL DESCRIPTIONS OF THE LIFE IN CAMP........................... 72

XI. UNDER THE FIRE OF SHARPSHOOTERS—MADE ADJUTANT GENERAL—RIDING WITH GRANT INTO VICKSBURG...................... 88

XII. DANA BECOMES ASSISTANT SECRETARY OF WAR —WITH ROSECRANS AT CHICKAMAUGUA—HIS JUDGMENT SUSTAINED.............. 96

CHAPTER   PAGE

XIII. "GLORY TO GOD! THE DAY IS OURS"—A PORTRAIT
      OF STANTON—GENERAL SHERMAN WRITES
      DANA 104

XIV. LINCOLN'S SOLICITUDE FOR DANA'S SAFETY—
     WITH GRANT IN THE FINAL CAMPAIGN... 114

XV. A REMARKABLE GOVERNMENT SPY—SHENAN-
    DOAH AND SHERIDAN—INTERVIEW WITH
    ANDREW JACKSON..................... 121

XVI. PORTRAITS OF LINCOLN AND HIS CABINET—
     THE BARGAIN THAT MADE NEVADA A STATE
     —A PRESIDENT WITHOUT ILLUSIONS...... 130

XVII. DANA BUYS THE *Sun*—CHARACTER OF THE *Sun*
      UP TO THEN, AND CONDITIONS IN THE
      COUNTRY'S METROPOLIS............... 143

XVIII. WHAT THE READERS THOUGHT OF DANA'S
       PAPER—NOT POPULAR WITH THE POLITI-
       CIANS—SUNBEAMS AND FORKED LIGHTNING 152

XIX. MEN WHO HELPED DANA MAKE "THE NEWS-
     PAPER MAN'S NEWSPAPER"—DOC WOOD, THE
     GREAT CONDENSER.................... 164

XX. PERSONAL JOURNALISM—DANA'S DEFINITION
    —SOME ILLUSTRATIONS OF ITS OPERATION 175

XXI. DANA TURNS ON GRANT—BOSS SHEPHERD
     TRIES TO "RAILROAD" HIM TO A WASHING-
     TON JAIL—FUN WITH GREELEY......... 187

XXII. SLOGANS OF THE *Sun*—THE BEECHER SCANDAL
      —WAR ON HAYES—UNFORTUNATE HAN-
      COCK 207

XXIII. A COSTLY FIGHT ON CLEVELAND—ITS ORIGIN
       AND THE BITTERNESS IT AROUSED—BIRTH
       OF THE OFFICE CAT.................. 221

XXIV. VIEWS ON BRYAN—DANA'S INTELLECTUAL
      CURIOSITY—GERZONI, WHO FOOLED ALL THE
      NEWSPAPERS 232

XXV. ODD CHARACTERS DEVELOPED FOR THE *Sun's*
     CIRCUS—THE STAFF HELD TO RIGID STAND-
     ARDS 241

XXVI. INSPIRATION FOR THE WORKERS—OSCAR
      WILDE'S GHOST STORY—STIRRING INCIDENTS
      IN THE CONDUCT OF A GREAT INSTITUTION 253

CONTENTS

XXVII. THE FRUITS OF LOYALTY—MEN FORGOT FA-
TIGUE—THE FIRE AT THE HOTEL ROYAL... 262

XXVIII. LAFFAN, A NEW FIGURE IN THE *Sun* OFFICE
—A BRILLIANT WRITER, CONNOISSEUR OF
ART AND FINE LIVING................. 270

XXIX. A BULL IN THE CHINA SHOP, SMASHING TRA-
DITIONS AND, INCIDENTALLY, COURTING DIS-
ASTER 279

XXX. DANA TALKS ABOUT THE EDUCATION AND
TRAINING OF NEWSPAPER MEN, AND THE
ETHICS OF JOURNALISM—THE *Sun's* NOTICE
OF HIS DEATH...................... 286

Illustrations

FRONT END PAPER: LOWER NEW YORK AND THE HARBOR FROM THE BROOKLYN TOWER OF UNFINISHED BROOKLYN BRIDGE, AFTER A SKETCH BY C. E. H. BONWILL, HARPER'S WEEKLY, NOVEMBER I, 1873.

BACK END PAPER: SQUATTERS AND THEIR SHANTIES ON THE OUTSKIRTS OF CENTRAL PARK, NEW YORK CITY, AFTER A SKETCH BY D. E. WYAND, HARPER'S WEEKLY, JUNE 26, 1868.

DANA IN HIS FAMOUS CORNER OFFICE........*Frontispiece*

Facing Page

FASHIONABLE UNION SQUARE IN 1858............. 18

THE OLD NEW YORK SUN BUILDING, ONE-TIME TAMMANY HALL, AT FRANKFORT AND NASSAU STREETS, NEW YORK CITY............................. 40

STANTON AND CHASE IN SESSION WITH PRESIDENT LINCOLN 80

DANA, THE GIANT OF JOURNALISM................ 126

THE ULYSSES GRANT WHO WAS ANATHEMA TO DANA... 168

GROVER CLEVELAND AS SEEN BY DANA IN THE DAYS OF "RUM, ROMANISM AND REBELLION".............. 208

CHARLES ANDERSON DANA, FROM THE BRONZE PLAQUE BY AUGUST SAINT-GAUDENS.................... 272

Foreword

ONE DAY near the close of the first half of the last century a man standing in the doorway of the one-time Tammany Hall, at the corner of Frankfort and Nassau streets, saw a Greek god crossing City Hall Park. New York has long had the reputation, here and there among certain good people, of being the favorite abiding place of the Devil, but no one up to then—or since—so far as I know, ever mentioned it as the habitat or even occasional resort of any kind of divinity. Least of all would any one in his right mind have thought of it as appealing to any member of the Greek pantheon, one and all of whom have ever been notoriously critical and fastidious about their environment, for at this time the metropolis of the country was certainly not a beauty spot. Nevertheless, the man on the old Tammany Hall steps thrilled with the belief that he was witnessing this miracle, and open-mouthed he stood staring at the vision.

It was one of those rare and brilliant days which have made New York the favorite winter resort of not a few seasoned globe-trotters, a day to win approval of gods and men. A friendly sun was shining from an unclouded sky, giving no excuse for optical illusion. A salt-laden wind, not cold yet vitalizing, was driving in from the ocean to give vim and snap to the air, quickening the blood and clearing the brain of every man. Just such a day as in old Athens stirred the philosophers to new inspiration and their students to exceptional receptivity.

The god was moving directly towards Printing House Square, and therefore approaching nearer every moment to his startled beholder. Tall, as gods should be, imposing in figure as in carriage, virile in movement, stepping with firm yet buoyant tread. But what impressed this witness more than anything else was the head. Large, with extraordinary elevation of brow, and framed in wavy golden curls and a blond beard. When this majestic figure had crossed Park Row, threading its way through the crush of carriages, wagons and trucks with a truly godlike contempt for plunging horses and swearing drivers—you see this was long before the arrival of the more menacing motor cars—it was seen that his eyes were as blue and effulgent as a god's should be. Altogether the beau-ideal of a god in his most radiant period; not a Jove nor a Wotan, nor any of the other old ones, but Apollo at his best.

I heard all about this marvelous happening in the spring of 1902—more than a half century later—when I was seated at the desk of the business manager of the *New York Sun*, then housed in that same old Tammany Hall building. I was bending over some papers when a strange voice at my elbow caused me to look up. Beside me stood a short, slight old man, of unmistakable New England origin, his rather prominent features in a setting of scraggly whiskers.

"I am Oliver Dyer," he said, "and many years ago I was an editorial writer on this paper."

Then he plunged into his recital, his voice carrying the thrill of excited memories, and concluding thus:

"That was Charles A. Dana, just returned from Paris."

There you have an ardent admirer's portrait of the great editor at thirty. Probably in all the world there never was a single individual who would have scoffed at it as wholeheartedly as Dana himself. And yet it was probably not so exaggerated.

When Dana Was
THE SUN

I. DANA, THE LAUGHING PHILOSOPHER, AND HIS *Sun* THAT SHONE FOR ALL.

> But bless ye, Mr. Dana! may you live a thousand
> years,
> To sort o' keep things lively in this vale of human
> tears;
> An' may I live a thousan', too,—a thousan' less
> a day,
> For I shouldn't like to be on earth to hear you'd
> passed away.
> And when it comes your time to go you'll need no
> Latin chaff
> Nor biographic data put in your epitaph;
> But one straight line of English and of truth will
> let folk know
> The homage 'nd the gratitude 'nd reverence they
> owe;
> You'll need no epitaph but this: "Here sleeps the
> man who run
> That best 'nd brightest paper, the Noo York Sun."
> —*Closing lines of Eugene Field's poem,*
> *"Mr. Dana, of the New York Sun."*

THERE are still men in newspaper offices throughout the
land who will echo the sentiments of the poet, to whom
Charles A. Dana was a joy and an inspiration, the incarna-
tion of all the qualities that should go to the making of a
great editor. And there are survivors of the host who bought
and read his paper, and chortled with glee over its wit and
its railleries and the subtleties which made it unique among
the journals of all time. For more than a quarter of a century it was the ambition of the former to found or be
associated with a replica of Dana's *Sun,* and even today

3

there are old fellows who ask wistfully if that cannot be done, freely confessing that something vital passed out of their lives when the great editor laid down his pen.

As well wish for the moon to play with! The *Sun* was Dana, and Dana was the *Sun*. Though it continued to shine for quite a while after he had departed, that was because his spirit had descended upon a few of his intimate associates, and they were able to carry on while it lasted. But the ghostly glow could not endure for long, and with its fading passed vitality and buoyancy and it was no longer a living thing. Much as its departure has been regretted, its complete elimination was probably the wisest and happiest ending. Much better that than a slow and degrading deterioration. The new and different flower that sprang from its grave smells the sweeter for having its own tints and its own perfume, even though it adopted the old name.

The changing times call for their own interpreters. The great newspapers of today are great businesses, as much so as the public utilities, the steel trusts and the department stores. Their function is not to express the individuality of the editor, however brilliant and fascinating that may be, but to record the events and picture the complexities of our amazing civilization. Editorial genius today lies not in guiding but in finding the public taste. That, too, calls for definite talents, but they are the talents which would win equally in any other of the many fields of salesmanship.

Very likely Dana would be lost in the present competition. He might even appear ludicrous. One cannot afford to be dogmatic about one so able in so many ways. Perhaps he would have adapted his methods to the present day had he been confronted with its problems. Genius has a way of meeting exigencies as they arise. But, in the history of journalism, the loss would be tremendous had he lived at any other time than that selected for him by Fate. For business played a small part then in the making of a paper. The counting room was comparatively a small factor; the business manager, the advertising man and the circulation

expert only necessary evils. Certainly that was true while
Dana was making his great success. Less so, undoubtedly,
in his closing years.

And the reason is not obscure. Journalism was not then
a business. Neither was it a profession. It was high adventure, and that editor outshone his rivals who could most
impress the imagination of the readers. That Dana did it
better than any other was due to the fact that he possessed
that rare combination, a giant intellect and the sympathetic
understanding which makes for tolerance of human weaknesses. Likewise a positive mind and the high courage to
follow its dictation against every obstacle. Moreover, fortune as well as design had led him through unusual experience—as will be shown in these pages—to give him a surer
and juster measure of his world than was possessed by
other journalists, confirming his natural gift for sound and
definite judgment. As Mayo W. Hazeltine wrote, "It could
be said of him with incomparably more truthfulness than
it was said of Ferdinand Lassalle that he came to journalism armed with all the learning of his epoch."

And, whatever his opponents might say of him, they
could never accuse him of hesitation or wobbling. Straight
over the barriers he rode, heedless of every obstacle, indifferent to the cost, minding his own counsel and none other.

What device appeared upon his banner? The *Sun*—and
Charles A. Dana. It was the high day of Personal Journalism. The pretentious folderol of later days, that the editor
was inspired only with a yearning for the public weal and
orthodox righteousness, would have brought only a smile of
derision to the man whose very soul revolted at the sight
of hypocrisy in high or low, and who turned his sharpest
weapons upon the holier-than-thou and the would-be reformers of mankind. Instinctively the laughing philosopher,
habitually using wit and raillery as his choicest weapons,
he could bite to the bone when Pretence entered the ring.

Yet he was far from indifferent to the opportunities
inherent in the control of a great newspaper. America was

then in the making and life was crude, with most of the newspapers reflecting the provincial tone and spirit, and none so well equipped as he to correct, to chasten and to guide. Informed, traveled, fresh from the inspirational contacts of the War of the Rebellion, in which he had played no minor role, of broad scholarship and artistic instincts in all matters of taste and culture, he was likewise gifted with a rare power of expression, which enabled him to reach his end without descending to dogmatism. Always seasoning wisdom with the spice of wit, and never a touch of the pedant. Under his régime no writer dared to be arrogant.

Still, it was his paper, the organ to express his will, his wishes, his views. Some editors used the license of the period to hoist the black flag, and exerted their power to extort wealth, indifferent to aught else. That was not true of Dana, though there were enemies to make the charge; the denial of which lay not in his words but in his readiness to adopt policies which could not result otherwise than in pecuniary loss. The newspaper proprietor of today would be thought bereft of his senses if he followed Dana's course in any one of a number of crises. Yet he was never in doubt about the ultimate cost of his quixotic acts. That he accumulated a fairly large fortune—for those days—was due entirely to the prestige he achieved, and in spite of repeated challenge of every dogma of business expediency.

A veritable bull in the china shop for affronting those who could add to his prosperity. Big advertisers were tolerated, and no more. Popular heroes were his particular target. Even his readers were turned away by the thousand when it was his fancy to charge their gods. Millions of dollars were sacrificed by the exuberant indulgence of his will. But he had a high old time all along, and never once lowered his banner. He was the last as well as the greatest of the exponents of personal journalism, and his career was the more joyous and picturesque for his giving so free a rein to his high-mettled individuality.

II.
A TYPE THAT CANNOT BE KEPT DOWN—WITH A GIFT FOR LANGUAGES AND A CRAVING FOR KNOWLEDGE, A DRYGOODS CLERK, UNAIDED, LAYS THE FOUNDATIONS OF SCHOLARSHIP—DAYS AT BUFFALO, CAMBRIDGE, SCITUATE—ADMITTED TO THE BROOK FARM COMMUNITY.

DANA was an exquisite in many things, the sort of man popularly described as a born aristocrat. No better dressed man walked the streets of New York. Even in his last years his waistcoat and his scarf showed a refined taste for delicate nuances in color. His bearing and tread were those of the conscious conqueror. Where did they come from?

Anderson Dana, his father, was a dire failure, one of those pathetic types who feel themselves competent to decide the fundamental problems of life yet are unable to earn a livelihood. A small merchant in a small town in western *Hinsdale* New Hampshire when Charles was born in the summer of *August* 1819, he failed and took to farming in New York state. The farm was infested with malaria and to this the mother succumbed after she had borne three more children. Defeated, he took refuge with a relative of the wife, and the children were divided among other relatives.

The Danas were not all like that. Among the numerous descendants of that Richard Dana who had come from England in the early days there had been quite a few outstanding individuals. Along with the ruck of soldiers, sailors, farmers, lawyers and small-town merchants there had been a governor, a general, a judge and an author. The Denisons, from whom sprang Ann, the mother, were of excellent repute, and she appears to have been a woman of unusual character. On neither side, however, was there any individual to whom could be traced the talents of the future editor. For the curious in matters of heredity there may be

7

a bone to gnaw on in the fact that somewhere in the misty annals of the Danas there had been an admixture of Italian blood. Though it missed expression elsewhere it may have been that which caused the boy to take to writing verse at the age of eight, gave him his remarkable facility in acquiring languages, his love for music and his fervid response to every new manifestation of the beautiful in art and nature.

At nine he was on the farm of Uncle David Denison in the Connecticut River Valley. There was a school in the winter time, and he found in the small home library a treasure-trove, a Latin grammar. Rather amusing, as well as impressive, is the picture presented of this child undertaking unaided to master the fundaments of that language which has been the terror of so many older boys, even with the guidance of able instructors. It is the old story of talent forging ahead undeterred by difficulties which overwhelm the herd. Already there was in evidence an eager brain, avid of information of every kind, whether the same was to be found in books or woodland walks, in the many operations on the farm, in contacts with man or beast, or while lounging on the grassy bank of some trout stream, gazing at the tumbling waters, which inspired in him poetic fervor. In the school he was in a class with boys six to eight years his senior.

Three years later he had left the farm and was launched in life upon his own resources. A husky, self-reliant lad of twelve, he was now a clerk in the general store of Staats & Dana, of which William Dana, another uncle, was the junior partner, in the thriving city of Buffalo. The delver into the mysteries of Latin, and composer of odes to babbling brooks, was facing the realities of practical existence. With industry, economy and a fair streak of luck he might arrive at the success of his employers, open a shop of his own, if not in this big city at least in the suburbs, acquire a reasonable competence and become a substantial citizen of his community.

What was it that disturbed the natural trend and took him out of the path so obviously marked for him? Other boys have had a taste for books and scribbling without thereby being deflected from their practical vocations, and apparently this one was pursuing his tasks with the full determination to succeed at them. In course of time he became quite adept in salesmanship, according to one authority. To be sure, he spent much time in a neighboring bookshop, thumbing the leaves of books he could not afford to buy, and the leisure of his evenings was given to such further pursuit of Latin that presently he was reading the classics, to be followed by similar progress with Greek.

Yet this facility with languages was not permitted to remain a vehicle for ornamental education only. Among the customers of Staats & Dana were Indians, members of the Six Nations, and the women could speak hardly any English. The opportunity to better the trade with them, through being able to talk freely with them, suggested itself early and the ambitious clerk did not hesitate to tackle their tongue. That this necessitated visiting their reservation and becoming acquainted with a new species of humans, and different habits of living, was no drawback to one consumed with intellectual curiosity.

Buffalo was even then a city of importance, and much was going on there socially and otherwise which might intrigue a young man, but the usual pleasures did not attract this one. Before he has reached the age of eighteen, however, we find him a member of the Coffee Club, whose members were interested in literary and artistic matters and included some of the best minds in the city. Surely there must have been even then something unusual in his personality to give him entrée into such a circle. It is not the usual thing for salesmen of drygoods and notions to march with those who abide in an environment of culture and refinement.

Nevertheless, there he was, and not a member on sufferance, either. Before he was twenty he was reading a paper on early English poetry which impressed his hearers both by its message and by the evidence it gave of wide reading. Friendships had been formed which ripened into intimacy and some of them endured throughout the lives of the participants. No doubt these did much to influence him finally to a determination to forsake commerce and fit himself for some kind of professional career. Dr. Austin Flint, already a promising physician and destined to achieve the highest honors in his profession later on in New York, did much in this direction.

A description of Dana at this time portrays a tall, handsome youth, with agreeable manners and something less definable which impressed the cultivated with whom he came in contact. Already he showed a fastidious taste in dress and habits. With none of the instincts of the beau or the fop, his appearance alone commanded attention.

For a brief moment soldiering attracted him. There was excitement in the towns along the border in the time preceding and during the "Patriot Rebellion" of '37. Like many another youth who had grown up during the years following the second war with England, Dana was strongly American and sympathetic with any move against British rule in Canada or elsewhere. He joined the City Guard and became a non-commissioned officer. Undoubtedly he made a striking figure in uniform. But the excitement passed and something more important intervened. There was a serious panic throughout the land, people were unable to pay their debts and merchants unable to collect what was due them. Among these unfortunates was Staats & Dana. They had to give up and the young clerk was out of a job. After a brief try elsewhere he finally abandoned commerce and set out for Cambridge to secure a conventional education in the classic halls of Harvard, chosen above all other colleges because his friend, Dr. Flint, was one of its alumni.

He had prepared himself entirely unaided for the examinations, which he passed without difficulty, and at the end of the first year he stood seventh in a class of seventy-four. But now the lack of money began to tell. There were not the opportunities to make a living open to students then which make this fairly easy today, and the millionaires who were to provide scholarships for the talented later on were not yet born. Teaching was practically the only means, and from time to time Dana quit his studies to raise the wind by this method. He found his opportunity at a school in Scituate, where he had on an average of sixty-five pupils, mostly "unruly sailors", whom he brought into "tolerable subjection" by flogging.

Dana wrote a friend it was "wearisome business". He taught by day and read and studied at night. However, it was not all serious reading. In fact, a serious eye-strain, which was to affect his whole after life, came after sitting up a whole night reading *Oliver Twist* by the flickering light of a tallow dip. So severely was he affected that for a time there was fear of actual blindness. It meant a radical change in his plans as well as habits. Never again would he be able to read by artificial light.

It was now out of the question to finish his college course. Prof. Felton, professor of Greek and later President of Harvard, wrote him a long letter, in which he mentioned a fund from which he might borrow to tide him over, and urged him to resume his regular studies. It was a flattering letter and should have stiffened the young student's resolve, if that were needed. But the injured eyes, together with the lack of money, made resumption impossible. The record shows he reached his junior year only. In 1861 he received from Harvard the honorary degree of bachelor of arts as of the class of 1843.

For a time he flirted with the idea of going to Germany. In a letter to a Buffalo friend named Barrett he wrote:

"My purpose of going to Germany grows fixed and definite. I am told I can live there at a university for fifty dollars a year, and can earn something besides by teaching

English. If at the end of my junior year I can get hold of two or three hundred dollars, I shall go, and then, God willing, I shall write you letters from Germany."

That ambition came to naught with the founding of the Brook Farm Community. The Transcendentalists were then at the summit of their intellectual and spiritual turmoil. In the *Dial*, a magazine influenced largely by Emerson, and conducted not for profit but for uplift, appeared the glowing outpouring of their mental wrestlings. Those who had communed with Cousin, the French philosopher, and the Germans, Kant, Fichte, Schelling, Hegel and Schleiermacher, were concerned with developing in the New World a new idealism of living. The inner circle, composed of the coterie surrounding Emerson, and including the intellectual élite, such as Margaret Fuller, Alcott and Thoreau, met in the select drawing rooms of Boston and its environs and discussed before hushed and reverent disciples their theories for revising the universe. Everybody seems to have been tense with the feeling that they were about to witness the birth of something which would lift mankind out of the mire to ethereal heights.

Among them was the Rev. George Ripley, who was of the stuff that martyrs are made of. Imbued with an irresistible desire to put into practical effect those lofty theories of altruism which fell in graceful, flowing phrases from the eloquent tongues of poet and philosopher, this fine, earnest, high-minded minister surrendered his assured position as the pastor of one of the churches of Boston, and cast himself adrift on a sea of idealistic communism. While his friends pondered, wrote and talked he decided to act. With a small body of fellow spirits he proposed to draw away from established society and organize a new way of living which should put into effect some of the more fundamental of the fine theories they had all been advocating.

At twenty-one most young men who have minds to exercise are likely to be concerned more or less with the riddle of the universe, and young Dana was no exception. Up to now he had worried chiefly over questions of theology. To Dr. Flint he had written at the end of 1840:

"I feel now an inclination to orthodoxy, and am trying to believe the real doctrine of the trinity. Whether I shall settle down in Episcopacy, Swedenborgianism or Goethean indifference to all religion, I know not. My only prayer is, 'God help me!'"

There was a brief period when he thought he had a call to the pulpit. The Danas had all been rock-ribbed Puritans, very much like the thousands of other conscience-burdened New Englanders whose forbears had left the Old World rather than forego the privilege of regulating the beliefs and habits of their neighbors. Gen. Ben Butler wrote of some of the New Hampshire Puritans who had left their asylum in Holland because they found there entire freedom of worship, which irked them beyond endurance. And, having traveled more than three thousand miles to found homes in a wilderness, where every man might be held strictly within the discipline they adored, why should they have tolerated the presence among them of the unregenerate? They didn't. All along the line the Danas appear to have been in good standing in the Congregational church. When Charles was about to enter Harvard he received this admonition from his father, who had been shocked at the news that the son was attending Unitarian meetings:

"Is it possible that the smooth sophistry of its supporters and advocates, and the convenient latitude of its doctrines have so beguiled you that you have lost sight of the odious and abominable courses and unfaith to which they unavoidably lead? If so, I do not suppose anything your father could say would produce any alteration, still I would raise a warning voice and say ponder well the paths of thy feet lest they lead down to the very gates of Hell!"

But it was Harvard that rocked the old man on his foundations—"When there, if you finally take that course, hope must be at an end. I know that it ranks high as a literary institution, but the influence it exerts in a religious way is most horrible. . . ."

Poor old man! Truly the son was a lost sheep. In that same letter to Dr. Flint he expressed the view that speculative opinions and creeds were of little consequence. In the end he veered off from all church ties.

The same attitude of uncertainty manifested itself in respect to Ripley's venture. "Whether the true way to reform this dead mass-society be to separate from it and commence without it, I am in doubt," he confided to Flint. However, it seems to have dawned upon him presently that Ripley was pointing the way to his own escape from a serious dilemma. The experiment he had indicated to Barrett, "to practise an art of which I am wholly ignorant— to wit, the art of living without means," had not been successful, and was less likely to be so now, in the bad state of his eyes.

Brook Farm offered an ideal refuge. Even though Dana could not subscribe whole-heartedly to the dreamer's theories, he was sympathetic, as he was to all the aspirations of the Transcendentalists.

Brook Farm, according to Ripley, proposed "to insure a more natural union between intellectual and manual labor than now exists; to combine the thinker and worker, as far as possible, in the same individual; to guarantee the highest mental freedom, by providing all with labor adapted to their tastes and talents, and securing to them the fruits of their industry; . . . and thus to prepare a society of liberal, intelligent and cultivated persons, whose relations with each other would permit a more wholesome and simple life than can be led amidst the pressure of our competitive institutions."

Had it been invented especially to suit his case it could not have met Dana's wants better. In July, 1841, he wrote Ripley, whose lectures he had attended, asking on what terms he might join. Ripley's reply, while indicating clearly his wish to have the young man, mentioned practical obstacles. They were full up and unable for the time being to squeeze in another recruit. If he could wait a bit—but he did not have to. Somehow they did make room for him.

III. AN EXPERIMENT IN COMMUNISM BEFORE LENIN WAS BORN — HAWTHORNE — THE YOUTHFUL DANA HOLDS THE BALANCE IN THIS ADVENTURE IN IDEALISM—THE MECCA OF CELEBRITIES.

IF EVER an enterprise was put under way which offered all the objections to lifting oneself by his own bootstraps, it was Brook Farm. At West Roxbury, a small village nine miles from Boston, Ripley had found a charming tract of land. Away from all unpleasant contacts, and cosily nestled in an amphitheatre of picturesque hills, it stretched in pleasant fields and sunny uplands, with airy groves to invite the contemplative. A brook like a silver thread wound its way among the varied shades of green.

Ripley's ancestors had been farmers, and he was not ignorant of what was required, but his esthetic instincts must have been in the ascendant. The character of the soil, unfit for cultivation without great expense, the fact that its remoteness—it was four miles from a railroad station—made it difficult to get the products to market or supplies to the farm, were all brushed aside. Here the reformers of society would be undisturbed. A vision of the morally and intellectually élite gathered in earnest discourse, remote from all defilement, while the pleasant country noises acted like a Greek chorus for their inspired eloquence, probably absorbed all his mental energies.

Once accepted all that the member was required to do was work for his living. A year's board for a year's work. Everybody was paid for his labor and all received the same. Not more than one dollar a day, and not more than ten hours' work. Moreover, the employment was to be adapted to the capacities, habits and tastes of the individual. Not many corporations start with so brave a readiness to assume burdens and obligations. It is not surprising that it should have looked alluring to the young man with weakened eyesight and empty pockets.

John Thomas Codman, who wrote a history of Brook Farm, has these comments to make on Dana:

> He was strong of purpose and lithe of frame, and it was not long before Mr. Ripley found it out and gave him a place at the front. He was about four and twenty years of age, and he took to books, languages and literature. Social, good-natured and animated, he readily pleased all with whom he came in contact. . . . His voice was musical and clear, and his language remarkably correct. He loved to spend a portion of his time in work on the farm and the tree nursery, and you might be sure of finding him there when not otherwise occupied. . . . Enjoying fun and social life, there was always a dignity remaining which gave him influence and commanded respect. If you looked into his room you saw pleasant volumes in various languages peeping at you from the table, chair, bookcase, and even from the floor, and they gave the impression that for so young a person he was remarkably studious and well-informed.

Thomas Wentworth Higginson made this brief comment:

"He was the best all-round man at Brook Farm, but was held not to be quite so zealous or unselfish for the faith as some others."

Yet there never was any question about his loyal service. Not only efficient but tremendously industrious.

Of the members of the Transcendental Club hardly any joined. Having inspired the ingenuous Ripley to embark upon the shining waters of altruism the great ones stood on the shore waving their handkerchiefs and exclaiming *bon voyage*. Emerson, who must have led Ripley to believe he would join, remarked coolly that he believed real estate at Concord to be a better investment than that at Brook Farm. Thoreau, George Bancroft, Margaret Fuller, James Freeman Clarke and the Rev. William Ellery Channing were among the shining lights who had applauded when Ripley rhapsodized over his proposed venture, but none of them would come aboard. Alcott, another whose adherence had been counted on, backed off when he learned that everybody would have to work at Brook Farm, a condition which violated his deepest convictions and most cherished instincts.

Hawthorne made at least a try at it, arriving in a heavy snowstorm, which is described in "Blithedale Romance". There were about twenty in at the start—Ripley's wife and sister; William B. Allen, who became the head farmer; and the Minot Pratt family, including a wife and three children, so that there was quite a domestic atmosphere. Pratt, who had been a foreman printer, developed a talent for farming, but his esthetic spirit refused to allow the flowers turned up by the plow to perish, and he would stop to plant them along the paths.

Publicity was not wanting, and all New England paused to watch and wonder, while new recruits came along to lend distinction and spread the interest: Father Hecker, who was declared one of the greatest of the sacred orators of his time; Abby Morton (Mrs. Diaz of the William Henry books); Francis Barlow, later one of the editors of the *New York Tribune*, and a general in the Civil War; George Duncan Wells, a lawyer of distinction and commander of a regiment in that war; George Partridge Bradford, ex-minister and a distinguished teacher. When Bradford left he confessed he would not have raised a finger to save the life of Dana, so jealous had he been of the latter's ability to lure into his German class the girls he wanted to teach.

In a talk at the University of Michigan many years later Dana mentioned some other Brook Farmers of a different type: "An English girl, who had been a domestic, and a very superior woman she was"; also an Englishman, who came from his service as valet to an English baronet staying

Fashionable Union Square in 1858.

(*From a Rare Engraving.*)

at Boston, and who proved "to be one of the most interesting members of the society". Among the later recruits was George William Curtis.

The Brook Farmers, besides farming, made shoes, britannia ware—which did not sell well—and had a sash and blind factory; but lack of capital kept them from buying lumber long enough ahead to allow it to season, so their product failed to stand up for long. The chief reliance was the school. Here the brain was trained from babyhood to university exams, or, as the pronouncement put it, from the "first rudiments to the highest culture". A course of six years prepared the youth for college.

Nothing gives a better idea of Dana's advancement in learning than his success as a teacher. He had himself had only desultory training, with two years of intermittent attendance at Harvard, yet his pupils stood out among the college entrants. Specifically, his subjects were Greek and German. The German class was full of pupils who yearned not only to discover the beauties of German literature, but who admired the scholarly young tutor, even though he was far from lenient. The hand which had wielded the switch at Scituate was restrained here, but apparently he was convinced that indulgence was fraught with danger to discipline. After all, he was not so much older than his students and could maintain his position only by a high appearance of dignity. Perhaps that explains the carefully cultivated beard. An eye-witness declared that "the shame of the youth who entered Dana's classroom with an unlearned lesson differed in quality from that which he felt in other classrooms under the same circumstance".

In general there was a lack of formality in the school. The pupil was expected to give an hour or two daily to manual labor on the farm or about the buildings, the rest was up to him. "It frequently happened," observed a critic, "that a teacher who was digging on the farm would leave his work to meet an appointment with a pupil; but the pupil, being absorbed in the pursuit of woodchucks, would either forget his appointment altogether or put in an appearance an hour later." This was doubtless exaggerated, for the school won a high reputation. There were students from far points, including Florida, Havana and Manila.

The spirit of the community was all that could be asked and there was no lack of gaiety when the day's work was done. Picnics, boating on the Charles, and other rural sports for holidays, while the piano was thumped energetically for dances. There was also singing and instrumental music, games, readings, charades, tableaux and plays on a portable stage. Ten o'clock was closing time, and the doors were locked. Said Dana to a youth discovered playing whist in a cottage to which he did not belong after the sacred hour:

"And how do you expect, sir, to enter the house when you know the doors are locked at ten?"

"Oh, I always get in at the pantry window," replied the incorrigible.

One suspects he detected the smile lurking behind the auburn beard. Youngsters have a faculty for sensing each other's pretensions.

Somebody coined a word for the outside world. There dwelt the "Civilisés". Brook Farm was a thing apart. To make this apparent to the casual eye, the indwellers dressed differently. Brown or blue holland tunics for the men, according to individual fancy, with black belts; also full beards, which were not the mode just then. At the entertainments the younger ones had tunics of black velvet. In their working hours—and they had their full share of hard work—the women wore short skirts and knickerbockers. Always they wore their hair flowing, usually with broad hats. At times the hair was intertwined with wild vines and gay berries. Col. Higginson speaks of the men wearing "picturesque little visorless caps, exquisitely unfitted for horny-handed tillers of the soil". Dana maintained his independence. He refused the tunics and would not curl his hair.

"Appliances to reduce the irksomeness of the trivial round

were few; a pump was the main dependence for water, and duly appointed carriers visited daily each house and supplied the empty pitchers, sometimes attended, in stormy weather, by a youth who carried an umbrella. Curtis occasionally trimmed lamps and Dana organized a band of griddle-cake servitors composed of four of the most elegant youths of the community." Youth helped maiden in preparing the vegetables for the market, and also helped wash and clean the dishes. Well-bred women scrubbed floors and scraped plates, and gentlemen and scholars hoed potatoes and cleaned out stables. The really nasty work was performed by a group of volunteers, who called themselves— The Sacred Legion.

Hawthorne was carried away by the spirit of the place. He wrote his sister: "The whole fraternity eat together, and such a delectable way of life has never been seen on earth since the days of the early Christians."

He enjoyed pork and beans for his Sunday breakfast and feasted on pan-dowdy and brewis. That is, on deep-dish apple pie, according to the New England mothers, and the Yankee version of *pot au feu*. There was no liquor and hardly any of the men used tobacco. Of course, none of the women. Far from Bohemia, indeed, unless this may be called a Puritan version. Sex appeal seems to have been conquered. Never once was there a breath of scandal, and yet all the world must have been watching for it.

The author of "The Scarlet Letter" arrived in April and by August his enthusiasm had vanished. No longer did he speak of the toil that "defiles the hands, indeed, but not the soul" but—"Oh, labor is the curse of the world, and nobody can meddle with it without becoming proportionably brutified! Is it a praiseworthy matter that I have spent five months in providing food for cows and horses?" He raised such a row he was relieved of all manual labor, made a trustee and chairman of the Finance Committee, where Dana and William Allen, the head farmer, did the work.

Emerson may have had him in mind when he remarked:
"The country members naturally were surprised to observe that one man ploughed all day, and one looked out
of the window all day—and perhaps drew his picture—and
both received at night the same wages."

Naturally enough, perhaps, remembering that he had
not kept faith with Ripley, Emerson was inclined to be
critical. "He never refers to Brook Farm without convey-
ing to the finest sense the assurance that some one is laughing behind the shrubbery," said Lindsay Swift. While
admitting that it was a pleasant place where lasting friendships were formed, Emerson found the impulse "without
centripetal balance" and the members suffering from "Intellectual sansculottism". Their cherished dream of unity
as the basis of a new society he called "an Age of Reason in
a patty-pan" and a "French Revolution in small". Yet he
was an occasional visitor and repeatedly delivered formal
lectures to the Brook Farmers. William Henry Channing
called Brook Farm a "republic of lovable fools". Curtis,
presumably at the close of his stay, wrote his father: "No
wise man is long a reformer, for wisdom sees plainly that
growth is steady, sure, and neither condemns nor rejects
what is or has been. Reform is organized distrust." Perhaps
one should make allowance for the fact that it is an almost
irresistible impulse for those to whom witty or felicitous
phrases come easily to spill them. Such is the basis of most
unforgettable criticism. Speaking of the experiment in later
days at the University of Michigan, Dana said:

"It was joked about in the newspapers. The newspapers
were great in joking then, as they have been since."

All of which served to keep Brook Farm in the public
eye. Visitors, famous and otherwise, poured in until there
was danger of its being swamped. Often the members were
put to it to find accommodation for ruthless ones who descended upon them without warning and demanded that
they be fed and bedded. Four thousand registered in one

year. Some of the names have survived—Horace Gree-
ley, Henry James, Parke Godwin, Charles Sumner, Robert
Owen, John A. Andrew, later Governor of Massachusetts,
W. W. Storey, Margaret Fuller, Rev. Theodore Parker,
Albert Brisbane, James Russell Lowell, Elizabeth Peabody.

IV.
ON THE VERGE OF DEEPER RADICALISM WHEN FATE INTERVENES—DANA'S ROMANCE ON THE EVE OF DISASTER—MARRIAGE—THE BEGINNING OF A NEW ADVENTURE—SUB-EDITOR OF THE *New York Tribune.*

AT THE END of two years all but six of the original Brook Farmers had disappeared, but others had flocked in and there were now seventy. However, the finances were not flourishing, which must have worried the young financier Dana quite a little. He, at least, had clear vision and few of Ripley's illusions. Of course, the extraordinary feature of the venture was the fact that it had been able to exist at all, considering that the control lay with rhapsodic visionaries, flouting every principle of logic, daring the most absurd experiments, veering off from the practical as much as possible; yet they were still going without even a visit from the sheriff.

But a new influence came along which wrought a mighty change. Albert Brisbane, the American sponsor for Fourier, the French Socialist, captured Ripley as a convert, and Brook Farm became one of the phalansteries of Fourierism. A lot of these were being established around the country and Horace Greeley gave them the powerful support of the *New York Tribune.*

Dana must have swallowed hard, but, having overcome his scruples, he took up the new burdens as manfully as he had the old. With Ripley and Minot Pratt he put his signature to the new constitution, which was published in the *Harbinger,* a new weekly, which filled much the same role held previously by the now defunct *Dial.* Jan. 18, 1844 appeared a fervid challenge to existing civilization, and an outline of the new crusade.

Whether because he had convinced himself, or was influenced by the enthusiasm of Ripley, Brisbane and others, Dana now threw himself with the ardor of a convert into the task of persuading the world that Fourierism was the magic means to create a new world. Practically on the farm, and with fluent pen in the *Harbinger*, he labored mightily towards this end. A new building, the Phalanstere, was erected to carry out that part of the Fourierist theory which called for the living together under one roof of the diverse types of humanity which were expected to unite to make the perfect human family. Intellectuals and horny-handed sons of toil, instructors in the classics and *belles lettres* with shoemakers and carpenters and others whose grammar and modes of expression could not be according to the dictates of culture. To be sure, they would not have to be social intimates, and the original habit of independence for everybody was to be maintained, but the purpose never-theless was to impress upon all Fourier's principle that the labor of the one was as worthy and ennobling as that of the other.

One valuable result for Dana was a closer intimacy with Greeley. There was correspondence back and forth. Greeley was skeptical about Brook Farm. "I do not deny," he wrote, "the advantage of your plan for a community of which every member shall be actuated solely by a true Christianity or a genuine manfulness—a disposition to bear others' bur-dens, and to count it happiness to do and suffer for the indolent and unthankful"—but wasn't there danger that at least one serpent might enter this Garden of Eden and prove as fatal as did the one of old? Would even the most ideal nature stand the strain of seeing his own idealism only confirming the worldly in selfishness?

There is reason to suspect that Dana had fallen into the extravagances of a loyal and fervid press agent. He must have laid it on thick to get that sort of reply from Greeley. In the light of after events the skeptical attitude of the latter, opposing a seemingly gushing sentimentality on the part of Dana, can only be regarded as highly amusing.

Dana's side of the correspondence appears to have been
lost, but one cannot resist the suspicion that it was keyed
to appeal to the known emotionalism of its recipient. At
all events, the acquaintance thus begun ripened into closer
relations. Greeley wrote occasionally for the *Harbinger* and
the way was opened for the approach to metropolitan journalism when Dana was ready for that.

It must be admitted that the editorials and articles which
appeared over Dana's signature in the *Harbinger* gave little
indication of the subtlety and wit which marked the writing
of the editor of *The Sun*. As yet the scalpel was not fitted
to his grasp, which seemed to find a hammer quite convenient. In the issue of Aug. 16, 1845, there is a review of
"A System of Latin Versification", of which the author
was Charles Anthon, Professor of Greek and Latin at
Columbia, which makes one marvel that something did not
happen to the critic. After a series of reflections upon the
scholarship as well as the writing of the author, there are
charges of plagiarism and this final summing up: "Our
purpose is simply, in plain words, to say that Dr. Anthon is
a humbug." Apparently the victim of his scorn was using
the scholarship and industry of various European writers
as his sources for compiling a number of text books without credit to the real workers. There was the sort that
would rouse the ire and scorn of the Dana of later years,
but what fun the older man would squeeze out of the process of de-hiding the culprit!

Dana's industry, considering his many other duties, was
enormous. He and Ripley wrote most of the editorials which
appeared in the *Harbinger*, and beyond that Dana contributed endless reviews, translations from the German—
especially verse—and some original poems. In all two hundred and forty-eight of his effusions appeared in the weekly
in two years.

Five years had passed when the Great Experiment came
to an abrupt and unanticipated end.

"It didn't pay," said Dana later. "We kept a good school,

with a most extensive range of instruction, but we didn't have scholars enough, or get enough money from them. There wasn't enough money coming in."

But the actual cause of destruction was the carelessness of the carpenters at work on the phalanstery. One night in the spring of 1846, while the dance was going on as usual, somebody saw flames in the new construction. His cry of "Fire!" was thought to be a jest, but it proved real enough. Before anything could be done the destruction was complete. Ten thousand dollars were lost—for the crowning joke of Fate was that the insurance had been allowed to lapse the day before!

In "Blithedale Romance" Hawthorne wrote: "Often in these years that are darkening around me, I remember our beautiful scheme of a noble and unselfish life, and how fair in that first summer appeared the prospect that it might endure for generations, and be perfected, as the ages rolled by, into the system of a people and a world." Mayo W. Hazeltine wrote of "that band of wistful reformers of society, whose Brook Farm experiment was a failure more illustrious than many a brilliant, self-seeking success." Dana himself at the zenith of his career said:

"Every person who was at Brook Farm looked back upon it with a feeling of satisfaction. The healthy mixture of manual and intellectual labor, the kindly and unaffected social relations, the absence of everything like assumption or servility, the amusements, the discussions, the friendships, the ideal and poetical atmosphere which gave a charm to life, all these combine to creat a picture towards which the mind turns back with pleasure as to something distant and beautiful, not elsewhere met with amid the routine of this world. In due time it ended and became almost forgotten; and yet it remains alive, and the purposes that inspired it still dwell in many minds."

The actual blow which forced the termination fell upon him like a tragic stroke of fate. He was absent at the time, having gone to New York to take the final step in what

was for him the most perfect of all the romantic features of
the life at Brook Farm. On the day preceding the fire he
was standing before a minister with one to whom an admirer referred in these glowing terms: "Those charming
black eyes and raven hair, and the quick, nervous, volatile,
lovely owner of them, with her Southern accent."

Married March 2, 1846
Eunice Macdaniel had come to Brook Farm with her
widowed mother, a brother and sister, from Maryland. She
had the ambition to become an actress, which may have
been transmitted to the granddaughter who has achieved so
distinguished a place on the stage of today, Ruth Draper,
but romance intervened. The happy couple went back to
West Roxbury expecting to take up their respective roles,
she as a member of the housekeeping group, only to find
themselves adrift upon the world.

The courageous sons of New England were more ready
to marry without due provision for the future then than they
would be now, and the American girl of that day was likewise inclined to place her faith in Providence rather than a
bank account, but the situation of these two looked particularly precarious. Dana made strenuous efforts to keep
Brook Farm going. Fortunately, the damage was beyond
repair. Otherwise, more valuable years might have been
wasted. Presently he was assistant to the editor of the *Daily
Chronotype*, a Boston journal read by Congregational ministers, receiving a salary of four dollars a week, later increased to five.

In the background, however, remained that acquaintance
with Greeley, so carefully nurtured from the beginning. It
proved to be all that had been hoped for. In February of
1847 the following year he was on the *Tribune*, receiving ten
dollars a week, which was quite a salary for a sub-editor in
those days. Greeley himself received only fifteen.

V. ASSOCIATION WITH HORACE GREELEY—NEW YORK AT THE CLOSE OF THE 'FORTIES—EUROPE IN THE THROES OF REVOLUTION LURES DANA ABROAD.

CURIOUSLY enough, shortly after his arrival Greeley made him city editor. It was like throwing a small boy into the river to sink or swim. A city editor is supposed to know above all everything knowable about his city—its moods, fancies, whims, likes and dislikes, all that makes its character and distinguishes it from other aggregations of humanity. John Bogart, later on to be held up to the admiration of all the craft as the best city editor New York ever knew, declared solemnly that in his judgment a city editor should be a product of his city, familiar from birth with all the nuances which made up its tone and color, responsive to every breath and aspiration, reacting by instinct to every indication of change or development. Who else but a born New Yorker could appreciate the sentiment which inspired the rival fire companies to fight like wild cats for the possession of the water mains while the flames merrily wrought destruction? What other could understand the frigidity with which the average citizen regarded his next-door neighbor, while his purse was ever open at a tale of suffering? What was more, asserted the master, a city editor must live in the heart of the town, on the very hub of the great revolving wheel, where he might always look down all the spokes and be in touch with whatever was going on. And here was a young man, fresh from the most secluded countryside and a life apart from the usual, thrust into this most difficult role!

The city editor is one of the most important of the directing powers of a newspaper. He is responsible for all that may occur within the city itself or its immediate environs— that is, for what interests the overwhelming majority of the readers of his paper beyond all else that may be printed in it. More particularly was that true at this time, when the average New Yorker cared mighty little about events abroad, and of all that was transpiring in these United States only what was going on in Washington—that is, in national politics—would receive from him more than a passing glance. But he did demand all the details of the latest set-to between the Bowery B'hoys and the Dead Rabbits, as well as all the gossip of the higher circles of East Broadway.

Possibly Greeley may have reasoned that a young man fresh from the rural life would have a keener zest and more ardent curiosity concerning the various manifestations of the town than one to whom these had become familiar by long association. Unquestionably he had discovered that Dana was peculiar in his eagerness to learn about everything, absorbing information wherever it might lie like a sponge, and probing relentlessly and with infinite patience for that which was not easily attainable. At all events, the new city editor must have satisfied, for within the year his salary had been raised to fourteen dollars.

New York was then, as it has remained, the great metropolis to all Americans, the abiding place of all the marvels that made the fame of ancient Bagdad, the Superb. For the stranger, at least, romance lurked in every doorway, and vice, horrible yet fascinating, stalked in all the byways. Life was freer, bolder and wickeder than anywhere else. Crowds, the rapid pace and the everlasting struggle, whether for supremacy or mere existence, seemed to create a different sort of being from those who ambled through life in the smaller town. One had to be alert in making contacts. For the outlander there was always a thrill of excitement in the very atmosphere of the Colossus.

A colossus in those days, small as it would seem to us now, the New York of 1847 certainly had much about it to arouse the lively interest of one so eager to see and to interpret as Dana. Even though Broadway was developed for only about four miles from the Battery, and must have had almost a rural aspect under its canopy of Lombardy poplars, it was nevertheless the greatest and busiest street on the American continent. In its upper reaches it was still given over to fine residences, but lower down it was alive with rapidly moving crowds, all intense and absorbed after the New York manner, the roadway a confused mass of vehicles—omnibuses, hackney cabs, gigs, phaetons, tilburies and trucks. Even then it was a real adventure to make a crossing, and part of the joy of the pedestrian was to listen to the verbal encounters of drivers caught in a seemingly inextricable tangle.

Distinctly a real city, with a city's extremes of wealth and poverty, of broad-minded tolerance and unreasoning prejudices, of enlightened idealism and unbelievable degradation, of luxury and misery jostling shoulders, of progress and decadence. A lot of the right-living but an undue proportion of idle rich and vagabond poor.

Already society was preening itself, the descendants of small merchants of the colonial days talking magniloquently of birth and inheritance, and aping slavishly so far as they knew them the ways of English aristocracy. From the windows of fashionable clubs pretentious men gazed with conscious vacuity over the heads of the passers-by. They lived in East Broadway and the streets immediately adjacent, in Washington Square and Waverly Place, and some of the other streets included in the vague borders of what we call Greenwich Village, in streets whose names have disappeared—Albion Place and Depeau Place; in Second Avenue, "a home for the rich when Fifth Avenue was parvenu"; on scattered estates on the edge of the town.

They dined at two and supped at seven, except when they entertained formally, when dinner came at five and supper after the dance, at eleven, when everybody ate stewed oysters, boned turkey and cranberry jelly, with plenty to drink of every variety of wine and hard liquor. There were homes of the elect where one might have those precious Madeiras, imported by knowing forbears in cask and left to ripen into priceless heirlooms. These homes might be survivals of the Dutch period, or Georgian, or modifications of the latter, "with heavy blond decoration in stone along and above the eaves, portals of some magnificence and rounded fronts of brick." There were also the beginnings of the brown stone invasion which made uptown New York monotonous and depressing later on.

Society had taken up the polka, against which Mr. Bennett—the elder, of course—let loose all his heaviest guns, denouncing it as an importation from immoral Hungary for the debauching of innocent America. The reputation of the *Herald* and its editor was not of the best, but it is always the penny dreadful that shouts the loudest for the protection of virtue. In this instance the onslaught was ignored by those at whom it was aimed. Just as Greeley's attacks upon horse racing and prize fighting were as the idle wind. Somehow the habits of the people, whether of high or low degree, were beyond the influence of the editorial pen.

In vain did the *Tribune* break out in verse on the occasion of the fight between Sullivan and Hyer:

> What means this strange and barbarous tale
> Which makes such stir in every street?
> Why throng these crowds, with visage pale,
> With eager ear, and hurrying feet?
> It is a sweet and pleasant story
> That men by men like dogs are handled,
> That human flesh, all bruised and gory,
> Is thus deformed, and gashed, and mangled,
> While gaping brutes stand by to see,
> And gloat on human misery ——

The remainder is even worse. But over in the Five Points, on Cherry Hill and along Water Street, prize fights were of daily occurrence, with such trimmings as eye gouging and ear biting. Ruffians wore hob nails in their heavy shoes so that they might finish their foes once they had them on the ground. Pistols, knives and bludgeons were carried openly and used without compunction or fear of consequences. For the innocent stranger to enter certain streets, not to mention the dives which infested them, was to invite certain robbery and not infrequently death. Bodies of the victims, stripped even of their clothes, were flung into the gutters or floated out through the sewers to the East River. When the Brewery, an infamous haunt of thieves and murderers in the heart of the Five Points, was torn down later search was made for the skeletons of unwary strangers said to have been dragged in from the streets and buried in its cellars. Rarely did the police invade these streets, and then only in force. Eugene Sue's *Mysteries of Paris* do not seem so exaggerated after reading the history of the Five Points, of Cow Bay and Gotham Court and all the other rendezvous of cutthroats and harlots. Inveighing against public prize fighting seems amusing then.

But Greeley was set in his views. At the celebration of the fiftieth anniversary of the *Tribune* in 1891 Dana told how Greeley would not allow horse racing to be reported. "But one day there was a horse race of enormous interest, involving much more than the usual event of the sort. It was the race between Boston and Fashion, the one champion of the North and the other of the South, and there was a feeling everywhere that it represented in a way the growing animosity between the two sections—a sort of premonition of that enormous and dreadful conflict which later covered the land with·devastation and sorrow."

The feeling in the *Tribune* office may be imagined. Here was something more than a horse race. It was almost a political event, and the whole public was on edge with excitement. Yet Greeley was the boss and the rule stood. Any man who ever worked in a newspaper office can realize that there was murder in the hearts of the subordinates, down to the newest office boy. The *Tribune* would be the laughing stock of the whole country, a byword in every crossroads weekly. "Finally," said Dana, "the man who was to report it, or who ought to report it, went to Mr. Greeley and said,

'Mr. Greeley, we ought to report that horse race. It will not do for the *Tribune* to appear day after tomorrow without any account of that event in which the whole public mind is absorbed.'" Still Greeley balked and hedged and it was only after a delay which tried the soul of the reporter that he finally gave way in these words: "I guess you will have to do it. *We have to report hangings anyway.*"

Like many another genius Greeley was not always logical. The exhorter and special pleader, which he was primarily, is naturally stiff-necked and rarely pliable. As events were to prove, he and his city editor could not indefinitely trot in double harness, nor would the latter be able to keep step as a wheel horse in a tandem.

Greeley had announced his journalistic principles in the first issue of the *Tribune*, six years before the advent of Dana, in the following terms:

> The *Tribune*, as its name imports, will labor to advance the interests of the People, and to promote their Moral, Social and Political well-being. The unmoral and degrading Police Reports, Advertisements, and other matters which have been allowed to disgrace the columns of our leading Penny Papers will be carefully excluded from this one, and no exertion spared to render it worthy of the hearty approval of the virtuous and refined, and a welcome visitant at the family fireside.

Carrying this lofty promise to the counting room he refused at the beginning even to accept advertisements of the theatre, and only the insistence of his partners overcame this self-sacrifice. Even then he refused to notice the stage in the news columns and if it appeared in the editorials, it was only to be excoriated and held up to scorn and condemnation as one of the devices of the Devil. Old Bennett must have had many a hearty laugh at the gyrations of Horace.

All this was foreign to Dana. Even though he was still under the influence of the Brook Farm idealism there never had been any evidence of Puritan narrowness of vision. In fact, even while he was fitting himself for the job into which he had been thrust so unexpectedly, he was finding time to contribute articles to the *Harbinger* about the new opera just started in the precursor to the Metropolitan Opera House, the Astor Place Opera House, organized by social leaders, with the frank purpose of providing a place of amusement specially designed for the aristocrats and purveying to them almost exclusively. Then as today the subscribers were all important and the herd were put in their place. Even more so, in fact, for the rules barred entrance to men who did not wear full evening dress, smooth-shaven faces, white waistcoats and white gloves, and even then the non-subscriber had to put up with hard uncomfortable seats, with the stage obscured by the enormous central chandelier, while the favored ones sat on luxurious lounges and deeply cushioned seats and had a perfect view of every part of the stage. One may imagine the uproar in the penny press, for here was a bold invasion of European practices at a time when the mere mention of anything transatlantic brought jeers if not curses from *hoi polloi*. But they were bold fellows, these aristocrats, and carried the war into Africa in no uncertain fashion by refusing free seats to the press! That this created more stir than even the snobbery goes without saying.

However, Dana was not influenced by all the uproar. The event for him was the fact that he might now listen to the operas of which he had thus far heard only such excerpts as might be given at the public concerts in Boston, and his articles in the *Harbinger* were devoted entirely to consideration of the music and the performance.

Apparently the post of city editor did not please him altogether, and it is not unlikely that the limitations to his scope, due to Greeley's views of what was fit to print, had much to do with this. Imagine a Dana, of all newspapermen, unable to picture what was going on in its true colors,

but ever having to denounce wickedness and support the
virtues in all sobriety.

There were a score of happenings which the Dana of the
Sun-to-be would have delighted to make the talk—and the
laugh—of the town, but which could not be treated thus
after the manner of the *Tribune*, whose downright method
of attack brought no smile to the cheek of the reader—and
was not intended to. Perhaps it was an inner revolt against
his restraints which disaffected Dana at this time. Yet this
is not certain. Up to now he had not shown the colors
under which he would ride and be known in his greater
days. At all events he was not willing to keep on and he
never returned to the city editor's desk.

Early in 1848 he notified Greeley that he was about to
sail for Europe with the purpose of reporting the great
events unfolding there. Greeley appears to have been convinced that the young man was foolish. What did he know
about European matters? Nothing. He would have to learn
practically everything before he would be equipped to
write anything.

It is curious that Greeley, a practical journalist, should
have taken this attitude. If there is any one talent which a
good reporter must have, it is the ability to absorb the
fundamental facts of anything, however foreign to his previous understanding, almost by contact. Not all reporters,
by any means. The great majority, as in every other calling,
are numbskulls and never get anything straight. But that
rare bird, the real reporter, has sources of penetration which
seem like magic to the average—and Dana was all his life
a real reporter. That was why he understood Greeley so
well and, cutting off further argument, asked him what he
would pay for a weekly letter? Greeley offered ten dollars
and Dana accepted.

But that was only one string to his bow. Then and there
Dana initiated the plan on which all later syndicated articles
appeared. The *Philadelphia American,* the *New York Commercial Advertiser*—an evening paper,—the *Harbinger* and

the *Chronotype* were appealed to and responded favorably. Altogether he was assured of forty dollars a week, which was reduced to thirty-five when the *Chronotype* gave up the ghost. Dana, of course, had to pay all his expenses. Even at that his success seems remarkable when one considers the purchasing power of money then, when one could obtain room and board at a leading hotel at Saratoga in the height of the season for two dollars a day, the swell Astor House charged only a dollar for its rooms and a dollar bought the best seat at the opera.

'Forty-eight was the year of the revolutions abroad when, as if actuated by a common impulse, the peoples of the whole continent rose against selfish and unreasonable masters with a wild determination to get for themselves some of the joy of life which had been held as the preserve of the rich and the aristocrats. Though the first impulse came from the Polish rebellion against Austria two years earlier it was the uprising in France against Louis Philippe which made the conflagration, and it was to France that Dana made his way as rapidly as the slow means of travel permitted. In June he reached Paris.

VI.

IN THE BLOOD-RUNNING STREETS OF PARIS—UNDER ARREST—LOUIS NAPOLEON—WITH THE REBELS OF BERLIN—OPTIMISTIC YOUTH CANNOT SEE THE CLOUDS BEHIND THE RAINBOW.

THEY were raising barricades and killing men in the streets. Everybody was suspect. No wonder then that a striking-looking foreigner—Oliver Dyer's young Greek god —should attract attention as he rushed about eager-eyed and inquisitive, appealing now to the representatives of constituted authority and again to the opposition. As a good reporter Dana was making a first-hand investigation of the bloody contest between the National Guard, representing the Assembly, and the supporters of the red flag, Socialists and what not. The shooting was no play business. Officially thirty thousand were killed. Dana found the figures exaggerated. There were not more than twelve thousand, he declared. Still, when even twelve thousand are wiped out in street fighting, only the temerarious care to hang around. But it was part of the job he had undertaken, so he rushed from barricade to barricade, and from one side to the other, determined to know just how the account stood.

The French are normally skeptical but, being also decidedly logical, they can sometimes be bluffed. At the height of the sensational review by the Cour de Cassation, the highest legal tribunal of France, of the proceedings which had culminated in the verdict against Captain Dreyfus, several workmen entered the courtroom with ladders and a scaffolding, which they set up deliberately. Then a tall, distinguished-looking man mounted the structure bearing a strange apparatus, waved his hands to command attention, waited calmly until he had received it, and then proceeded to take a photograph of the courtroom. With the same absence of precipitation he descended and walked off. The workmen removed the encumbrances and the legal proceedings were resumed.

Could any Frenchman conceive that any human being would have the monumental impudence to precipitate himself without authority into the sacred precincts of the court, interrupting the solemnest official undertaking of the century for the mere gratification of the readers of a newspaper in a foreign country? No one more daring than the Frenchman—or more impudent, for that matter; but everything in its place. So it had been taken for granted in this instance that the photographing was for the Government archives and, while the good taste of the officials responsible might be questioned in under-the-breath criticism, it was permitted to pass. When it became known later that the intruder was a Russian artist-reporter named Valerian Gribayedoff, whose bravado had led him to obtain this "scoop" for the papers he represented, all official France stood aghast. In the meantime the offender had disappeared, which was a relief, as to have proceeded against him would only have aroused a storm of ridicule.

It was this same sense of the fitness of things which must have prevailed against interfering with Dana at the time of his daring wanderings along the firing lines, but after a time somebody must have awakened to the fact that he had no sanction to be there, and one night a loud summons at his door called upon him to open in the name of the law. At the threshold stood a squad of the National Guard under the command of an officer of decided truculence. Why had monsieur been so dilatory in responding to his summons, and who was monsieur, anyhow? By what authority was he asking all sorts of impertinent questions of all sorts of people, and circulating in forbidden precincts?

Dana's replies were received with incredulity, and only increased the suspicion that he was a conspirator working with the enemies of order. Without further ado his belongings were hauled out and subjected to minute search. This had not proceeded far before unquestionable incriminatory evidence was discovered. One can see the sergeant with it in his hands, the soldiers crowding around and ready to put an end to the criminal if he so much as moved a finger.

By unlucky chance Dana had an improved gunlock in his baggage, which he had brought to oblige a friend who wished to sell it in Europe.

Not so easy to make this clear to his inquisitors, any more than to convince them that American custom permitted reporters to wander at will in search of information. In fact, it took earnest intervention on the part of the official representatives of the United States to clear his skirts.

However, this was but a slight interlude, after all. Besides the fighting there were the debates in the Assembly. No previous experience can prepare any one for the devastating effects of French oratory, and he must have a cool head who can penetrate beneath its insidious eloquence, its moving rhythms, its overwhelming outpouring of well-sounding words. Even the baker, the plumber or the errand boy is an orator in Paris, almost irresistible in his flow of musical language, so what must have been the effect of days of attention to the élite of the talkers of France! Only by holding tight to his purpose could the recent graduate of Brook Farm have withstood their numbing influence.

In his first letter to the *Tribune* he made clear the various proposals for improving the lot of the workingman, which was the subject of the moment.

It was the workingman who was making difficult the restoration of order, for the prostration of business had thrown him out of work. For the first time, too, he had become articulate and made demands. Moreover, he was spilling his blood and that of those who would resist him to maintain these demands. He was strong enough to make the other classes listen, and among them were quite a few who felt there was justice in his outcry. These talked of the duty of the Government to encourage associations of work-

The Old New York Sun Building, One-time
Tammany Hall, at Frankfort and Nassau
Streets, New York City.

(*From Frank Leslie's Illustrated Newspaper,
May 16, 1868.*)

ingmen with their former employers by allowing them to undertake public works without the bonds required of individual contractors. It was the duty of the nation, declared these orators, to elevate the workingman and emancipate him from the wage system. There were many high-sounding phrases about the selfishness of the bourgeoisie and the misery of the laborers.

Dana had not neglected the leaders of the latter, with whom he was most sympathetic, but he was keeping a clear head amid all the outpourings of sentiment. The lack of constructive plans for carrying out the alluring promises did not escape him, any more than the underlying violence of class hatreds. Moreover, the treasury was empty and there was almost complete stagnation of trade and manufacture. While allowing a certain degree of sincerity in the efforts to make the lot of the worker more tolerable he was frankly skeptical of results. "There is a long way between such transient emotions," he wrote, "and the perception of the fact that the emancipation of labor is the especial duty and destiny of this nation, and that it depends on the wealthy to say whether this be done peacefully and with benefit to all, or whether by refusing to do it they will bring on a new and more desperate phase of the revolution."

Other problems were in the melting pot. A new constitution had to be framed, for France was to be a republic now, and the organization of parliament, the questions of franchise—should this be universal or limited—freedom of conscience in matters of religion, the status of secret clubs and societies—the usual instrument of those who were against the powers in being, all these problems were being fought over in endless heated discussions.

There was a debate between Thiers and Proudhon over the latter's proposal to end all the ills of the laboring men by abolishing rent and interest, which was to have an echo later on when Dana was writing editorials for the *Tribune*. Proudhon, like our own Henry George, was convinced that he had discovered the way to the millennium, but the bourgeois in control of the Assembly met his proposals with derision, his being the only vote in their favor.

July, August and September passed with the Assembly still spouting fervid orations, while artillery thundered and bullets whistled in the streets of Paris, and Dana trying to picture it all in comprehensive letters to America. It was a generous assignment for one man. After an effort to portray the leading men of the Assembly—Cavaignac, Hugo, Lamartine, De Tocqueville, Thiers among others—he would turn to a description of unofficial life. The streets were filled with beggars, not professionals but even respectable citizens driven to this last resort by the sudden reversal of normal conditions.

"Young men stop you in the streets to ask assistance, and respectably-dressed women, duly veiled, entreat the passers on the sidewalks to buy some ornament which is their last resource against starvation." The Government was supplying a dole to more than two hundred thousand.

Some of Dana's comments on the leaders make good reading even now.

> The essence of Lamartine's oratory is sentiment, imagination. It is not the reason he addresses, and logic is not one of his weapons, but there is something electric, something inspired in his words which makes you forget reason, forget everything, indeed, but the magnificent periods that seem to envelop you like an atmosphere of the finer and more exciting quality. His oratory absorbs you, carries you away, magnetizes and delights you. You are revived, elevated, ennobled by its influence. Your mind afterward works more freely, as if it had been bathed in some invigorating and expanding element. He has not argued with you, has not convinced, has not instructed you, but you come from hearing him with a new faith in truth and in humanity, with clearer insight, and with fresh resolution and courage.

Comparing Proudhon with Robespierre, he said of the former: "He is a logician with the French passion for theatrical effect. Robespierre was a man of profound sincerity. Proudhon is a man of unequalled skill in dialectics. Robespierre was a man of ideas. Proudhon is a man of mental conception. Robespierre spoke to convince; Proudhon to startle. But the man of '48 is of his times, as the man of '93 was of his." Departing from the men to express his judgment of what was to follow from the present situation he added: "Robespierre made violence the instrument of liberty. Is it the destiny of fraternity to pass through the same companionship and through similar strains? I cannot believe it. There will be great and trying difficulties, but the passion which raged then can hardly be kindled now, besides history does not repeat itself."

In September Louis Napoleon suddenly loomed very large upon the political horizon. He had been elected to the Assembly by large majorities in five departments and the significance of this made a profound impression. Already the word Emperor was whispered in the *couloirs*. The Napoleonic tradition was still potent and the interminable wranglings of the politicians were exasperating to a nation struggling through the murky waters of financial and industrial chaos with no rescuing ship in sight. Everybody was annoyed with leaders whose solution of the unemployment problem went no further than to hire men to carry earth from one side of the river to the other and then take it back again. If that was what a Republic signified, then it was about time to look for a strong man.

"Louis Napoleon in ordinary circumstances," wrote Dana, "would pass for nothing more than a hare-brained and very foolish young man; now he is magnified into a danger to the Republic, and the people vote for him because he is made a greater man than he is."

This was Dana's description of his first appearance in the Assembly:

He was instantly the sole object of attention of every person in the House except the unlucky orator who happened to be in the Tribune; even the elegant and massive lorgnette of ivory that President Marast wields with such consummate skill was gracefully levelled upon him. He bore the quizzing with calmness and courage. He was dressed in black with a bad-looking moustache—at least that was the verdict of the ladies in the gallery. He is rather undersized and seems worn with dissipation. As soon as his election was proclaimed he read a speech about two minutes long in which he took the oath of allegiance to the Republic and his constituents. All parties joined in applauding it.

Three months later—having in the meantime made a study of conditions in Germany during a visit to Berlin—he was an eye-witness of the inauguration of Napoleon as President of the Republic. He was still skeptical. "I have no faith in the sincerity of Louis Napoleon's adherence to the Republic," he wrote to the *Tribune*. "His history is marked with examples of falsehood too glaring to allow any confidence to be placed in his protestations even were he a man of sufficient intellect and character to be capable of genuine sincerity. There is no doubt he would much rather be Emperor than President."

In Berlin he had gone about as in Paris, talking with everybody, mixing with the great and with the people in the streets, watching the fighting between the guards of Frederick William, the Prussian King, and the champions of a liberal government, the deceptive fraternizing of the former with the latter and the promising launching of the conference at Frankfort, which seemed to contain the seeds of a speedy growth of liberalism for Germany.

All Europe was in ferment. Vienna, in the control of those who had forced the abdication and flight of Metternich, was being besieged by soldiers of Ferdinand under Prince Windischgrätz. All Italy was aflame with desperate and bloody insurrections against the hated Austrian domination, and there was loud talk of a united Italy. Under the spur of Kossuth's impetuous oratory Hungary had torn itself loose from the Dual Monarchy and Bohemia was in uproar, with the Czechs demanding independence and the Germans waiting upon the theorists at Frankfort.

The outpouring of fervid republican sentiment in speeches and articles in newspapers, magazines and books influenced Dana to believe that Germany, even more than France, must do away with thrones and tyrannies. The German character he found "eminently fraternal" and it was in Germany, he thought, that "the question of the age" would be decided. The will to believe must have been dominant and he failed to see that the various kinds of Herr Doktor who were acclaiming or denouncing in the tribune at Frankfort were fundamentally too sentimental to permit even their love of liberty to override their inherent devotion to nationalism. The racial spirit was to decide in the end—Jellachich's Croats undermining the Magyars, the latter against the Italians, the Germans and the Czechs ready to fly at each other's throats. Well did the clever diplomats of Austria utilize the national jealousies to set the revolutionaries against each other and even, in the end, to bring the Russian bear to support their cause. The beginnings had indeed been most promising, but the times were not yet ripe for the overthrow of kings. Even while the fervent believer in fraternity was proclaiming his faith that the uprisings would not be without some permanent results for good, and that the day of absolutism was surely drawing to a close, the old tyrants were preparing plans for the punishment of the audacious challengers of their powers which measure before the world the enormity of their offense.

"The impulse given to the heart and mind of Christendom by the year 1848 will wake after its ruins are rebuilt. This impulse is everywhere in new and more vigorous life, in all countries of Europe . . ."

The prisons and the scaffolds would for some time tell a different story.

VII. BACK TO GREELEY, STILL AN UNTAMED RADICAL—BADGERING POOR HORACE—THE EDUCATION OF AN EDITOR.

THERE can be no question of the value of his experience for the career which was still in its beginnings. He had seen Europe at a time when few Americans ventured to cross the sea, and the broadening influence of contact with the older civilizations was not only underestimated but even scoffed at. The jeer of ignorance which is not unknown even today at everything not appurtenant to "God's Own Country" was far more common then. American chauvinism was what every politician knew he could rely upon in making appeal to prejudice, even surer of response than partisan attack or assaults upon the prosperous. Nothing more popular than to dwell upon the decadence of Europe —with especial emphasis upon England, of course—and to hold up in contrast the red-blooded virility of all Americans.

At the very moment of Dana's return to New York— where he arrived in March, after a voyage so long delayed his ship had been thought to be lost—the city was seething with hot antagonisms over just such a discussion. The Forrest-Macready rivalry was about to reach its tragic culmination and had arrived at a tenseness which almost foretold what was about to happen. The underlying cause of the bitterness was realized all over the country, and it had become a topic of national interest, with comment in the newspapers everywhere.

Dana did not take part at first. Probably his mind was still possessed by the European concerns with which he had been busy, and which seemed to him far more important and interesting than the petty rivalry between an American and an English actor. His pen was still busy with analysis of the confused European situation.

46

The financier of Brook Farm set out to elucidate Proudhon's proposal for a bank of the people which was to make the workingman his own master and free him from the domination of the capitalist. In an editorial in the *Tribune*, afterward revised for the Rev. William Henry Channing's weekly, *The Spirit of the Age*, he expressed some views which must have made queer reading to him later on. In fact, a gentleman named B. R. Tucker re-published this article in pamphlet form in the height of the Bryan campaign of 1896 with the evident purpose of annoying the author, stating in a preface that there was strong evidence "to warrant the belief that Mr. Dana will greet my efforts to preserve them with anything but cordiality. . . . He who is today traducer in chief of all who stand for the people and are actuated by a desire for the people's welfare was once . . . as earnest a defender of the people's interests and as ardent an admirer of the people's champions as is, for instance, the hairy Anarchist who pens this preface or the shaven Nebraskan (Bryan) whom politics has made, at the present moment, the most conspicuous target of Mr. Dana's most biting shafts."

Mr. Tucker flattered himself. The most that anybody could get out of Charles A. Dana in 1896 by telling him he no longer held to his former views was an indulgent smile, a smile that began in his eloquent eyes and lost itself in the twitchings under the heavy gray mustache. Frankly and openly he many times had registered his contempt for consistency of mind.

However, his sympathy with Proudhon was certainly strong at the time of his writing, even as was his distrust of the rich. "It is a notorious fact," said he, "that working people pay dearer for the necessaries of life than any class beside. . . . They pay in proportion far more for rents, fuel, lights, clothing and food than those who lie in perfumed chambers, whose meats are fat, whose drink is real and sparkling, and whose vesture is sumptuous and soft." Proudhon showed that capital was "essentially unproductive, and therefore rent and interest are robbery." The solution lay in making credit free to the workers, to whom it rightfully belonged, whereby they would escape having to give the larger part of their products for the use of capital. *"And let it be borne in mind that productive industry is the only real basis of credit.* You may set up any number of fictions in regard to the matter, but this is always the truth at the bottom."

No doubt about Dana's radicalism then. In an article for Channing's publication entitled "The European Revolution", appeared this:

> The history of the past and the examples of the present instruct us that the privileged and powerful, by whatever name they are called, do not yield their privileges except as they are compelled. . . . Let others give aid and comfort to despots. Be it ours to stand for Liberty and Justice, nor fear to lock arms with those who are called hot-heads and demagogues, when the good cause requires.

As Mr. Tucker had observed, he was thirty and in the full glow of that fraternalism which had been the inspiration of Brook Farm. It was not likely to grow less on the *Tribune* under the leadership of Greeley.

Nor is it to be forgotten that Dana had married a woman who was of the same faith, and that all his friendships had evolved from association with enthusiastic devotees of radical thought. It would take the experience of years to cool his ardor; for the clear vision, which had penetrated the unrealities of some of the theories of the leaders at Brook Farm, to discover the muddle-headedness of much that masqueraded as reform, and the insincerity of many who posed as the promoters of altruism.

Thus far he had lived more than most men with his books. The practice begun at Brook Farm of having always at his elbow a book of quotations, in which he wrote down, in the language of the author, those sentiments which he deemed worthy of preservation, was still continued and must have had a decided influence upon his outlook on life and its manifestations. Thucydides, Euripides, Virgil, Horace, Cicero, Goethe, Schiller, Heine, Carlyle, Coleridge, Swedenborg, Wordsworth, Fourier and a host of others contributed of their best, and surely one cannot live in daily communion with the idealists and not be affected thereby.

Presently he turned his attention to local affairs. The Forrest-Macready embroilment had passed beyond personal jealousy and rivalry and developed a principle worth discussing. Public clamor, excited by chauvinism skilfully manipulated by the leaders of the Native Americans, the party of the Know-Nothings, was making frenzied protest against the right of the Englishman to appear upon the New York stage. With all the accents of aroused indignation Dana assailed this contention, declaring that "his rights as a man were superior to other people's prejudices".

Along came the bloody riot before the theatre in Astor Place, with a scared militia shooting down defiant men and women, and the *Herald* had this to say:

"The late fearful riot has opened up a new and alarming subject of investigation, and that is how far the anarchical socialism of the *Tribune* . . . has operated in this community in unsettling the foundations of law and order and arraying the poor against the rich. . . . Do we now really see the beginning of socialism in America?"

Did Greeley come to the defense of his associate, or was it the latter who retorted:

> The most direct agency of disorder is yet to be spoken of. We mean the licentious, unprincipled and venal Press . . . which panders to depraved appetites, traffics in falsehood and calumny, speculates on dishonor, gloats over vice, and does its utmost to weaken the moral sense of the public and bring Law into contempt. Who will estimate the part which this branch of the newspaper Press has had in bringing about the Astor Place riots?

Slavery and the abolition movement were not as prominent in New York as in Boston, but the *Tribune* was losing no opportunity to denounce the one and bolster the other. Greeley was ready even then to consider disunion if necessary to get slavery out and thereby prevent its extension. In his eagerness to increase the opposition he went on the stump and spent much time at Washington trying to influence political pressure in Congress, exposing the tactics of the pro-slavery officials and politicians. He also went abroad for a time and during all his absence Dana was in control of the paper. It was in these years that the real editor was evolved, and evidence of his development is nowhere made more apparent than in Greeley's letters to his lieutenant.

There never could have been real sympathy between these two, even though they were in agreement on many of the great problems of the day. Dana was no less anti-slavery than his chief, but he was equally firm against secession. But it was in the more personal matters that there was a subtle antagonism. The exquisite young man could not but be offended at the manners and dress of the slovenly elder. Then the one was to a degree, at least, the product of college education, and convinced that the old-fashioned classical education, with Greek and Latin as its foundation, was indispensable to the making of the cultivated man; while the other had acquired what knowledge he possessed entirely through his own efforts and, as is often the case with the self-educated, was inclined to belittle the value of college training. As was not infrequently true then and even much later, college-bred men were the exception in newspaper offices, and even great editors had started as printers, what we now call compositors. These were inclined to sneer at the college graduate.

Later Dana said of Greeley: "He was a man of almost no education—indeed, of no education at all, except what he had acquired for himself. The worst school that a man can be sent to, and the worst of all for a man of genius, is what is called a self-education. There is no greater fortune for a man of extraordinary talent than to be thrown into contact with other youths in the conflicts of study and in the struggle for superiority in the school and in the college. That was denied to Mr. Greeley." As was always true of his public references to his former chief, Dana did not fail to give him credit for his great ability. "He knew no language but his own," he went on to say, "but of that he possessed the most extraordinary mastery. His wit and his humor flowed out in idiomatic forms of expression that were surprising and delightful, and that remained in the mind forever."

Just the same there was in Greeley the submerged resentment of the man of great talent who feels that the other chap has had advantages denied him. That book of quotations on Dana's desk may easily have been a constant provocative, with its inherent evidence of intimate acquaintance with the classics and fluency in the use of many languages, all practically a world unknown to the other. And it may well be that the younger man occasionally brought home to his chief this superiority in culture.

That he was inclined to indulge a sly humor at the expense of Greeley is indicated nowhere as fully as in the letters Greeley wrote him from Washington. As managing editor, with full control of what should and should not appear in the *Tribune*, it seems to be almost beyond doubt that Dana often thwarted the wishes of the absent chief. Somehow or other Greeley's own contributions would be suppressed. Sometimes it was the latter's fault, his negligent methods responsible for delays in mailing, but again it would be downright assertion of Dana's preference for some other topic. One can see Dana chuckling in advance with a sure premonition of the storm which will rage in Greeley when he sees the next day's paper, and the evidence of which will be made manifest in the opening words of Greeley's personal letter. "Dear Dana" and "Friend Dana" are contracted into just "Dana" or—subtly satirical—become "Fellow Citizen".

Poor man! He was having troubles enough of his own without being hamstrung in his own office. He was being threatened with personal violence, repeatedly confined to bed with illness, finding his pet aversions in politics triumphant, and here was that incorrigible Dana going his own headstrong way!

There was that damfool opera for instance. A musical critic named Fry had been allowed interminable space to argue the feasibility of maintaining opera in New York—despite the unsuccessful experiment with the Astor Place venture—thereby crowding out Greeley's own letter from Washington on matters of great political importance!

"What would it cost to burn the Opera House?" demanded Greeley. "If the price is reasonable have it done and send me the bill." Fry's whole "eleven columns of arguments", he declared, were based upon his conviction that success depended upon the playing of his (Fry's) compositions, and—"I don't believe three hundred people who take the *Tribune* care one chew of tobacco for the matter."

One of the "Fellow Citizen" letters ran thus:

> If you . . . allowed my letter on Hale's and Toombs's Kansas speeches . . . to be crowded out by the immortal scandal of the Griswold divorce case, why then you failed to consider fairly what is and what is not perishable. My letter would have been middling on Saturday while it will be sour as whey and flat as cold dish water on Monday; while the Griswold business would have been rolled as a sweet morsel under the tongues of all the old maids of New York any day you might see fit to print it. . . . Oh, my friend, the wisdom which teaches what should not be said, that is the hardest to acquire of all!

What pleading and what agony appear in these excerpts from various letters! "Now I write once more to entreat that I may be allowed to conduct *The Tribune* with reference to the mile wide that stretches either way from Pennsylvania Avenue. It is a small space, and you have all the

world beside." After repeated attacks upon his political
friends and allies: "I must give it up and go home. All the
Border Ruffians from here to the lowest pit could not start
me away, but you can do it, and I must give up. You are
getting everybody to curse me. I am too sick to be out of
bed, too crazy to sleep, and am surrounded by horrors."
Again: "Do send some one here and kill me if you cannot
stop this, for I can bear it no longer."

Some of the articles Dana permitted to be printed exacer-
bated Greeley's frazzled nerves. "I have labored many years
to give *The Tribune* a reputation for candor and generosity
toward unpopular creeds and races," he wrote, "and Stewart
(a brilliant but erratic contributor to the *Tribune*) will use
this up if you let him. It isn't one article on the Jews; he is
always slurring them, and this is not like *The Tribune*. I consider even his Irish articles, though partly true, impelled by
a bad spirit, and calculated to make us needless enemies.
Let us try to cultivate a generous spirit in all things."

There is no reason to believe that Dana was doing all
these things which irritated Greeley so intensely without
full knowledge of what they portended. Everything known
about him cries to the contrary. The fact was that the two
had entirely different theories of newspaper making. Greeley
stood for a plain, unvarnished opposition to all the vices
and an equally clear and unmistakable support of the virtues. No reader of his *Tribune* could for a moment be in
doubt as to the meaning of its policies. Powerful and force-
ful as were many of his editorials, bold and uncompromising
his attitude on many great problems of the day, there was
never any subtlety to give pause for thought or basis for
doubt. A simple, downright, homespun presentation, even
when clothed in eloquent phrases.

Dana, on the other hand, was beginning to use his own
wings and to make his flights after his own peculiar form
and manner. Out of his own consciousness he was evolving
the editorial attitude which gave substance and color to the
newspaper with which he finally became identified, and

which was based on far subtler reasoning and calculation than the simpler Greeley was capable of. Humor, keen and yet not too transparent—in truth, often sly and at times tinged with malice—had been discovered to be a far more potent weapon in the hands of him who knew how to use it than any other. With it had dawned the realization of the value of keeping the readers stimulated by occasionally jarring their equanimity. Whether it was the result of more prolonged experience in his profession, with its valuable instruction in the weaknesses of human nature, or whether it was by some other development of his psychological intuitions, he had come to the conclusion that the average mentality was too sunk in complacency and needed an occasional blow between the eyes to keep it interested.

Some years before the quoted letters from Greeley—in fact, only a year after his return from Europe—he expressed his conviction in a letter to James S. Pike, a prominent correspondent and later Minister to the Netherlands. Referring to a contribution from Pike to the *Tribune* he wrote that it had "stirred up the animals, which you as well as I recognize as one of the great ends of life". There was the philosophy which would be nailed to the mast of his ship of journalism throughout the rest of his career. A dangerous one for incompetents to handle and capable of much mischief when used by the unconscionable. Likewise obnoxious to such as dear old Horace, nor would it apply today when the need of commanding immense circulations in order to achieve financial success rules out all subtle methods of approach. But it worked splendidly in all the days when Dana's *Sun* shone in the journalistic skies.

VIII.
SLAVERY AND SECESSION TAKE FIRST PLACE IN NEWSPAPER DISCUSSION—DANA FORCES GREELEY TO COME OUT AGAINST REBELLION—GREELEY DISCHARGES DANA.

DANA had become a stockholder in the _Tribune._ In a letter to Pike suggesting that he do likewise, and become a regular contributor to the paper, he laid bare the secrets of ownership and salaries paid to the principals. "We regular stagers don't get very large salaries in proportion to our remarkable merits. Greeley has fifty dollars a week; Snow, thirty dollars; I, twenty-five dollars; Taylor, twenty dollars; Cleveland, sixteen; Ripley, fifteen. All these fellows are proprietors."

Altogether the _Tribune_ stock consisted of one hundred shares and at this time Greeley owned twenty-five and Dana five. He had contracted to buy five more and said he stood ready to invest fifty thousand dollars for additional shares. How he had secured his capital for investment and from what source he expected the further sums he spoke of investing was never made clear, but it has always been easier to get loans for investment in going newspapers than for any other kind of enterprise. Not from banks, of course, but from capitalists who do not apply cut and dried rules to all their ventures. The same type of Maecenas that stood patron to a Beethoven in earlier days has always been ready to back a worth-while journalist, and perhaps never more so than in Dana's time. There was no hidden incentive, necessarily, though doubtless it did exist in some instances.

There was a playful tone in Dana's correspondence with Pike which was evidently habitual in his communications with all the contributors and which had a value in the making of loyalties which can hardly be estimated. It was a habit which extended over into later years with excellent results.

"Greatest and Best of Pikes," he begins. Along in the heart of his letter comes, "First and foremost, a thousand thanks for your articles. . . . They were great and good." Greeley was about to leave for Europe and he would be glad to have Pike's valuable assistance. "I hope you'll send me a rocket occasionally during the summer to flash up in our sky and save the country, not to speak of saving me from making a stupid paper. You see it must be better than when the Old Man is home, or they'll say Dana's a failure, which God forbid!"

Later on came another appeal: "KEENEST OF PIKES: What a desert void of news you keep at Washington! For goodness' sake, kick up a row of some sort. Fight a duel, defraud the Treasury, set fire to the fueling-mill, get Black Dan (Daniel Webster) drunk, or commit some other excess that will make a stir."

Dana had been doing very well when the panic of '57 fell upon the land. His industry was remarkable. In addition to his work for the paper he had compiled *The Household Book of Poetry*, for many years the best collection of the minor poems in the English language; had produced, with the aid of Ripley and a few others, *The American Cyclopoedia*, and never neglected his book of quotations. His income from the outside ventures had been gratifying, while his salary on the *Tribune* had been increased to forty dollars a week, and his share of the profits had been mounting. It had meant denying himself the pleasure of relaxation with the growing family, but he was building for the future. When the panic came he wrote William Henry Huntington, an old friend and also a *Tribune* correspondent at Paris:

> Last year I had eight thousand dollars income. Now I have my salary of forty dollars a week, and no great hopes of more. Of the first volume of the *Cyclopoedia* we are printing an edition of one thousand instead of

ten thousand, which we should have done. It promises well, however, for ultimate profit, and I believe will be recognized as a good book by the critics. *The Household Book of Poetry*, which should have paid me one thousand dollars in January, lies sound asleep in the hope of a blessed resurrection.

Still his buoyancy was not affected. "But we don't cry about it," he went on. "That is, I and the wife and the babies; but keep on having as jolly a time as ever, even without the luxuries of other days." His family life always meant a lot to him. He had previously written to Pike: "I have been busy going to Westport (Connecticut) to see my children—driving them about in old Bradley's one-horse wagon, rowing and sailing with them on the bay and Sound, gathering shells on the shore with them, picking cherries, lounging on the grass, gazing into the sky with the whole tribe about me! There's no delight like that in a pack of children—of your own. Love is selfish, friendship is exacting, but this other affection gives all and asks nothing. The man who hasn't half a dozen young children about him must have a very mean conception of life. Besides, there ought always be a baby in every house. A house without a baby is inhuman."

A many-sided man this, with moments of splendid exaggeration, but from other sources we know that his home life was uncommonly beautiful. Earlier there has been reference to his inability to read by artificial light, which meant that he had to be read to when the dark arrived. First his wife and later, as they grew up, the children read aloud to him, and there are descriptions of the family circle listening intently, with its head interrupting to illuminate obscure passages and to add from his own rich store of knowledge to the wit or wisdom of the author. For the listeners these interludes were the most enjoyable features of the readings.

In the meantime his editorial education was proceeding. The association with Greeley helped in many ways. For one thing Greeley was always in hot water, which meant plenty of fighting. Greeley was a good fighter, but apt to weaken when pushed hard, and one of the lessons Dana learned from watching his campaigns was that there must be no surrender, victory often arriving when defeat seemed certain. Reiteration, the most powerful weapon in the journalistic arsenal, might almost be said to have been Dana's invention. The constant repetition of some telling epithet or phrase, until it became almost maddening to those to whom it was applied, and a provoker of laughs—or anger, if it was meant to be that—to the general reader, was probably the most valuable contribution brought to the *Tribune*, but its possibilities were not realized until its inventor was free to use it without let or hindrance.

More than once the older editor was annoyed by the tenacity with which the younger clung to an issue. Once in a mêlée, he could not be stopped and, where Greeley was ready to compromise, his managing editor was only girding on his armor for a new assault. "Charge Dana not to slaughter anybody," Greeley wrote, "but be mild and meek-souled like me."

But there wasn't a chance of it. Mild and kindly enough where his opposition was not aroused, one could never think of Dana and meekness in partnership. He and Greeley could drag along together fairly well until it came to something fundamental and then wild horses could not restrain the younger and more virile. The test came with the appearance of Lincoln in the political arena, and the dramatic consequences of his being chosen the leader of the Republican party. More and more Greeley had been sounding the changes on the keynote of secession.

> The union of these States is in its nature irrevocable and only the earthquake of revolution can shiver it. Still we say, in all earnestness and good faith, whenever a whole section of this Republic—whether a half, a third, or only a fourth—shall truly desire and demand a separation from the residue, we shall earnestly favor such separation. If the fifteen slave states, or

even the eight cotton states alone, shall quietly, decisively say to the rest, "We prefer to be henceforth separate from you," we shall insist that they be permitted to go in peace. War is a hideous necessity at best—and a civil conflict, a war of estranged and embittered countrymen—is the most hideous of all wars.

If the Union be really oppressive or unjust to the South—nay, if the South really believes it so—we insist that a decent self-respect should impel the North to say, "We think you utterly mistaken, but you have the right to judge for yourselves; so go if you will."

Repeatedly this same view was expressed and emphasized, seemingly contradicting what Dana had written just prior to the election of 1860:

The Union . . . is a rock upon which thousands may make shipwreck of their own hopes, fortunes and even lives, but which will itself be unaffected by their criminal madness. Parties will rise and fall, factions may rave and cabals plot; but Saratoga and Yorktown are parts of our common country and so will remain forever.

Apparently Dana had been squelched by his superior, but the end was not yet. Greeley was away the following January, whether by design or not, when this appeared:

Stand firm! No compromise; no surrender of principle! No cowardly reversal of the great verdict of the sixth of November. Let us have the question of questions settled now and for all time! There can never be another opportunity so good as the present. Let us know once and for all whether the slave power is really stronger than the Union. Let us have it decided whether the Mexican system of rebellion can be successfully introduced in this country as a means of carrying an election after it has been fairly lost at the polls. It will be time enough to talk of redressing grievances of long standing and of minor consequences after this startling novelty has been disposed of. . . .

The *Tribune* had now a circulation through its weekly edition of over two hundred thousand and was a force to be reckoned with. It had been fighting slavery for years, had denounced the fugitive slave law and the Dred Scott decision, had waged a tremendous campaign to make Kansas and Nebraska free states and, merely as a matter of sound journalism, Greeley was definitely in the wrong. To permit secession was merely shifting responsibility. Slavery would be fastened indefinitely in the seceding states and the growing forces of opposition outside would be powerless forever after. It is not at all unlikely that letters to the paper about this time were hot reading for the weak-kneed editor. At all events there was a complete face-about after the firing on Fort Sumter.

> We are at war [thundered the *Tribune*]. Let us cease mere fending off and strike home. . . . There has been a good deal of discussion of the propriety of allowing the "Southern States" to separate themselves from the Union and set up an independent slave-holding government for themselves. But in the face of the glorious, the sublime uprising of the unanimous and devoted people, this idea has become obsolete. . . . The business of this nation to-day is the annihilation of rebellion and the preservation of the national integrity. . . . That this end will be attained through perils, sacrifices, discouragements, disasters even, we know; but it will secure a noble heritage of peace and prosperity to our country and our children. Through the Red Sea, not around it, lies the appointed way to the Land of Promise. . . .

Whether or not Greeley approved this fighting editorial, the keynote had been sounded and there was no retreat, but in May appeared a stirring demand for a move upon the rebel capital which paved the way for a definite rupture between the commander-in-chief and his first aid.

"Forward to Richmond! Forward to Richmond!" thundered the *Tribune,* and repeated the same demand day after day. The congress of the rebels must not be allowed to meet at its chosen site on its chosen date. The army of the Union must prevent it.

The author was Fitz-Henry Warren, a regular contributor, later a Major-General, but it was Dana who inserted it and was responsible for the reiteration. Greeley took full responsibility over his own signature after the defeat suffered at Bull Run, but at the same time let it be known he was neither the author nor had approved of the resounding phrase. "Henceforth I bar all criticism in these columns on army movements," he declared.

In spite of this, which might be regarded as in the nature of a public reproof, the two worked on together as previously, sometimes in full accord and sometimes in flat opposition on the policies of the war, but with no sign of personal disagreement. Then, without warning, Dana was informed that his services were no longer required.

In his *Recollections of the Civil War* Dana gave this account of his dismissal: "I had been associated with Horace Greeley . . . for about fifteen years when, one morning early in April, 1862, Mr. Sinclair, the advertising manager of the paper, came to me, saying that Mr. Greeley would be glad to have me resign. I asked one of my associates to find from Mr. Greeley if that was really his wish. In a few hours he came to me saying that I had better go. I stayed the day out in order to make up the paper and give them an opportunity to find a successor, but I never went into the office after that. I think I then owned a fifth of the paper—twenty shares; this stock my colleagues bought. Mr. Greeley never gave a reason for dismissing me, nor did I ever ask one. I know, though, that the real explanation was that while he was for peace I was for war, and that as long as I stayed on the *Tribune* there was a spirit there which was not his spirit—that he did not like."

This was penned a quarter of a century after the event. It varies slightly from the account he wrote his friend Huntington a fortnight after it:

On Thursday, March 27th, I was notified that Mr. Greeley had given the stockholders notice that I must leave, or he would, and that they wanted me to leave accordingly. No cause of dissatisfaction being alleged, and H. G. having been of late more confidential and friendly than ever, not once having said anything betokening disaffection to me, I sent a friend to him to ascertain if it was true, or if some misunderstanding was at the bottom of it. My friend came and reported it was true, and that H. G. was immovable. On Friday, March 28th, I resigned, and the trustees at once accepted it, passing highly complimentary resolutions, and voting me six months' salary after the date of my resignation. . . . On Saturday, March 29th, Mr. Greeley came down, called another meeting of the trustees, said he had never desired me to leave, that it was a "damned lie" that he had presented such an alternative as that he or I must go, and finally sent me a verbal message desiring me to remain as a writer of editorials; but has never been near me since to meet the "damned lie" in person, nor written one word on the subject. I conclude, accordingly, that he is glad to have me out, and that he really set on foot the secret cabal by which it was accomplished. And as soon as I get my pay for my shares (ten thousand dollars less than I could have got for them a year ago), I shall be content. Mr. Greeley himself resumes the active management of the paper, and I am left to begin the world anew.

Adrift at forty-three, with a sizable family and limited funds, in an upset world, was no pleasing prospect. It might well have dismayed better than an average man. Yet it was most fortunate in the light of subsequent events. Had he remained on the *Tribune* it is probable Dana would have succeeded Greeley in command when the latter succumbed. The *Tribune* would have prospered under his management, and it would have remained a great newspaper. But it would still have been the *Tribune*, and the world would never have known the *Sun* of Charles A. Dana.

Even a great editor cannot overcome the tremendous

inertia of a well-established, successful newspaper, with recognized policies, habits and traditions, and convert it into a reflection of his own personality. The character and nature of the *Tribune*, thoroughly defined both to its readers and to the workers in its vineyard, were what is known in the business world as its good will and could be deflected only at great risk as well as trouble. Many a good newspaper has gone to the scrap heap because its new controllers could not realize that the character of a paper is vital, its tap root, which may be nourished, improved in quality, strengthened and forced to new growth, whereby new branches will come into being and the foliage become more dense and vivid, but that it will not submit to the grafting thereon of something at variance with the old stock.

Then Dana himself was not yet altogether ripe for his real life's work. He certainly would be the better for the rough, disillusioning experiences which destiny had in store for him. In the hard school he was about to enter he would see human nature in the most trying of all crucibles, where the noblest idealism and the most sordid meanness would rise to the surface, and where the soul of man would bare its most intimate secrets. The professor of Brook Farm, the family man of Westport, the pundit of the editorial sanctum was about to become part of the great adventure of the war itself.

IX. CONTACTS WITH STANTON, SECRETARY OF WAR—A REPORTER FOR THE UNITED STATES GOVERNMENT, ASSIGNED TO "COVER" GENERAL GRANT.

SEVERAL efforts to deflect him came to naught. One was a suggestion from Washington that he might have a diplomatic position, but to be abroad with the war raging at home was unthinkable. Then came a proposal from the Treasury Department that he buy cotton in occupied portions of the South and bring it North, where it could help fill the demand in our mills or in the market, which was besieged by England's cotton importers, cut off from their usual supplies by the Union blockade of southern ports. But he put both of these aside and went to Stanton.

The new Secretary of War had reason to welcome this recruit. One of the most impressive editorials written by Dana for the *Tribune* had been a glowing tribute to Stanton's patriotism and ability. It had been more than that, for it had made clear the state of semi-treason existing in the Department itself and in the society of Washington and Baltimore. Subtle phrases here and there indicated that the rod was in pickle for the traitors:

"Edwin M. Stanton yesterday entered upon the full discharge of his official responsibilities as Secretary of War, and was formally presented to all the military officers in Washington—*the number having been considerably larger than it will be a few days hence.*"

Officers and clerks in the War Department who declared their purpose to resign whenever "the war for the Union is perverted into a war upon slavery" were put upon notice that this Secretary would make short shift of the treason that "skulks within our own lines". Warning was also served upon the society of Washington and Baltimore which "have been from the outset nests of treason so rampant and

intense that it has never condescended to disguise its animus
and scarcely its complicity with the avowed and militant
rebels." Conspiracy lurked "in many if not the most of the
houses of patrician traitors" in Baltimore, and the Secretary must be prepared for the "spitting, face-making and
other feline demonstrations of rage and spite with which
their ladies salute the Union officers stationed among them".
Rotten supplies had been sent to the front, orders from the
War Department betrayed, officials were guilty of pecula-
tions. In a thundering wind up the *Tribune* had called for
rawhide and rope for the purveyors of spoiled food, and
others to be hanged or shot; drum head court martials and
fifteen minutes to prepare!

Stanton had promptly expressed his appreciation in a personal letter in which he said that the facts mentioned by
Dana were new to him but that he proposed to correct them
speedily.

"As soon as I can get the machinery of the office working, the rats cleared out, and the rat holes stopped we shall
move. This army has got to fight or run away; and while
men are striving nobly in the West, the champagne and
oysters on the Potomac must be stopped. But patience for
a short while only is all I ask, if you and others like you
will rally around me."

In his enthusiasm for the new spirit created by Stanton,
Dana continued to write in praise until the Secretary feared
that the officers responsible for the victories in the West
might feel that they were not receiving their share of approval, and Stanton was impelled to write a letter disclaim-
ing any credit for them:

> The glory of our recent victories belongs to the gal-
> lant officers and soldiers that fought the battles. No
> share of it belongs to me. Much has recently been said
> of military combinations and organizing victory. I
> hear such phrases with apprehension. They commenced
> in infidel France with the Italian campaign, and re-
> sulted in Waterloo. Who can organize victory? Who

can combine the elements of success on the battlefield?
. . . What, under the blessing of Providence, I conceive to be the true organization of victory and military combination to end this war, was declared in a few
words by General Grant's message to General Buckner:
"I propose to move immediately on your works."

Immediately upon receipt of this Dana wired the *Tribune's* Washington correspondent to wait upon Stanton and
ask him whether he meant to "repudiate the *Tribune*?" The
same sensitiveness which was to influence later on his relations with other public men—sometimes with ill results to
himself—caused him to misconstrue Stanton's purpose.
Fortunately the latter promptly wrote again, explaining sat-
isfactorily, and suggesting that the first letter should not be
published, "as it might imply an antagonism between myself
and the *Tribune*". Thoroughly disarmed, Dana published
the original without comment. If anything, the relations between the two had been improved by this incident, demonstrating as it did that both could show the magnanimous
spirit on occasion.

<u>Dana's first work for the War Department was as a
member of a commission to audit the claims made at Cairo,
Illinois.</u> There had been charges of gross frauds in these
claims which amounted to more than half a million dollars.
The commission disallowed about a third, but mostly because of error or because the claimants were shown to be
supporters of the rebels.

"There was a great deal of curiosity among officers in
Washington about the result of our investigation," Dana
wrote, "and all the time that I was in the city I was being
questioned on the subject. It was natural enough that they
should have felt interested in our report. The charges of
fraud and corruption against officers and contractors had
become so reckless and general that the mere sight of a man
in conference with a high official led to the suspicion and
often the charge that he was conspiring against the Government. That in this case, where the charges seemed so well-

based, so small a percentage of corruption had been proved was a source of solid satisfaction to everyone in the War Department."

While waiting for his report to be received he met General Grant at a dinner at Memphis. He found the General a man of "simple manners, straightforward and unpretending". Victor at Fort Donelson and Shiloh, he was nevertheless rather under a cloud, his opponents having spread the report that he would have been defeated at Shiloh had not Buell appeared, an assertion hotly denied by the staff officers with whom Dana spoke at this time.

It looked as though Dana was to continue in the Department, evidence that his first assignment had pleased. He had returned to New York and was occupied with personal affairs when he received a telegram asking him to report to Stanton. This time he was offered the post of Assistant Secretary of War and accepted. Unfortunately he was indiscreet enough to mention the fact to a newspaper friend, and it got into the New York papers the next morning—before official announcement had been made. Stanton promptly withdrew the appointment. In his book Dana made a bald statement of the fact, but it is not likely that the matter ended so simply. Still they must have parted amicably, for not long thereafter Stanton gave him letters to various commanding officers, commending him to their courtesy, as he was about to embark in the business of purchasing cotton on his own account for Northern consumption, his partners being Roscoe Conkling and George W. Chadwick. The undertaking was of short duration. In less than three weeks Dana wrote Stanton from Memphis suggesting that no private purchaser of cotton should be allowed in the occupied regions, but that the purchases should be by the army quartermasters at a fixed price, to be resold at public auction in designated cities outside the lines. His desire to make a fortune had been overcome by what he had seen.

"The mania for sudden fortunes," he wrote Stanton,

"has to an alarming extent corrupted and demoralized the army. Every colonel, captain or quartermaster is in secret partnership with some operator in cotton; every soldier dreams of adding a bale of cotton to his monthly pay."

He modified his imputation of corruption on the part of the army after a talk with Grant, but this was not altogether whole-hearted. From other sources there has been substantiation of the assertion that some of the officers, at least, were not above making a profit at this time. The temptation must have been tremendous, and consciences were probably salved by the fact that the Government was favorable to the securing of the cotton.

As soon as he could get away Dana went to Washington, where he discussed the subject with both Lincoln and Stanton, and enlarged upon his plan to have the Government take control, pointing out that the profits would far exceed the cost, and have the further desirable result of cutting down the returns to the rebel producers. The result was the issue of a proclamation by the President prohibiting all commercial intercourse with the rebels, except under the regulations prescribed by the Secretary of the Treasury, and, though this was evaded to some extent throughout the war, the situation was greatly improved.

Not long thereafter he was back in the War Department. Stanton wanted him to go to Grant and report on the latter's conduct, so that Stanton and the President might "settle their minds as to Grant, about whom there were many doubts". In a personal letter Stanton wrote that "having explained the purposes of your appointment to you personally, no further instructions will be given unless specially required". A formal document notified the army paymasters that he had been appointed "Special Commissioner of the War Department to investigate and report upon the condition of the pay service in the Western armies", and called upon them to furnish information upon any matters "as fully and completely and promptly as if directly called for by the Secretary of War". To the generals everywhere this letter of instruction made clear his authority:

> General: Charles A. Dana, Esq., has been appointed a special commissioner of this department to investigate and report upon the condition of the pay service in the Western armies. You will please aid him in the performance of his duties, and communicate to him fully your views and wishes in respect to that branch of the service in your command, and also give to him such information as you may deem beneficial to the service. He is especially commended to your courtesy and protection.

So he was back at his old job, the job which to every worth-while newspaper man is the most intriguing, and which many a great editor looks back to with regret; once more he was a reporter, an investigator, a prober into dark corners, only now his employer was the United States. He was to be the eyes and to a certain extent the brains of his country. His loyalty must be to the Nation, which made the assignment far more difficult than if it had been to a newspaper.

Reporters are after all like other men. With due devotion to their papers they may still exercise human emotions. Many an interviewer has softened the asperities which might fairly have been drawn from his contacts with the interviewed. More often than the outside world imagines the reporter has saved reputations by suppressing the inanities and gaucheries he was invited to publish. Many great men have thus been rescued, for even superior intellects are only rarely gifted with the instinct for visualizing the spoken word in print. The understanding reporter has it, and out of sympathy and pity he is moved now and then to omit what would make a good story. No doubt Dana had passed up many such opportunities in his contacts with the statesmen and the warriors of France and Germany.

But now there could be no suppressions. The future of the country was at stake, and much might depend upon the completeness of his report. The nation had been sadly injured by the failure of those in control to understand the failings of a supposedly great general in the East. Battles had been lost, thousands of soldiers killed and wounded, the war prolonged because McClellan had been retained in command. It was the realization of this that had prompted Dana's appointment. It was up to him to be the eyes of Lincoln and of Stanton, to use his best judgment and discretion in selecting for report of the actions of Grant whatever might help to make a true and significant portrait. He must be alert, penetrating, cold-blooded and yet entirely fair. Personal predilection or dislike must be ruthlessly suppressed. The treatment he received must not be permitted to weigh as much as a fledgling's feather in the balance. It was as important to discover latent virtues as to detect hidden faults, to make clear that Grant was the man of the hour—if he was that—as to show that there was real basis for the charges made by Grant's detractors, should that appear. He could not for a moment forget he was the agent of a nation in agony. It was an assignment to try the soul and the nerves of any man big enough to understand all its implications.

Both Lincoln and Stanton must have pondered deeply before making their selection, and the event proved they had made no mistake. With all his enthusiasms, proneness to like much or detest intensely, Dana invariably showed a cool head in whatever he undertook. Quick to perceive the heart of a problem, his brain and not his nerves took command in reaching for it.

It was so now. Coolly and calmly he mapped out his program. A special cipher was created which should thwart the spies in the War Department as well as the enemy and the curious outside. It was Dana's own invention and it was good enough to last unchanged through the war; only once, so far as was ever known, was it penetrated. Then he started for Memphis, going by way of Cairo and Columbus. Memphis proving unsatisfactory for his purposes, he was presently on the way to Milliken's Bend, where Grant had his headquarters.

X. THE CAMPAIGN BEFORE VICKSBURG—DANA COMPILES A PORTRAIT GALLERY OF THE LEADING OFFICERS FOR LINCOLN AND STANTON—WRITES HIS LITTLE GIRL DESCRIPTIONS OF THE LIFE IN CAMP.

GEN. JAMES HARRISON WILSON, who wrote a life of Dana twenty years ago, is authority for the assertion that Dana's real mission was known by the members of Grant's staff even before his arrival, which indicates how little chance there was of keeping any secret in the War Department. In fact, Wilson, who was then Inspector General of Grant's army, and Adjutant General Rawlins, who was not only chief of staff but also Grant's closest personal friend and most efficient adviser, met together in solemn session to discuss what should be done about it. There had been rumors that Dana had absolute authority to remove Grant. Whether or no, the General's fate would depend upon the character of Dana's reports. Should they extend to this potential enemy the velvet hand, or ——

It was finally decided to place all the cards on the table. He was to have access to everything, favorable and unfavorable, official or personal. Dana was not unknown to them by reputation and they were convinced there was neither wisdom nor value in trying to keep him in ignorance of anything. With plenty of enemies about to bring to him both truth and exaggerations, the worst tactics would be to arouse his suspicion by attempted concealment. A wise decision and fully endorsed by Grant.

Dana relieved the tenseness by the same attitude of frankness. After all, he had nothing to conceal. He was there to report, not to create trouble. If they were on their jobs, and showed the ability expected of them, Washington would hear of it with celerity and due emphasis. If they were wanting, that too would go forward, but they could not blame him for their defects. They alone were the architects of their own fortunes. What they could rely upon was fair and even generous construction of every act performed in the spirit of loyalty. In fact, Dana was soon convinced that he was dealing with men of ability and entire devotion to their duty, and that of none was this truer than of Grant himself.

Their relations were cordial from the beginning, when Grant with the utmost frankness made clear to him his campaign against Vicksburg, with its ultimate object of opening the Mississippi. Once satisfied that he was the right man in the right place, and that his detractors were unjustified in their allegations, Dana settled down into a state of patient watchfulness, alert for the opportunity to inform his superiors of anything which called for their attention, but at the same time permitting himself to appreciate his new surroundings and contacts.

There was plenty to impress one so avid of new sensations and new experiences. Here he was in the midst of great undertakings, whose results must have far-reaching consequences, with his fingers on the very pulse of every operation. The intimate of the creators and doers, and himself no inconsequential figure. Early he became convinced that Grant was mistaken in entrusting to General McClernand the attack on Grand Gulf, preliminary to Grant's bringing his army across the Mississippi from New Carthage. General Sherman, Admiral Porter and other leading officers were of the opinion that McClernand was not equal to it. But Grant would not budge. To Dana he said that McClernand was the senior officer, that he had supported the plan with enthusiasm when Sherman had been doubtful and critical, and that his corps occupied a position which made the advance naturally fall to it. Finally, and here was an argument which would have stilled further discussion from most men, McClernand was a special favorite of the President, who had known him for some time and believed in him.

Nothing could be more typical of Dana than to disregard this warning. Satisfied that McClernand was unreliable, opposition only increased his zeal, and promptly after his interview with Grant a dispatch went forward to Stanton, detailing all the circumstances and concluding with the following:

"I have remonstrated so far as I could properly do so against intrusting so momentous an operation to McClernand."

But Stanton agreed with Grant, for back came this reply:

"Allow me to suggest that you carefully avoid giving any advice in respect to commands that may be assigned, as it may lead to misunderstanding and troublesome complications."

Dana accepted the rebuke and refrained thereafter from offering suggestions, but he had the satisfaction—if such it was—of seeing his warning justified. With everybody else moving according to plan, McClernand failed to coöperate. His corps was not ready at the crucial moment, and, in flat opposition to orders, he was arranging to take his bride and her servants along with him. The afternoon preceding the night chosen for his attack he was reviewing a brigade of troops from his state, accompanied by artillery salute, in defiance of Grant's order that no ammunition be used for any purpose except firing against the enemy. In the end the plan was changed, as the gunboats found it impossible to silence all the batteries at Grand Gulf.

Dana was in the midst of everything, often accompanying Grant, and even amid all the excitement of night marches, of watching the boats floating down the Mississippi past the batteries of Vicksburg, of the fighting between the batteries of the rebels and the gunboats, his interest in the personality of the commander kept him watchful of every significant act. One pitchdark night, as they were riding together, he saw the General's horse give a nasty stumble. He expected to see him go over the horse's head, as the movement was so unexpected.

"I watched intently," he records, "not to see if he was hurt, but if he would show any anger." He was especially curious about Grant's self-control because in the three weeks of daily intimacy he had never once seen any exhibition of temper. "His equanimity was becoming a curious spectacle to me. When I saw his horse lunge my first thought was, 'Now he will swear.' For an instant his moral status was on trial; but Grant was a tenacious horseman, and instead of going over the animal's head, as I imagined he would, he kept his seat. Pulling up his horse, he rode on, and, to my utter amazement, without a word or sign of impatience." At the end of the war, although he had seen him in many crises and trying moments, he had still failed to hear Grant swear.

Nor did he find him without sense of humor. At Port Gibson Dana found himself with only an old farm horse to ride, having in fact been forced to struggle along on foot for quite a distance, after separating from Grant. One day a Confederate officer was brought before Grant. With him had been captured a very good horse. Said the prisoner:

"General, this horse and saddle are my private property; they do not belong to the Confederate army; they belong to me as a citizen, and I trust you will let me have them. Of course, while I am a prisoner I do not expect to be allowed to ride the horse, but I hope you will regard him as my property, and finally restore him to me."

"Well," Grant replied, "I have got four or five first-rate horses wandering somewhere about the Southern Confederacy. They have been captured from me in battle or by spies. I will authorize you, whenever you find one of them, to take possession of him. I cheerfully give him to you; but as for this horse, I think he is just about the horse Mr. Dana needs."

According to Wilson, Grant was greatly impressed with Dana. The latter's breadth of knowledge and, more particularly, his ability to converse fluently with every foreign-speaking soldier with whom he came in contact, was a source of never-ending wonder to the general. One day Grant introduced Dana to a Seneca Indian, who was a member of his staff, and Dana promptly addressed the Indian in his own tongue, which happened to be identical with that the former had learned while clerking at Buffalo. The conversation was long and animated, the Indian being naturally delighted to find one with whom he could talk freely. Grant never quite got over that surprise and recurred to it frequently in commenting on Dana's remarkable mentality.

Apparently all the important officers took to the War Department's agent, and the latter found many among them for whom he developed both liking and admiration. For Sherman especially he had at once a warm regard.

"Sherman impressed me as a man of genius and of the widest intellectual acquisitions," he recorded.

Wilson set down this impression of Dana:

> In the full vigor of life, an excellent horseman and athlete, entirely without timidity or fear, he was a helpful and encouraging influence upon all with whom he came in contact, and with no one more than with General Grant, who adopted towards him the most friendly and cordial manner and seemed to take special pleasure in his company both in camp and on the march. In fact, Dana was in a certain sense a revelation to Grant as well as to those of us who were younger. He was not only genial and unaffected and sympathetic in his manners, but far and away the best educated and most widely informed man that any of us had up to that time ever met.

And all the time he was taking note of things as well as men with the apprehension of the trained journalist, to whom the seemingly insignificant is often more pregnant and of greater import than that which fills the eye of the superficial observer. Books being no longer at hand from which to cull the wisdom of the sages, he was storing up what was worth remembering from his contacts with men and his environment. The poet in him was keenly awake to the beauty of his surroundings.

"Grant's big army was stretched up and down the river bank over the plantation," he noted before they had left Milliken's Bend, "its white tents affording a new decoration to the natural magnificence of the broad plains. These plains, which stretch far back from the river, were divided into rich and old plantations by blooming hedges of rose and Osage orange, the mansions of the owners being inclosed in roses, myrtles, magnolias, oaks, and every other sort of beautiful and noble trees."

One night he and one of the staff officers were guests at a stately mansion over which presided a typical Southern lady who did not carry her partisanship into personal relations with the enemy whom the fortunes of war had forced upon her hospitality. Her cook had a reputation even among the aristocrats of the vicinage, and the dinner to which her guests sat down was something not soon forgotten by one of them, at least.

There were other details to impress the journalist. The luxury and charm of this beautiful home were only typical of all the great surrounding properties, for here were rich and fruitful lands and abundant slaves. The owners lived like feudal lords, and actually bore titles taken from their enormous estates. In contrast was the condition of the human chattels, and Dana went away more confirmed than ever in his hatred of slavery and all its trappings.

To one of his children he painted this picture of his life in camp:

All of a sudden it is very cold here. Two days ago it was hot like summer, but now I sit in my tent in my overcoat, writing, and thinking if I were only home instead of being almost two thousand miles away. Away yonder, in the edge of the woods, I hear the drum-beat that calls the soldiers to their supper. It is only a little after five o'clock, but they begin the day very early and end it early. Pretty soon after dark they are all asleep, lying in their blankets under the trees, for in a quick march they leave their tents behind. Their guns are all ready at their sides, so that if they are suddenly called at night they can start in a moment. It is strange in the morning before daylight to hear the bugle and drums sound the reveille, which calls the army to wake up. It will begin perhaps at a distance and then run along the whole line, bugle after bugle and drum after drum taking it up, and then it goes from front to rear, farther and farther away, the sweet sounds throbbing and rolling while you lie on the grass with your saddle for a pillow, half awake, or opening your eyes to see that the stars are all bright in the sky, or that there is only a faint flush in the east, where the day is soon to break.

Living in camp is queer business. I get my meals in General Grant's mess and pay my share of the expenses. The table is a chest with a double cover, which unfolds on the right and on the left; the dishes, knives and forks, and casters are inside. Sometimes we get good things, but generally we don't. The cook is an old Negro, black and grimy. The cooking is not as clean as it might be, but in war you can't be particular about such things.

The plums and peaches here are pretty nearly ripe. The strawberries have been ripe these few days, but the soldiers eat them up before we get a sight of them. The figs are as big as the end of your thumb, and the green pears are big enough to eat. But you don't know what beautiful flower gardens there are here. I never saw such roses; and the other day I found a lily as big as a tiger lily, only it was a magnificent red.

He saw the army brought across the Mississippi, witnessed the penetration of the enemy country, with its consequent cutting off of communication with the North as well as with supplies. Grant had boldly decided to live off the country while he closed in on Vicksburg and threatened the State capital. For ten days Dana could not get a dispatch through to Stanton.

Life was not nearly so comfortable as he had described it to his child. Many nights he was sleeping on the ground in the rain after being all day in the saddle, and it was a luxurious experience to have the refuge of a church, with the Bible from the pulpit for his pillow. Along with Grant and his staff he had left behind everything not absolutely essential, limiting his personal baggage to his tooth brush, and using the space in his saddle-bags, as they did, for food, to guard against possible scarcity. But never was he more enthusiastic for the cause, and in a letter to his friend Huntington he wrote:

> It may be that the future will justify you, Greeley, Gen. Scott and John Van Buren in your idea of "letting the wayward sisters go". But I judge that it will be long before the body of the American people will adopt that notion. The strongest sentiment of this people is that for the preservation of the territorial and political integrity of the nation at all costs, and no matter how long it takes. In other words, they prefer to keep up the existing war a little longer, rather than to make arrangements for indefinite wars hereafter, and for other disruptions. Let us have it out now and settle forever the question, so that our children may be able to attend to other matters.

In his eagerness to see success he permitted his ardor to again overcome discretion in his comments on the conduct of McClernand, only now they bore welcome fruit. In a letter dated May 5, 1863, and signed by Stanton, appeared the following:

> General Grant has full and absolute authority to enforce his own commands, and to remove any person who, by ignorance, inaction, or any cause, interferes with or delays his operations. He has the full confidence of the government, is expected to enforce his authority, and will be firmly and heartily supported, but he will be responsible for any failure to exert his powers. You may communicate this to him.

Lincoln had finally become convinced. It may be imagined that not even Grant was more gratified with this message than was the man who bore it to him as promptly as possible.

With communications reopened Dana sent frequent dispatches, outlining the movements of the campaign and Grant's plans for the immediate future. It had been necessary to make changes repeatedly as unexpected obstacles were revealed, more particularly in the character of the ground and the various waterways which had been thought practicable. But Grant was making personal surveys and meeting each situation as it arose, devising new plans as rapidly as the old proved unpractical, never baffled or failing in invention.

Dana was now constantly at his side and able to report the glorious victories which enabled the army to move forward to its various objectives. Alert for straws to tell the wind he saw what seemed even then to foretell the end. In the entire territory through which they were passing there were no men capable of bearing arms, only old men or children. The half million in the Southern army, ten per cent of the entire white population, had drained the country of its fighting youth. Soon there would be an end to what could be drawn on for soldiers. That this was realized among them was shown by the appearance of men who had sympathized with the rebellion, even some who had fought for it, and who now were ready to lend their aid to Grant in order to finish the war as soon as possible, and thus avoid the total ruin of the South.

"Slavery is gone," Dana quoted them as saying, "other property is mainly gone, but, for God's sake, let us save some relic of our former means of living."

Jackson had been taken and Grant turned back to face Pemberton coming out from Vicksburg under orders to attack the Union army. Dana was present both at the taking of Champion's Hill, where Pemberton occupied a formidable position, and the following day at the battle at the bridge of the Big Black, where the Confederates met an-

Stanton and Chase in Session with President Lincoln. Under the First, Dana Served as Assistant Secretary of War.

(*From the Painting by Frank B. Carpenter.*)

other defeat and burned the bridge to cover their retreat into Vicksburg.

Grant had four new bridges constructed the same night and within twenty-four hours the town was so thoroughly invested that Dana felt justified in predicting in his dispatch to Stanton that it would be taken that day. He was mistaken. The assault he had anticipated was not delivered until two days later and then it was repulsed, though without heavy loss. It remained for McClernand to cause a more serious mishap through misleading reports. Asking for reenforcements, he asserted that he was in possession of two of the enemy forts. Believing this to be true, Grant sent a division to his support and at the same time ordered new attacks by Sherman and McPherson. But McClernand had taken no forts and the second attack was far more costly than the first. Grant decided that he would have to proceed with a regular siege and the army settled down to this under his dispositions of the various corps.

The Union forces were admirably located from the point of view of the health and comfort of the men. "The high wooded hills afforded pure air and shade," Dana recorded, "and the deep ravines abounded in springs of excellent water, and if they failed it was easy to bring it from the Mississippi. Our line of supplies was beyond the reach of the enemy, and there was an abundance of fruit all about us. I frequently met soldiers coming into camp with buckets full of mulberries, blackberries, and red and yellow wild plums."

With only the occasional incident to report while the army was thus stationary, Dana began a series of portraits of the officers with whom he was in contact for the information of Stanton and the President, which were so highly appreciated that when he stopped with the top-notchers he received a dispatch from Stanton begging him to continue with the lesser officers.

Grant, Sherman and McPherson, whom he considered the Big Three of the Vicksburg campaign, were all from

Ohio, which may have had something to do in creating the spirit of cordiality and confidence which held them together, and to which Dana attributed much of the success achieved in their combined endeavors. There was neither jealousy nor bickering, and "in their unpretending simplicity they were as alike as three peas".

"Grant," said Dana, "was an uncommon fellow—the most modest, the most disinterested, and the most honest man I ever knew, with a temper that nothing could disturb, and a judgment that was judicial in its comprehensiveness and wisdom. Not a great man, except morally; not an original or brilliant man, but sincere, thoughtful, deep, and gifted with courage that never faltered; when the time came to risk all, he went in like a simple-hearted, unaffected, unpretending hero, whom no ill omens could deject and no triumph unduly exalt. A social, friendly man, too, fond of a pleasant joke and also ready with one; but liking above all a long chat of an evening, and ready to sit up with you all night, talking in the cool breeze in front of his tent. Not a man of sentimentality, not demonstrative in friendship, but always holding to his friends, and just even to the enemies he hated."

There is no mention, it will be observed, of drinking, although that had been one of the complaints against the General. Yet they were in a hard drinking country. In a letter to Huntington, Dana said: "This is an awful country for drinking. I calculate that on an average a friendly man will drink a gallon in twenty-four hours. I wish you were here to do my drinking for me, for I suffer in public estimation from not doing as the Romans do."

Not only as a great soldier but as a brilliant man Sherman appealed to him. He had broad information, was a clever talker and liked to have about him people who could keep his intellectual pace, though he remained always genial and unaffected.

Major General J. B. McPherson, although then only thirty-two, Dana set down as one of the most efficient of the commanders. "A handsome, gallant-looking man, with rather a dark complexion, dark eyes, and a most cordial manner." An engineer officer of great natural ability and extraordinary acquirements, graduating at the top of his class at West Point, yet without any pretensions and always offering a pleasant hand-shake to the visitor.

About McClernand Dana was unequivocal. His friend, General Wilson, was of the opinion that the former would have fitted into his proper place had he not been led to believe that the President intended him for the high command, and gave him credit for both patriotism and courage, but Dana's judgment of him by this time was that he had not the qualities necessary for commander of even a regiment.

Vicksburg

In the first place, he was not a military man; he was a politician and a member of Congress. He was a man of a good deal of a certain kind of talent, not of a high order, but not one of intellectual accomplishments. His education was that which a man gets who is in Congress five or six years. In short, McClernand was merely a smart man, quick, very active-minded, but his judgment was not solid, and he looked after himself a good deal. It was a great thing to get McClernand into the war in the first place, for his natural predisposition, one would have supposed, would have been to sympathize with the South. As long as he adhered to the war he carried his Illinois constituency with him; and chiefly for this reason, doubtless, Lincoln made it a point to take special care of him. In doing this the President really served the greater good of the cause. But from the circumstances of Lincoln's supposed friendship, McClernand had more consequence in the army than he deserved.

In a letter dated July 12th Dana described for Lincoln and Stanton the generals of division and brigade under Grant. Short, pithy paragraphs, each summing up the characteristics of the man considered, they must have entertained and amused as well as informed, and will serve as a verbal portrait gallery of the leaders in the Vicksburg campaign for all time. The writer did not hesitate to express his opinion of the capacities or weaknesses of those he passed under review.

Brigadier General A. P. Hovey "is a lawyer of Indiana, and from forty to forty-five years old. He is ambitious, active, nervous, irritable, energetic, clear-headed, quick-witted, and prompt-handed. He works with all his might and all his mind; and, unlike most volunteer officers, makes it his business to learn the military profession just as if he expected to spend his life in it. He distinguished himself most honorably at Port Gibson and Champion's Hill. . . . He is a man whose character will always command respect though he is too anxious about his personal renown and his own advancement to be considered a first-rate man morally, judged by the high standard of men like Grant and Sherman."

General A. J. Smith was "an old cavalry officer of the regular service. He is intrepid to recklessness, his head is clear though rather thick, his disposition honest and manly, though rather given to boasting and exaggeration of a gentle and innocent kind."

Of Hovey's principal brigadiers, General McGinnis and Colonel Slack: "McGinnis is brave enough, but too excitable. He lost his balance at Champion's Hill. . . . Slack is a solid, steady man, brave, thorough and sensible, but will never set the river afire. His education is poor, but he would make a respectable brigadier general."

General M. K. Lawler "weighs two hundred and fifty pounds, is a Roman Catholic, and was a Douglas Democrat, belongs in Shawneetown, Ill., and served in the Mexican War. He is as brave as a lion, and has about as much brains; but his purpose is always honest, and his sense is always good. He is a good disciplinarian and a first-rate soldier. He once hung a man for murdering a comrade, without reporting the case to his commanding general either before or after the hanging, but there was no doubt the man

deserved his fate. Grant has two or three times gently reprimanded him for indiscretions, but is pretty sure to go and
thank him after a battle."

General Lauman "got his promotion by bravery on the
field and Iowa political influence. He is totally unfit to command—a very good man but a very poor general." General
Kimball "is not so bad a commander as Lauman, but he is
bad enough; brave, of course, but lacking the military instinct and the genius of generalship." General W. S. Smith
of the Sixteenth Corps "is one of the best officers in that
army. A rigid disciplinarian, his division is always ready
and always safe. A man of brains, a hard worker, unpretending, quick, suggestive, he may also be a little crotchety,
for such is his reputation; but I judge that he only needs
the opportunity to render good services."

Logan, the "most prominent division general of the Sev-
enteenth Corps, was a man of remarkable qualities and
peculiar character. Heroic and brilliant, he is sometimes
unsteady. Inspiring his men with his own enthusiasm on
the field of battle, he is splendid in all its crash and com-
motion, but before it begins he is doubtful of the result, and
after it is over he is fearful we may yet be beaten. A man
of instinct and not of reflection, his judgments are often
absurd, but his extemporaneous opinions are very apt to be
right. Deficient in education, he is full of generous attach-
ments and sincere animosities. On the whole few can serve
the cause of the country more effectively than he, and none
serve it more faithfully."

In our day Logan might be said to be afflicted with an
intermittent inferiority complex. After the battle of Champion's Hill Dana came upon him and found him greatly
excited and fully convinced the Union army had been defeated. "Why, General," protested Dana, "we have gained
the day." Logan would not be brought around. "Don't you
hear the cannon over there?" he retorted. "They will be
down on us right away! In an hour I will have twenty
thousand men to fight." Not that he had any thought of

giving way. His idiosyncrasy never controlled his performance.

At Grant's headquarters there was a General Sullivan whom Dana found "doing nothing with more energy and effect than he would be likely to show in any other line of duty. He is a gentlemanly fellow, intelligent, a charming companion, but heavy, jovial and lazy."

Dana's only criticism of Grant was based on his indulgence for his staff. There were a few good men. Lieutenant Colonel Rawlins, Grant's Assistant Adjutant General, was invaluable. An old friend and fellow townsman, he watched over Grant as a mother might watch a wayward child. At the beginning of the war he had made Grant promise on his word of honor he would not touch liquor while it lasted, and every time Grant violated his promise Rawlins was at him relentlessly. Dana found him industrious and conscientious, never losing a moment or allowing himself any indulgence "except swearing and scolding", but curiously enough, as he was a lawyer by profession, unable to write English correctly without a great deal of careful consideration. Perhaps he had overcome this when he came to wear the official shoes then worn by Stanton.

"Grant's staff," wrote Dana, "is a curious mixture of good, bad and indifferent. As he is neither an organizer nor a disciplinarian himself, his staff is naturally a mosaic of accidental elements and family friends. It contains four working men, two who are able to accomplish their duties without much work, and several who either don't think of work, or who accomplish nothing no matter what they undertake."

Besides Rawlins, Dana approved of the Judge Advocate, Major Bowers; of his later friend Wilson, then Inspector General; of Lieutenant Colonel Kent, the Provost Marshal General. These were the four workers. Then there was an astonishing Chief Commissary, Lieutenant Colonel Macfeely, who never seemed to be doing anything but be "a jolly, agreeable fellow", yet no one ever found fault with his department, which was one "of the most efficacious parts" of the great machine. Lieutenant Colonel Bingham, in charge of the Quartermaster's Department, was another genius who could do much with little effort, but in his case it was not laziness but physical weakness that was responsible for his lack of exertion.

But there were two colonels, nameless in the "Recollections", who aroused Dana's ire. They were both personal friends of Grant and his aides-de-camp. One was a "worthless, whiskey-drinking, useless fellow, the other decent enough, but neither of them worth his salt for service". In truth, all of Grant's aides-de-camp were practically worthless. Sometimes on the battlefield Grant sent orders by them, but otherwise they were "idle loafers".

"If General Grant had about him a staff of thoroughly competent men," Dana summed up, "disciplinarians and workers, the efficiency and fighting quality of his army would soon be much increased. As it is, things go too much by hazard and by spasms; or, when the pinch comes, Grant forces through, by his own energy and main strength, what proper organization and proper staff officers would have done already." The chief trouble lay in that weakness of Grant which made him "unwilling to hurt the feelings of a friend".

XI. UNDER THE FIRE OF SHARPSHOOTERS—MADE ADJUTANT GENERAL—AN ADVENTURE WITH GRANT—RIDING WITH GRANT INTO VICKSBURG.

ALTHOUGH he must have been under fire many times Dana never had a closer call than one day when he went alone to the top of a hill overlooking Vicksburg. As he stood there surveying the besieged city he heard something go "whizz, whiz" by his ear. What in the world could it be? he asked himself. The place was so desolate it took him some moments to realize that he had been observed by the rebel sharpshooters, and that these were bullets intended to cut off his further usefulness.

"When I did realize it," he said, "I immediately started to lie down. Then came the question, which was the best way to lie down? If I lay at right angles to the enemy's line the bullets from the right and left might strike me; if I lay parallel to it then those directly from the front might hit me. So I concluded it made no difference which way I lay. After remaining quiet for a time the bullets ceased. . . ."

There were other adventures, for he was not content with writing dispatches. He wanted to be helpful, and wanted to keep himself informed by personal observation, and every day he made a round of the trenches, which were between six and seven miles long. Sometimes this occurred at night and once his tour was so late the men were all asleep on their guns, and he was impressed by the grotesque positions into which they had curled themselves. Once, when he was riding with Wilson, they were fired on by rebel sentries, and the bullets hit their orderly.

"I like living in tents very well," he wrote his little daughter, the mother of Ruth Draper. "Every night I sleep with one side of the tent wide open and the walls put up all around to get plenty of air. Sometimes I wake up in the night and think it is raining, the wind roars so in the tops of the great oak forest on the hillside where we are encamped, and I think it is thundering till I look out and see the golden moonlight in all its glory, and listen again and know that it is only the thunder of General Sherman's great guns, that neither rest nor let others rest by night or by day."

There were more serious thoughts to occupy him. Grant was worried lest Johnston should attack him in the rear, and it was known that the Confederate commander was gathering troops for that purpose. Grant appealed to Banks, who was besieging Port Hudson, to come to his aid, and offered to coöperate with him or serve under him; Banks being his senior in rank. He also telegraphed General Halleck, the General in Chief, insisting that he must have assistance. That was as far as he felt he could go, but Dana was giving invaluable aid in his dispatches to Stanton, urging the prompt supply of reinforcements.

At Grant's request he started for Port Hudson to impress upon Banks the importance of coming to Grant's assistance. Passing through the Chickasaw Bayou into the Yazoo, and thence into the Mississippi to Young's Point, he went overland across the peninsula to get a gunboat south of Vicksburg. As he was going down the river he met a steamer bearing one of Grant's previous messengers to Banks, who was returning with the latter's reply. Not only had he refused Grant's request but was asking Grant to come to his aid. Thereupon Dana returned and immediately forwarded another dispatch to Stanton. Early in June came the following reply:

War Department, June 5, 1863

Your telegrams up to the 30th have been received. Everything in the power of this Government will be put forth to aid General Grant. The emergency is not underrated here. Your telegrams are a great obligation, and are looked for with deep interest. I cannot thank you as much as I feel for the service you are now rendering. You have been appointed an assistant adjutant general, with rank of major, with liberty to report to General Grant if he needs you. The appointment may be a protection to you. I shall expect daily reports if possible.

Edwin M. Stanton
Secretary of War

C. A. Dana, Esq.,
Grant's Headquarters near Vicksburg

Washington had awakened to the fact that its valuable correspondent needed protection. As any good reporter, Dana had given no thought to the matter. He was out on a job and his mind was full of that. But the fact remained that he was assuming an unusual danger. Had he been captured he would have been rated as a private citizen in the enemy lines and it would have been well nigh impossible to have secured his release. Certainly not if the Confederates had any idea of the importance of the work he was doing. Hence this appointment to the army after which it would be possible to arrange for his exchange.

From this time on Grant utilized Dana more than ever, and the latter accompanied him frequently on his surveys of outlying posts. On one occasion they were together on Grant's personal boat, intending to steam to Satartia from Haynes's Bluff. General Wilson's somewhat cryptic account of this expedition suggests that Grant was not his usual self, and a reference to a letter written by Rawlins to Grant, remonstrating with the latter in connection with this incident, suggests the nature of his illness. "It is a curious circumstance," Wilson added, "that neither Grant nor Dana ever made to the other the slightest reference to the peculiar features of the excursion, nor, so far as the records show, did Dana report them to Stanton. On the other hand, nothing can be more certain than that every circumstance connected with it became known at once to the leading officers of Grant's army."

Dana's own account of it lends to it the most innocent air possible. "Mr. Dana," said Grant, at breakfast one morning, "I am going to Satartia today; would you like to come along?"

Dana was willing, and they were soon on horseback, riding with a small cavalry guard to Haynes's Bluff, where they took the steamer.

"Grant was ill and went to bed soon after we started," Dana records. Apparently he had been all right on the ride and this would seem to have been a sudden development. "We had gone up the river to within two miles of Satartia," the account continues, "when we met two gunboats coming down. Seeing the General's flag, the officers in charge of the gunboats came aboard our steamer and asked where the General was going. I told them to Satartia.

" 'Why,' said they, 'it will not be safe. Kimball (our advance was under the charge of Brigadier General Nathan Kimball) has retreated from there, and is sending all his supplies to Haynes's Bluff. The enemy is probably in the town now.'

"I told them Grant was sick and asleep, and that I did not want to awaken him. They insisted it was unsafe to go on, and that I would better call the General. Finally I did so, but he was too sick to decide. 'I will leave it with you,' he said. I immediately said we would go back to Haynes's Bluff, which we did. The next morning Grant came out to breakfast fresh as a rose, clean shirt and all, quite himself.

" 'Well, Mr. Dana,' he said, 'I suppose we are at Satartia now.'

" 'No, General,' I said, 'we are at Haynes's Bluff.' And I told him what had happened.

"He did not complain. . . ."

Although there were many alarms, now Johnston coming to attack on the east and again invasion by Kirby Smith from the west, and no reinforcements forthcoming, Grant did not budge. Dana's admiring comments present a picture of a bulldog standing alert with jaws set and teeth showing, immovable but ready for any development.

On June 10th the longed-for assistance began to arrive and the last hope of Vicksburg was gone. Soon Grant had eighty-five thousand men hemming it in. Dana relaxed to give a pen portrait of General Herron, the first of the new commanders to arrive:

> Herron was a first-rate officer, and the only con-summate dandy I ever saw in the army. He was always handsomely dressed; I believe he never went out with-out patent-leather boots on, and you would see him in the middle of a battle—well, I cannot say exactly that he went into battle with a lace pocket-handkerchief, but at all events he always displayed a clean white one.

The siege went forward rapidly now, the trenches being brought ever closer. Grant was considering another general assault, and again he was halted by the dilatoriness of Mc-Clernand, whose trenches were mere rifle pits, which would not allow the passage of artillery or the assemblage of any considerable number of men. Whether Grant would have acted upon this cannot be said, for the final attack upon his patience came in the form of a newspaper article containing McClernand's congratulatory address to the Thirteenth Army Corps, in which he claimed for himself all the glory of the campaign, insisted that for several hours he had held the two forts, as he had reported, and charged that it was the failure of other officers and troops to support him which had forced him to let go, and with them had failed the cer-tain capture of Vicksburg. When the paper containing this reached the army there was a furore. McClernand was re-lieved and sent back to Illinois to await orders and General Ord took his command.

The protracted defense of Vicksburg is a part of the history of the war and Dana was among the many who were deceived into thinking it would fall long before it did. In his dispatch of June 14th he asked Stanton to telegraph him whether he should proceed to General Rosecrans after the surrender. Actually it was the third of July when Pemberton opened negotiations with Grant. Dana reported the previous day Grant had told him that if he had to wait until the 6th he would storm the city. So many lives were spared.

There was quite a lot of criticism of Grant for paroling the enemy, especially after the Confederate Government repudiated the parole, but when the terms were made he had to be persuaded by the other officers to depart from his original demand for unconditional surrender. Dana seemed to think the terms wise in all respects, giving the reasons advanced by McPherson, who proposed them. It would have absorbed all the steamboat transportation to send the prisoners North, besides using a large part of the army to guard them. As it was, the surrender was in itself a cause of demoralization and would release the whole of Grant's army for offensive operations against Johnston and Port Hudson.

Dana rode into the conquered city at the side of the conqueror and noted that the latter was far more gracious than the defeated commander. In fact, the manner of the latter had been discourteous from the beginning. Dana had been present at the first meeting between the two generals, he, together with the members of Grant's staff, being seated on the ground before Grant's tent, while Grant, McPherson and General A. J. Smith conferred apart with Pemberton and his two assistants, General Bowen and Colonel Montgomery.

Pemberton appeared much excited and the onlookers could see that he was decidedly impatient with Grant.

> It must have been a bitter moment for the Confederate chieftain [Dana remarked]. Pemberton was a Northern man, a Pennsylvanian by birth, from which state he was appointed to West Point. . . . In the old army he fell under the spell of the influence of Jefferson Davis, whose close friend he was. Davis appears

to have thought Pemberton was a military genius, for he was jumped almost at a stroke, without much previous service, to be a lieutenant general, and the defense of the Mississippi River was given over to his charge. His dispositions throughout the entire campaign, after Grant crossed at Bruinsburg, were weak, and he was easily overcome, though his troops fought well. . . . Penned up and finally compelled to surrender a vital post and a great army to his conqueror, an almost irremediable disaster to his cause, Pemberton not only suffered the usual pangs of defeat, but he was doubly humiliated by the knowledge that he would be suspected and accused of treachery by his adopted brethren, and that the result would be used by the enemies of Davis. . . . As the event proved, it was indeed a great blow to Davis's hold upon the people of the South. These things must have passed through Pemberton's mind as he faced Grant for this final settlement of the fate of Vicksburg.

Apparently his ruffled emotions controlled him when he had to meet the formal sacrifice, and were outwardly exhibited to Grant in "more marked impertinence than at their former interview". To Dana's delight "Grant bore it like a philosopher, and in reply treated Pemberton with even gentler courtesy and dignity than before".

No sooner were the formal ceremonies over than Dana slipped from his horse to roam about the town, once more the reporter seeking facts and impressions. If Pemberton had been petulant all the other officers looked like men who had been crying all night. In fact, one Major, commander of a regiment from Missouri, could not control his feelings and burst into tears as he followed his disarmed men back to their lines.

But the soldiers generally were joyous. They had enough of the war, they declared freely, and now they were going home. The Confederacy was done for. Many of them wanted to take the oath of allegiance to the Union.

Enormous supplies of foodstuffs, clothing and ammunition remained, some of it concealed, and the defenses were still in excellent condition. Undoubtedly Pemberton's state of mind would not have been bettered had he heard Grant remark grimly that there was enough ammunition to have kept up the defense for six years at the rate it had been used.

Thus ended Dana's experience with what he considered one of the most brilliant campaigns of the war.

XII. DANA BECOMES ASSISTANT SECRETARY OF WAR—LINCOLN CALLS HIM "THE EYES OF THE GOVERNMENT AT THE FRONT"—WITH ROSECRANS AT CHICKAMAUGUA—URGES THE REPLACING OF ROSECRANS—HIS JUDGMENT SUSTAINED.

WHILE Grant was following up his victory with his usual alertness and energy, directing Sherman to move against Johnston and lending aid to Banks at Port Hudson, Dana was on his way back to Washington. His mission was finished and he was possessed with longing for that refuge in Connecticut where a lonely family was waiting to welcome him. He had a fortnight of it and the temptation to continue was strong enough to make him listen to an invitation to enter business with a Mr. Ketchum, a banker, and one George Opdyke, a merchant, but he surrendered to Stanton's veto, and returned to Washington, this time as Assistant Secretary of War. Shortly thereafter he was on his way to Chattanooga, to observe and report on the movements of Rosecrans against Bragg. As the President observed, he was again to be "the eyes of the government at the front".

It proved an exasperating experience. To Dana's clear mind the grant of power to one so palpably unfit as Rosecrans was little short of a crime. Even while he was on his way there came information of an act which made him wonder what sort of a general this could be. Rosecrans had sent a telegram to the clergy of the country that he expected a great battle that day and desired their prayers.

Leaving the railroad at Bridgeport on the Tennessee River, Dana proceeded on horseback through a wild and magnificent region of rocks and valleys, arriving at Chattanooga in the middle of September. He was greeted by Rosecrans with a tirade of abuse against the Government, which he declared had done everything possible to thwart his plans and prevent his success.

Not a satisfactory introduction, but Dana held him by saying quietly he had no authority to listen to complaints against his superiors, his mission being limited to ascertaining what could be done to aid in achieving success. Never before had so many dispatches from Dana poured into Washington. There was plenty to report—the dispositions of the men made by Rosecrans, the threatening danger of a concentration of the Confederates against the loosely-joined forces of the Union army, and finally the vagaries of a commanding general who united unconquerable obstinacy with extraordinary lack of essential qualifications.

One mitigating condition gave ground for hope. At sight of the energy displayed at Thomas's headquarters, the fine condition of his troops, and realizing for the first time the tremendous difficulties Thomas had overcome in bringing his army across the Cumberland mountains, Dana's faith revived.

Realizing the danger of sudden attack upon the precarious line of communications, he sent an urgent dispatch to Stanton, asking that a strong column be sent forward from Corinth, in northeastern Mississippi. The job of the moment was to concentrate the Union forces. It took an all-night march of Thomas's troops to bring about the new dispositions. He had barely headed the enemy off from Chattanooga.

Battle began on the 19th. It was in a forest, so little could be seen of what was happening, but the telegraph was working well and Dana sent eleven dispatches that day. They were fairly optimistic. Rosecrans had everything ready "to grind up Bragg's flank". At half-past four Dana did not dare to say victory was complete, but it seemed certain. Far more consequential was the announcement of Longstreet's arrival.

Rosecrans failed to realize this. At the council of war

held that night he "began by asking each of the corps commanders for a report of the condition of his troops and of the position they occupied; also for his opinion of what was to be done. Each proposition was discussed by the entire council as it was made. General Thomas was so tired—he had not slept the night before and had been in battle all day —that he went to sleep every minute. Every time Rosecrans spoke to him he would straighten up and answer, but he always said the same thing, 'I would strengthen the left,' and then he would be asleep, sitting up in his chair".

When it was all over Rosecrans gave his orders. Thomas's corps was to remain on the left, with his line somewhat drawn in; McCook was to close on Thomas, and Crittenden was to have two divisions in reserve to support either, if needed. The conference closed with hot coffee and the singing of the "Hebrew Maiden" by McCook. There had been no reference to Longstreet.

After a night much disturbed by cold winds blowing up through the cracks of the floor on which he had sought slumber, Dana was out at daybreak to accompany Rosecrans on a survey of the front. McCook's line was elongated to a mere thread, whereupon Rosecrans rebuked him severely, although McCook had merely followed his written instructions.

The battle opened on Thomas's front about nine o'clock. Dana was on the right, where Rosecrans had taken command. At noon, being hot and exhausted, Dana got off his horse and went to sleep in the grass. He was wakened by a terrific racket.

> Never in any battle I had witnessed [he wrote] was there such a discharge of cannon and musketry. I sat up on the grass, and the first thing I saw was General Rosecrans crossing himself—he was a very devout Catholic. "Hello!" I said to myself, "if the General is crossing himself, we are in a desperate situation."
>
> I was on my horse in a moment. I had no sooner collected my thoughts and looked around toward the

front, where all this din came from, than I saw our lines break and melt away like leaves before the wind. Then the headquarters around me disappeared. The graybacks came through with a rush, and soon the musket balls and the cannon shot began to reach the place where we stood. The whole right of the army had apparently been routed. My orderly stuck to me like a veteran, and we drew back for greater safety into the woods a little way. There I came upon General (Horace) Porter—Captain Porter he was then—and Captain Drouillard, an aide-de-camp infantry officer attached to General Rosecrans's staff, halting fugitives. They would halt a few of them, get them into some sort of a line, and make a beginning of order among them, and then there would come a few rounds of cannon shot through the tree tops over their heads and the men would break and run. I saw Porter and Drouillard plant themselves in front of a body of these stampeding men and command them to halt. One man charged with his bayonet, menacing Porter, but Porter held his ground, and the man gave in. That was the only case of real mutiny that I ever saw in the army, and that was under such circumstances that the man was excusable. The cause of all this disaster was the charge of the Confederates through the hiatus in the line caused by the withdrawal of Wood's division, under a misapprehension of orders, before its place could be filled.

I attempted to make my way from this point in the woods to Sheridan's division, but when I reached the place where I knew it had been a little time before, I found it had been swept from the field. Not far away, however, I stumbled on a body of organized troops. This was a brigade of mounted riflemen under Colonel John T. Wilder, of Indiana. "Mr. Dana," asked Colonel Wilder, "what is the situation?" "I do not know," I said, "except that this end of the army has been routed. There is still heavy fighting at the left front, and our troops seem to be holding their ground there yet." "Will you give me any orders?" he asked. "I have no authority to give orders," I replied; "but if I were in your situation I should go to the left, where Thomas is."

Dana rode over Missionary Ridge, struck the Chattanooga Valley and made for the town. The whole road, between twelve and fifteen miles, was filled with fleeing soldiers, with here and there pieces of artillery, caissons and baggage wagons, all in the greatest disorder. He reached Chattanooga around four o'clock, to find Rosecrans already there, and doing what he could to resist the entrance of the enemy, whom he expected every minute.

Naturally, Dana was excited and his first dispatch to Stanton began:

"My report today is of deplorable importance. Chickamauga is as fatal a name in our history as Bull Run."

Fortunately, Thomas's iron courage and clear head saved the day. Drawing his troops into horseshoe form, he held off the repeated assaults from Longstreet, repulsing every onslaught with dire results to the enemy. "Thomas seemed to have filled every soldier with his own unconquerable firmness, and Granger (who had come up from Rossville), his hat torn by bullets, raged like a lion wherever the combat was hottest with the electrical courage of a Ney." When night put an end to the fighting Thomas still held the ground he had occupied in the morning.

It was a trying situation which followed. Rosecrans, unsobered by his disaster, continued to fritter away time in pleasant trivialities, vacillating between tenaciously holding to stupid decisions and failing to arrive at those which the situation demanded. He gave up Lookout Mountain, which practically commanded the town, against the pleadings of other generals, and interfered with those who were ready to work out of the debacle. Chattanooga had been prepared for a siege, but supplies were getting low and the roads, almost impassable with mud, were under the fire of snipers. It looked as though they might be starved into surrender, and rations for man and beast had to be cut.

WHEN DANA WAS THE SUN 101

Dana was keeping the wires hot. Whatever faith he had had in Rosecrans was gone. In a later summing up, he wrote this estimate of his character:

> While few persons exhibited more estimable social qualities, I have never seen a public man possessing talent with less administrative power, less clearness and steadiness in difficulty, and greater practical incapacity than General Rosecrans. He had inventive fertility and knowledge, but he had no strength of will and no concentration of purpose. His mind scattered; there was no system in the use of his busy days and restless nights, no courage against individuals in his composition, and, with great love of command, he was a feeble commander. He was conscientious and honest, just as he was imperious and disputatious; always with a stray vein of caprice and an overweening passion for the approbation of his personal friends and the public outside.

Dana was suggesting two men to take his place—Grant or Thomas, and the latter was the man the army itself was hoping for. In reply to his recommendation of Thomas, Dana received this telegram from Stanton:

"I wish you to go directly to see General Thomas, and say to him that his services, his abilities, his character, his unselfishness, have always been most cordially appreciated by me, and that it is not my fault he has not long since had command of an independent army."

An agreeable errand for Dana. He lost no time in taking the message to Thomas's headquarters. The hero of Chickamaugua was too affected to reply for some moments. He confessed he would like to have an independent command, one he could himself "organize, discipline, distribute and combine", but he wound up with the flat assertion he did not want a command which would expose him "to the imputation of having intrigued or of having exercised any effort to supplant my previous commander."

Dana may well have thought generals were no better than

prima donnas, and that too much modesty ceased to be a virtue. Here he was making an effort to get the best man for a difficult job, with no interest in personalities, and the first crack out of the box came an interference which had no business to exist where the interests of the country were concerned. Four days later the incident was seemingly closed by a message from Thomas. The latter had heard rumors he was slated for the place of Rosecrans and could not consent to accept such an appointment, or do anything which would give countenance to the suspicion that he had intrigued against his commander. His message concluded with the declaration that he had perfect confidence in the fidelity and capacity of Rosecrans, which put out of court any appeal to patriotic duty.

In the meantime things were getting no better. By the middle of October the situation appeared desperate. On the 19th Dana received a dispatch asking him to meet Stanton in Louisville. He started at once, but not before he had wired his opinion that Rosecrans would abandon Chattanooga unless ordered to the contrary.

The roads were not safe and in a fearful condition as he turned his horse toward Waldon's Bridge. Ten days earlier he had suffered a tumble on this same road, when the bank had given way and the horse had pitched down some fourteen feet, carrying him along and rolling over him repeatedly on the way down, besides planting his hind foot on the back of his head. The road was even worse now, besides being jammed with struggling teams trying to get supplies to Chattanooga. Two days earlier five hundred teams had been forced to halt between the mountain and the river. There was no forage for the unfortunate animals, already half starved, and now the road was strewn with their bodies.

Finally he secured a train to take him to Nashville, but eight miles from that city it struck something and came to an abrupt halt. A tie had been inserted to throw the train down an embankment. Fortunately it broke off without doing any damage.

When the train reached Nashville it was halted and one of Grant's aids came aboard, much to Dana's surprise, as he did not know Grant was in Tennessee. Dana went over to the General's car.

"I am going to interfere with your journey, Mr. Dana," said Grant. "I have got the Secretary's permission to take you back with me to Chattanooga. I want you to dismiss your train and get in mine."

On the way he told how he had been appointed to the command of the Military Division of the Mississippi, with permission to leave Rosecrans in command of the Army of the Cumberland or to assign Thomas to it. He had chosen to do the latter, and had telegraphed Thomas to take charge. That occurred on the night of the 19th, after Stanton had received Dana's dispatch indicating Rosecrans's purpose to abandon Chattanooga. Rosecrans had been shifted to St. Louis, with command of the Army of the Missouri.

Grant was on crutches at that time, having injured his leg through the fall of his horse at New Orleans, so Dana pushed on ahead from the railroad terminus to call on Thomas.

"Mr. Dana," said the latter, "you have got me this time. There is nothing for a man to do in such a case as this but to obey orders."

Dana noticed with satisfaction that already a change had come over the headquarters, "order prevailing instead of universal chaos".

XIII. WHEN THE SOLDIERS COULD NOT BE HELD BACK FROM DOING THE SEEMINGLY IMPOSSIBLE—"GLORY TO GOD! THE DAY IS OURS"—A PORTRAIT OF STANTON—GEN. SHERMAN WRITES DANA ABOUT GOOD PEOPLE IN WAR-TIME.

THINGS were doing immediately when Grant arrived, "wet, dirty and well". Gen. Smith had discovered a way of breaking the grip of the besiegers and Grant lost no time in making use of it. In the meantime it became apparent the enemy were meditating an assault upon Burnside, to drive him out of East Tennessee, and Grant sent Dana to report on that situation. He started Nov. 9th, and here is what he wrote that little daughter at home about his plans:

> I expect to go all the way on horseback, and it will take about five days. About seventy horsemen will go along, with their sabres and carbines to keep off the guerillas. Our baggage we shall have carried on pack mules. These are funny little rats of creatures, with the big panniers fastened to their sides to carry their burdens in. I shall put my bed in one pannier and my carpet bag and India-rubber things in the other. Colonel Wilson, who is to go with me, will have another mule for his traps, and a third will carry the bread and meat and coffee that we are to live on. At night we shall halt in some nice shady nook where there is a spring, build a roaring fire, cook our supper, spread the blankets on the ground, and sleep with our feet toward the fire, while half a dozen of the soldiers, with their guns ready loaded, watch all about to keep the rebels at a safe distance. Then in the morning we shall first wake up, then wash our faces, get our breakfasts, and march on, like John Brown's soul, toward our destination. How long I shall stay at Knoxville is uncertain, but I hope not very long—though it must be very charming

in that country of mountains and rivers—and then I shall pray for orders to take me home again.

He must have been in a happy mood when he wrote that, although he knew very well there was no chance of what he indicated in his last line coming to pass.

He found Burnside "rather a large man physically, about six feet tall, with a large face and a small head, and heavy side whiskers. [As Wellington became known for his boots to even those who recked not of his military genius, so for many years that type of whiskers made the name Burnside familiar to every urchin in the land.] He was an energetic, decided man, frank, manly and well educated. He was a very showy officer—not that he *made* any show; he was naturally that. When he first talked with you, you would think he had a great deal more intelligence than he really possessed. You had to know him some time before you really took his measure."

He was more fearful of having to retreat than the circumstances were found to warrant, and Dana reported that only by Wilson's intervention in the name of Grant was he prevented from executing a move which might easily have proved costly. Dana concluded that there was a reasonable probability that he would be able to hold his position and returned to make his report. They had left none too soon, for the rebels were taking possession of the country between Knoxville and Chattanooga. The return took four days and his first dispatch to Washington brought this reply from Stanton:

"I am rejoiced that you have got safely back. My anxiety about you for several days had been very great. Make your arrangements to remain in the field during the winter. Continue your reports as frequently as possible, always noting the hour."

The camp was buzzing with expectation of great events. Sherman had arrived at Bridgeport, the railroad terminus, and a plan was all ready whereby the enemy would be attacked from all sides. Sherman would make a night march, crossing the Tennessee, and getting out of sight behind the hills. Hooker was to deliver an attack on the head of Lookout Mountain simultaneously with Sherman's on Missionary Ridge. But, as Dana observed, it is almost impossible to execute a campaign as laid out, especially when it requires so many concerted movements as this one. There were hitches, there were blunders and the very heavens conspired, sending down a deluge of rain which almost stopped Sherman altogether. Three days after the date set by Grant for beginning the assault Sherman was still struggling to bring up his rear. However, there could be no further delay. The first encounter of the Battle of Chattanooga occurred on Nov. 23rd.

"It was the beginning of the most spectacular operations I ever saw," Dana reported, "operations extending over three days and full of the most exciting incidents."

Rarely can one see all that is going on in a battle. Usually the eye-witness grasps no more than an incident, which makes it possible for entirely truthful accounts to vary greatly. This time the whole field of operations was exposed to the watchers at Fort Wood. Facing them, in a great half circle, and high above on Lookout Mountain and Missionary Ridge, were the enemy. The problem was to drive them from these heights. This first engagement began at two o'clock and at half-past three Dana was filing his dispatch recounting the opening success.

The final assault and culminating victory of Lookout Mountain and Missionary Ridge were in Dana's judgment largely due to the soldiers themselves. They had been ordered to take the rifle pits at the foot of the Ridge and stop there, but they could not be held back.

> To the amazement of all of us who watched on Orchard Knob [said Dana], they moved out and up the steep ahead of them, and before we realized it they were at the top of Missionary Ridge. . . . No man who climbs the ascent by any of the roads that wind along its front can believe that eighteen thousand

men were moved in tolerably good order up its broken and crumbling face unless it was his fortune to witness the dead. It seemed as awful as a visible interposition of God. Neither Grant nor Thomas intended it. . . . The order to storm appears to have been given simultaneously by Generals Sheridan and Wood because the men were not to be held back, dangerous as the attempt appeared to military prudence. Besides, the generals had caught the inspiration of the men, and were ready themselves to undertake impossibilities.

Later he asked Sheridan how he came to do it. Sheridan replied that when he saw the men were determined to go he had no thought of stopping them. On the way he saw a Confederate General on horseback at the head of the Ridge. "I had a silver whisky flask in my pocket," said Sheridan, "and when I saw this man on the top of the hill I took out my flask and waved my hand toward him, holding up the shining, glittering flask, and then I took a drink. He waved back to me, and then the whole corps went up."

As Grant rode along the front that day the men went frantic with joy and enthusiasm and the fever communicated itself to the Government's reporter.

"Glory to God!" he wired to Washington, "the day is decisively ours."

The excitement continued far into the night, with Bragg retreating down the Chickamaugua Valley, burning his depots of supplies as he went, and Sheridan still fighting along the east slope of Missionary Ridge. Dana kept on informing Washington with frequent dispatches, for the clear moonlight enabled him to see almost as well as by day, and on the 27th Washington recorded its appreciation. Stanton was away and the President was ill, but both had received his messages "and esteemed them highly, not merely because they are reliable, but for their clearness of narrative and their graphic pictures of the stirring events they describe".

A week later Dana accompanied Sherman on his way to

relieve Burnside, then under attack from Longstreet. This accomplished he left for Washington, carrying with him a full exposition of Grant's proposed plan for a winter campaign against Mobile and the interior of Alabama. Those plans, although enthusiastically received by Stanton, and approved by Halleck, were not put into effect because the latter insisted upon Longstreet being driven out of Tennessee before anything else was undertaken. Dana, never enthusiastic about the General in Chief, was disgusted. His considered opinion, given later, was that had Grant not been interfered with he would have captured Mobile a year before it fell, would have opened the Alabama River, secured permanently all the gains made by the Union forces and released for duty elsewhere thousands of soldiers held in garrison. However, it was not to be and "the eyes of the Government at the front" were retained for a time at the War Department in Washington.

It was his first really good opportunity to study his chief at close quarters, and this pen-picture was the result:

Mr. Stanton was a short, thick, dark man, with a very large head and a mass of black hair. His nature was intense, and he was one of the most eloquent men that I ever met. Stanton was entirely absorbed in his duties, and his energy in prosecuting them was something almost superhuman. . . . One of the first things which struck me in Stanton was his deep religious feeling and his familiarity with the Bible. He must have studied the Bible a great deal when he was a boy. He had the firmest conviction that the Lord directed our armies. . . . There never was any cant in Stanton's religious feeling. It was the straightforward expression of what he believed and lived, and was as simple and genuine and real to him as the principles of his business.

Stanton was a serious student of history. He had read many books on the subject—more than on any other, I should say—and he was fond of discussing

historical characters with his associates; not that he
made a show of his learning. He was fond, too, of discussing legal questions, and would listen with eagerness
to the statement of cases in which his friends were
interested. He was a man who was devoted to his
friends, and he had a good many with whom he liked
to sit down and talk. In conversation he was witty
and satirical; he told a story well and was very com-
panionable.

There is a popular impression that Mr. Stanton took
a malevolent delight in browbeating his subordinates,
and every now and then making a spectacle of some
poor officer or soldier, who unfortunately fell into his
clutches in the Secretary's reception room, for the edi-
fication of bystanders. This idea, like many other false
notions concerning great men, is largely a mistaken
one. There were certain men in whom he had little
faith, and I have heard him speak to some of these
in a tone of severity. He was a man of the quickest
intelligence, and understood a thing before the half of
it was told him. His judgment was just as swift, and
when he got hold of a man who did not understand,
who did not state his case clearly, he was very impatient.

They got along together famously and only once did
Stanton show rudeness to him. It followed the reference
to Dana of the petition of a man from Virginia to recover
the money he had surrendered to the Government upon
being permitted to leave the Confederacy and come North.
It was the rule that such surrender of funds should take
place when a man passed the lines, and in his case he had
handed over between fifty and seventy-five thousand dollars
to Gen. Butler, who was then in command at Fortress Mon-
roe. The man came to Stanton a number of times, accompanied by Congressman Strouse, and they bothered the
Secretary. Finally the matter was referred to Dana, who
investigated and paid the money to the claimant against his
receipt from Butler. The following day Stanton sent for
him, and it was plain he was angry.

"Did you give that Jew back his money?" he demanded harshly.

"Yes, sir," said Dana.

"Well," he returned, "I should like to know by what authority."

Dana produced the papers in the case upon which appeared this endorsement: "Referred to Mr. Dana, Assistant Secretary of War, to be settled as in his judgment shall be best." Beneath this appeared Stanton's signature. He looked at it and the scowl melted into a laugh.

"You are right," he said. "You have got me this time."

Dana's special duty was the making of contracts for supplies for the army and this included about everything that fighting men could use. In that year he bought five million flannel shirts and drawers, three million pairs of trousers, seven million pairs of stockings, thirteen thousand drums, fifteen thousand fifes, hundreds of thousands of mess pans and camp kettles, besides equally large quantities of medicines, horses, mules, telegraph wire, guns, powder, coffins, forage, groceries and endless other things. Some of these supplies were purchased in the open market, some by contract and some had to be made by the Government. As might be expected there were plenty of attempts to defraud the Government, and a lot of political influence was used to save the scoundrels when they were caught.

One such incident was a swindle in the supply of forage to the Army of the Potomac. It was detected by Dana's colleague, Peter H. Watson, a distinguished patent lawyer. Watson was absent when a delegation of politicians came from Philadelphia to see what could be done for the swindlers. In the delegation was the President of the Philadelphia Corn Exchange. They came with cash to pay the amount of which the Government had been defrauded. This done they demanded the release of the prisoners and the restoration of the funds and papers seized when they were arrested. Dana refused, convinced that there were earlier frauds which might be cleared up by holding the men for further investigation. Then he telegraphed Watson to return.

Among the politicians was David Wilmot, author of the Wilmot Proviso, and at this time United States Senator. He appealed to Lincoln and finally induced the latter to go to the War Department with him and see what could be done with Watson. Wilmot remained outside while the President went into Watson's office. Watson listened while Lincoln explained the importance of preserving the powerful support which these politicians were lending to the Administration in its waging of the war. After all, the prisoners had refunded a large sum of money and their punishment was not as important as the safety of the cause. But Watson was unyielding. If the President wished the men released he had only to give the order, but it must be in writing—and he might as well understand that the facts would become public sooner or later. Lincoln took his hat and went out into the corridor, where Wilmot was waiting, confident of his success.

"Wilmot," said Lincoln, "I can't do anything with Watson; he won't release them."

Wilmot's reply, Dana remarked, was unfit for print—but it did not change Lincoln's attitude.

About this time came an eloquent and self-explanatory letter from Gen. Sherman, which ought to be duplicated many thousand times and held for distribution among the good, the kind and the unreasonable in future emergencies of the kind the General describes. It came from Nashville and was dated April 21, 1864.

> My Dear Friend: It may be parliamentary, but is not military, for me to write you; but I feel assured anything I may write will only have the force of a casual conversation, such as we have indulged in by the camp fire or as we jogged along the road. The text of my letter is one you gave a Philadephia gentleman who is going up to East Tennessee to hunt up his brother Quakers and administer the bounties of his own and

his fellow-citizens' charity. Now who would stand in the way of one so kindly and so charitably disposed? Surely not I. But other questions present themselves. We have been working hard with tens of thousands of men, and at a cost of millions of dollars, to make railroads to carry to the line of the Tennessee enough provisions and material of war to enable us to push in our physical force to the next step in the war. I have found on personal inspection that hitherto the railroads have barely been able to feed our men, that mules have died by the thousand, that arms and ammunition have laid in the depot for two weeks for want of cars, that no accumulation at all of clothing and stores had been or could be moved at Chattanooga, and that it took four sets of cars and locomotives to accommodate the passes given by military commanders; that gradually the wants of citizens and charities were actually consuming the resources of a road designed exclusively for army purposes. You have been on the spot and can understand my argument. At least one hundred citizens daily presented good claims to go forward—women to attend sick children, parents in search of the bodies of sons slain in battle, sanitary committees sent by States and corporations to look after the personal wants of their constituents, ministers and friends to minister to the Christian wants of their flocks; men who had fled anxious to go back to look after lost families, etc.; and, more still, the tons of goods which they all bore on their merciful errands. None but such as you, who have been present and seen the tens, hundreds, and thousands of such cases, can measure them in the aggregate and segregate the exceptions.

I had no time to hesitate, for but a short month was left me to prepare, and I must be ready to put in motion near one hundred thousand men to move when naught remains to save life. I figured up the mathematics, and saw that I must have daily one hundred and forty-five carloads of essentials for thirty days to enable me to fill the requirement. Only seventy-five daily was all the roads were doing. Now I have got it up to one hundred and thirty-five. Troops march, cattle go by the road, sanitary and sutler's stores limited, and all is done that human energy can accomplish. Yet come these pressing claims of charity, by men and women who cannot grasp the problem. My usual answer is, "Show me that your presence at the front is more valuable than two hundred pounds of powder, bread or oats;" and it is generally conclusive. I have given Mr. Savery a pass on your letter, and it takes two hundred pounds of bread from our soldiers, or the same of oats from our patient mules; but I could not promise to feed the suffering Quakers at the expense of our army. I have ordered all who cannot provide food at the front to be allowed transportation back in our empty cars; but I cannot undertake to transport the food needed by the worthy East Tennesseeans or any of them. In peace there is a beautiful harmony in all the departments of life—they fit together like the Chinese puzzle; but in war all is ajar. Nothing fits, and it is the struggle between the stronger and weaker; and the latter, however it may appeal to the better feelings of our nature, must kick the beam. To make war we must and will harden our hearts.

Therefore, when preachers clamor and the sanitaries wail, don't join in, but know that war, like the thunderbolt, follows its laws, and turns not aside even if the beautiful, the virtuous and the charitable stand in its path.

When the day and the hour come, I'll strike Joe Johnston, be the result what it may; but in the time allotted to me for preparation I must and will be selfish in making those preparations which I know to be necessary.

How Dana must have regretted his interference for the Quaker!

XIV.
LINCOLN'S SOLICITUDE FOR DANA'S SAFETY—WITH GRANT IN THE FINAL CAMPAIGN—A CRITICISM OF GRANT NOT SENT TO WASHINGTON.

DANA remained in Washington through the winter of 1863-4. Then he went back into the field again and once more it was with Grant. The prelude to that move was an incident which he loved to relate as indicating the nature of Lincoln. Shortly after Grant had been made Commander-in-Chief and had begun his eventful campaign against Lee there was a brief period when no word came from him and both Lincoln and Stanton were worried. Dana was at a reception when a messenger came to summon him to the War Department. He found there both the President and Stanton.

"Dana," said the President, "you know we have been in the dark for two days since Grant moved. We are very much troubled, and have concluded to send you down there. How soon can you start?"

"It will take me twenty minutes to go home and change my clothes and get the things I want, and get my horse saddled," Dana computed, "and then it will take twenty minutes to get a train. Besides, we must have an escort."

"Well," said Lincoln, "you are willing to go?"

"Why, yes," Dana replied. "I am delighted. I want to see it."

In little more than half an hour he had got into his camp clothes and had ridden over to the station where a train was waiting with steam up. A cavalry escort of a hundred men was already aboard. He got on, expecting the train to move at once, but nothing happened. Presently an orderly came up with word that the President wished to see him at the War Department. He rode back in hot haste to find Lincoln occupying the same chair.

"I have been thinking about this, Dana," he said, "and I don't like to send you down there."

"But why not, Mr. President?" asked Dana.

"You can't tell," Lincoln argued, "just where Lee is or what he is doing, and Jeb Stuart is rampaging around pretty lively in between the Rappahannock and the Rapidan. It's a considerable risk and I'm afraid to have you go."

"Mr. President," Dana returned, "is that the reason you called me back?"

"Yes," said Lincoln; "I don't like to have you go."

"Mr. President," said Dana, "I have a cavalry guard ready and a good horse myself. If we are attacked, we are probably strong enough to fight. If we are not strong enough to fight, and it comes to the worst, we are equipped to run. It's getting late, and I want to get down to the Rappahannock by daylight. I think I'll start."

"Well now, Dana," said Lincoln, with a little twinkle in his eyes, "if you feel that way, I rather wish you would. I really want you to go, but I couldn't send you until I felt sure that you were entirely willing yourself."

Dana remarked that Lincoln was probably the first general who had ever given orders in that way, and Lincoln said, "God bless you!" as they parted. It was all sincere on both sides and one can understand how Dana for once became a real hero-worshiper.

Dana now was thrown with officers unknown to him and, as usual, his psychological-reportorial instincts were aroused to add them to his portrait gallery. Meade, he was unable to accept as a great commander. Tall, thin, dyspeptic and frequently affected by spasms of nervous irritation, he was unpopular with his subordinates. An intellectual man, and agreeable enough to talk to when his mind was free, he was silent and indifferent to everybody when he was interested in anything in particular. His lack of cordiality was the subject of comment. Neither had he the self-confidence nor the tenacity of purpose essential to success in an independent commander, and was at his best under orders. For that reason he got along well with Grant, possessing that first virtue of a soldier—obedience.

Winfield Scott Hancock, Major General of the Second Army Corps, appealed to Dana. A splendid fellow, he declared, brilliant, "as brave as Julius Caesar", and always ready to obey orders, especially if these led to fighting. Hancock reciprocated in good will and there was real enthusiasm in their relations. Little did either reck then of their contact in the future, or its searing influence!

An old acquaintance came into view, recalling the days in Buffalo when Dana had been a sergeant in the city guard formed to resist the threatened McKenzie invasion. John Sedgwick, then second lieutenant in the Second Artillery of the United States Army, which had been sent to Buffalo, and Dana had come together and had become quite friendly. Now Sedgwick was Major General of the Sixth Army Corps of the Army of the Potomac. A very solid man he had become, "with no flummery about him. You could always tell where Sedgwick was to be found, and in a battle he was apt to be found where the hardest fighting was. He was not an ardent, impetuous soldier like Hancock, but was steady and sure." Two days after their reunion Sedgwick was shot through the head by a rebel sharpshooter while on a tour of inspection. It was all in the day's work, but the army had lost a good general and Dana one whose friendship he had hoped to cultivate.

Dana set down that in his opinion General Humphreys was the great soldier of the Army of the Potomac. He was chief of staff to Meade and not only a strategist, a tactician and an engineer of ability, but also a good fighter. Wearing a black felt hat, with the brim turned down all around, he had the appearance of a Quaker. It must have been startling to hear him break loose when he was aroused, for he was the loudest swearer of all those he-men with whom destiny had thrown Dana.

"The men of distinguished and brilliant profanity in the war were General Sherman and General Humphreys," was his verdict. "I could not mention any others that could be classed with them. General Logan was also a strong swearer, but he was not a West Pointer: he was a civilian. Sherman and Humphreys would swear to make everything blue when some dispatch had not been delivered correctly or they were provoked."

Dana was in a ticklish position through the months of awful fighting which followed. Though he clung to his previous judgment that Grant was the supreme general of the war, and therefore the man to have the high command, there were times when he knew that he was not at his best. Some of the fearful losses appeared unjustified, and though Grant was himself deeply moved by the results of some of his unavailing frontal attacks, he repeated them.

In his *Recollections of the Civil War* Dana said: "There are still many persons who bitterly accuse Grant of butchery in this campaign. As a matter of fact, Grant lost fewer men in his successful effort to take Richmond and end the war than his predecessors lost in making the same attempt and failing." He submitted official figures to prove this. They showed Grant's losses to be nearly twenty thousand less than the combined losses of McDowell, McClellan, Pope, Burnside, Hooker and Meade. But they were nearly one hundred and twenty-five thousand of killed, wounded, captured or missing and they occurred in eleven months. The question really was whether all these losses were justified. Dana's friend Wilson, who was with Grant, and was in command of a division during some of the bloodiest fighting, tells of a dinner in camp with Dana and Rawlins, during which they all discussed the campaign in utmost candor, and, while approving Grant's tactics in general, heartily condemned "the insane policy of butting into intrenchments", with such fearful losses as occurred at Cold Harbor. They were all agreed as to the cause.

Grant, who was now surrounded by officers of the regular

army, had come under their influence, and especially under that of an engineer who had come with him from the West. To him Rawlins attributed the cry of "Smash 'em up! Smash 'em up!" He was now the dominating adviser and Rawlins had been supplanted for the time being.

Being of this opinion, why did not Dana criticise Grant in his dispatches to Washington? The outstanding characteristic of his advices throughout had been their complete frankness. Nothing had been allowed to stand in the way of his expressing the truth, the whole truth and nothing but the truth, as he saw it. It was part of his nature to do his job thoroughly and to be uncompromising and unmoved by any considerations whatsoever. What was the motive for his reticence here? Wilson indicates it and thereby justifies it. It was a case of submitting to the lesser evil.

On the whole Grant was justifying his supremacy. His purpose to go on to Richmond and cut Lee off from his base of supplies was manifestly the thing to do, and even his critics were convinced he would finally accomplish it. To lessen the confidence of the Government in him at this time would certainly be a serious interference, without necessarily preventing the great losses that were the cause of criticism. The wise thing to do was to keep at Grant through every influence which could reach him and try to restore the sane ascendancy of Rawlins. And that is the course which was followed, with the hoped-for result.

There is no mention of all this in Dana's memoirs. In fact, he flatly declares that the outlook warranted the attack at Cold Harbor. "Sheridan took the same chances at Five Forks ten months later, and won," he declared. Luck was against Grant. There would have been no thought of his losses had he won.

Grant had accomplished one great thing. The legend that Lee was invincible was no longer paralyzing the efforts of the officers of the Army of the Potomac. Grant's boldness in maneuvering against him had destroyed that. But Grant confessed to Dana his disappointment in not being able to get Lee into open battle. Could that be accomplished the war would be ended. Lee had indicated that his real ability lay in defensive fighting. Yet, according to Dana, Grant deceived him by his march on Petersburg, when Lee was expecting him to be advancing on a new line between the James and the Chickahominy. Lee had been caught napping, and if Gen. Smith had not stopped too soon in his advance on the heights southeast of Petersburg that town would have been captured with little loss. There was just a hint, in Dana's comment on this movement, of Grant's sacrifice of valuable lives in frontal attacks. The operations at Petersburg were unsatisfactory, owing to the previous heavy loss in superior officers. The men fought as well as ever, but they were not directed with the same skill and enthusiasm. Dana had mentioned this loss of officers before.

But he was convinced Grant had shown great skill in getting the army from Cold Harbor to this point, "a far more brilliant evolution than McClellan's 'change of base' two years before over almost the same roads". And it was Beauregard and not Lee who saved the Confederacy for the time being by holding out at Petersburg against the Union attack.

The fright in Washington over what seemed to be a menacing invasion of the Confederate army brought Dana back there to be for a time "the eyes of Grant at the capital", as he had been those of the Government at the front. Grant had not been able to get satisfactory information from Washington and asked Dana to go there and report to him. He found Washington and Baltimore in a state of great excitement. From the former could be seen clouds of dust which were credited to the hostile cavalry. Every able-bodied man was being enrolled for the defence of the capital. Fifteen hundred employes of the Quartermaster's Department were armed and posted outside. Six boatloads of troops from Grant's army relieved the tension somewhat, but still there was great alarm. The lack of a central authority over the troops resulted in confusion. Dana telegraphed Grant that Stanton looked to him for more than advice or suggestions. Halleck would give no orders except as he received them, the President would give none, and it remained for him, as Commander-in-Chief, to end the deplorable situation.

As it turned out, much of the alarm was unwarranted. The Confederates, not realizing their opportunity, swung away after inflicting considerable damage on railroads, bridges and surrounding property. Calm was restored with the appointment of Sheridan to clean up Shenandoah Valley. General Meigs marched his "division of quartermaster's clerks back to their desks, and Admiral Goldsborough, who had marshalled the marines and sailors, returned to smoke his pipe on his own doorstep". Dana went back to the War Department to resume his investigations of alleged frauds and disloyalty. A new service put upon him was the supervision of spies.

XV. STANTON DISCOMFITS A DELEGATION OF DISLOYAL BALTIMOREANS—A REMARKABLE GOVERNMENT SPY—SHENANDOAH AND SHERIDAN—VISIT TO RICHMOND AFTER THE SURRENDER, AND INTERVIEW WITH ANDREW JOHNSON.

THE GOVERNMENT had to take chances with some of the men used for this unpleasant service, and it was not always possible to be certain about their trustworthiness. There was a pedler, called Morse by Dana, though that was not his real name, who traveled between Washington and Richmond, nominally playing the spy for both sides. At Washington he was believed to be hoodwinking the Confederates, and at Richmond they must have had the same faith in his deception of the Federals. He was presumed to be smuggling things into the Confederate lines—luxuries they could not get otherwise. These were always supervised by the Federal agents. When he came back he brought more or less valuable information. But once he was caught overstepping the line. The goods he was undertaking to transport contained uniforms and other military articles, and altogether they were valued at more than twenty-five thousand dollars. These were taken from him and he was locked up.

Investigation implicated a lot of leading Baltimore merchants and Stanton decided to make an example of them. Acting under his instructions, Dana ordered their arrest, and ninety-seven were lodged in jail. The result was a deputation from Baltimore to see the President. They came in a very high-hat mood, asserted that the men arrested were gentlemen and faultless citizens, and demanded not only their instant release but damages for the indignity to which they had been subjected. Lincoln directed them to see Stanton, and the latter was notified of what was in store for him. He sent for Dana, and said:

"All Baltimore is coming here; sit down and hear the discussion."

The deputation was ushered in, bank presidents, millionaire merchants, all the élite of the business world of Baltimore. They must have represented at least fifty million dollars. They sat down around the fire, and presently began speechifying. There was no ground, no justification for this outrage, whose wickedness transcended the power of description. After half a dozen had delivered themselves thus, Stanton asked the others, one after another, if they had anything to add. When all expressed satisfaction with the manner in which their errand had been presented, he began.

"He described the beginning of the war," said Dana, "for which, he said, there was no justification—being beaten in an election was no reason for destroying the Government. Then he went on to the fact that half a million of our young men had been laid in untimely graves by this conspiracy of the slave interest. He outlined the whole conspiracy in the most solemn and impressive terms, and then he depicted the offense that this man Morse, aided by these several merchants, had committed. 'Gentlemen,' he said, 'if you would like to examine the bills of what he was taking to the enemy, here they are.' When Stanton had finished, these gentlemen, without answering a word, got up and one by one went away. That was the only speech I ever listened to that cleared out the entire audience."

From the welter of many interesting experiences with the secret service there stood out that of a clerk in one of the departments who applied for the post of spy within the confederate lines. A prepossessing young man in the mid-twenties, well-spoken and intelligent, bearing an excellent character from his superiors, his asking for the most dangerous work in the army surprised those to whom he made application and caused comment in the War Department. The perilous nature of the service was even pointed out to him, but he was not to be dissuaded. All he asked was a horse and an order which would carry him safely through the Federal lines. Having received these he disappeared.

Several weeks later he reported back to the War Department. He had been in Gordonsville and Richmond, had won the confidence of the Confederate authorities, and was now carrying a letter from Jefferson Davis to Clement C. Clay, Confederate agent in Canada. This letter, he informed Dana, was only a letter of recommendation to Clay, and his official associate, Jacob Thompson, who had been Secretary of the Interior in the Cabinet of President Buchanan. It was to pave the way for the young man's employment as messenger between these two agents and their Government. He also reported upon the condition of the Confederate army, but there was nothing new in what he had to offer. Accepting his word, the letter was not opened and he was allowed to proceed to Niagara Falls and thence to Canada. Not long thereafter he was again in Washington, and again the message he bore was allowed to go unopened upon his assertion that it contained nothing of importance.

Months passed and the messenger went to and fro between Richmond and St. Catherine, stopping always at the War Department where now the letters were inspected and copies made. There was some difficulty in getting the English-made paper required to duplicate the envelopes, and some delay in imitating the seals, but the spy was apparently able to account to the Confederates for his slowness of passage by inventing accidents or attempted Federal interference.

One day he appeared much excited, declaring his letter this time was of great importance. It was found to be the outline of a plan to set fire to New York and Chicago. Incendiary machines, operated by clockwork, were to be placed in a number of the large hotels and places of amusement, to operate simultaneously, so that the fire departments would be unable to respond to all the calls, and the cities would be helpless while conflagrations swept them. It was confidently expected they would be greatly damaged if not totally destroyed.

The dispatch was carefully sealed again, and the messenger sent on his way, while special officers of the War Department hurried to New York and Chicago to warn the authorities. In New York General Dix was strongly inclined to believe this was a hoax, and John A. Kennedy, the Superintendent of Police, was of the same opinion. But the orders from the War Department had been peremptory, and on the day appointed for the attempt the military and the police were prepared to meet it. It happened that the Government's messenger was stopping at the St. Nicholas Hotel, one of those designated in the letter, and while he was dressing in the evening, preparatory to going to dinner, he smelled smoke and fire was discovered burning in an adjoining room. It had been started by a machine such as had been described in the letter, evidently set in operation by a lodger who had left some hours earlier. Similar fires were discovered elsewhere and in each case proved to be of similar origin. Thanks to their preparedness the military and the firemen were able to put them out before they had gained headway and without revealing the facts, which might have excited the populace.

Once again the young man turned up with an important message, this time from Clay to the Confederate Secretary of State Benjamin. It outlined the program for a formidable attack upon Vermont. An organization had been formed in Canada for this purpose and was only waiting for a suitable opportunity to descend upon Burlington. Coming after the attempt upon St. Albans and Lake Champlain, this one had been prepared with especial care and promised to be more serious. The Confederate estimate of the importance of this dispatch was demonstrated by the precautions taken against its falling into the hands of the Federals. It had been placed between the two thicknesses of the spy's reinforced trousers, and sewed up so that when he was on his horse it was held above the saddle.

Stanton was ill at home when Dana brought him the letter. "This is serious," he declared. "Go over to the White House and ask the President to come here." It was Sunday and Lincoln was getting ready to go to church, but he obeyed the summons at once.

He and Stanton considered the situation in all its aspects. To retain the letter would put an end to the spy's service, and yet it was highly desirable not to let it go, as it proved the use by the Confederates of the territory of a neutral nation to fit out a warlike expedition against the United States. It was finally decided to keep it and, as further evidence of its genuineness, which would refute any doubts which might be raised by the British Government, it was agreed that it must be taken from the spy while he was acting as the dispatch bearer of the Confederate Government.

"We must have the paper for Seward," declared the President. "As for the young man, get him out of the scrape if you can."

So the paper was taken back to the War Department, where it was again sewed up in the trousers, and the spy was ordered to start at dusk on the road he was accustomed to take in passing the Federal lines, and to be at a certain tavern outside Alexandria at nine o'clock in the evening, stopping there to water his horse. At the same time word was sent to the officer in charge of the defenses of that town to be at the tavern to arrest a Confederate dispatch-bearer, concerning whom the War Department had received information.

Around midnight the prisoner was brought in and the officer in charge reported that while he had offered no resistance he had been most abusive in his language, denouncing the United States in violent terms and boasting of his attachment to the Confederacy.

Dana, always interested in the exposition of individual character, was greatly impressed by the bearing of the prisoner. Patient, scornful and undaunted, his lips firmly closed except when he made terse response to some questions, he carried out his role with the skill and finesse of a trained actor. "If Mr. Clay and Mr. Benjamin had been present," Dana commented, "they would have been more than ever certain that he was one of their noblest young men." Through all the details of the search of his person he never once lost his pose or indicated even to the observant Dana that he was playing a part. The letter having been discovered, and a report of the seizure drawn up and signed, the prisoner was taken to the Old Capitol Prison.

Secretary of State Seward received the dispatch and the report for use in London and several days later the warden of the prison was instructed to let the prisoner escape, yet maintain the appearance of an effort at prevention. Shortly thereafter he walked into Dana's office.

"Ah," said Dana, "you have run away."

"Yes, sir," he answered.

"Did they shoot at you?"

"They did, and didn't hit me; but I didn't think that would answer the purpose, so I shot myself through the arm."

And so he had. Dana saw the wound, which was through the fleshy part of the forearm, due care having been taken to prevent the bullet's hitting any bones. Yet it did not look trivial. What was more, it had received no attention nor would he permit it to be dressed, being determined to use that fact to impress the Confederates. Sure enough, within a few weeks he was back again from Canada, and again bearing dispatches. To help along his deception the War Department had inserted advertisements in a number of the leading newspapers, offering two thousand dollars reward for his recapture. Apparently he was able to evade would-be winners of this prize as well as he did detection of his duplicities. After the war he received a post in one of the departments, but held it only a short time. Evidently clerical work proved too tame after the excitements of his military service. "He was one of the cleverest creatures I ever saw,"

The ☀ Sun.

MONDAY. OCTOBER 18, 1897.

CHARLES ANDERSON DANA, Editor of THE SUN, died yesterday afternoon.

Dana, the Giant of Journalism

Below: As viewed by the *Chicago Daily News* Staff, 1888. Eugene Field is the pigmy fingering his pistol holster.

Above: As viewed by Dana himself, 1897. This brief death notice reflected his express wish.

said Dana. "His style of patriotic lying was sublime; it amounted to genius."

In October Dana was sent down the Shenandoah Valley to bear to Sheridan his commission as Major General. It was a marked compliment on the part of the War Department to do this with special ceremonial. Stanton did not usually employ his chief aids to carry commissions to generals.

The next morning, riding with Sheridan through the lines, Dana was struck by the evidence of personal affection shown by the rank and file.

> Everybody seemed personally to be attached to him. He was like the most popular man after an election—the whole force everywhere honored him. Finally I said to the General: "I wish you would explain one thing to me. Here I find all these people of every rank—generals, sergeants, corporals and private soldiers; in fact, everybody—manifesting a personal affection for you that I have never seen in any other army, not even in the Army of the Tennessee for Grant. I have never seen anything like it. Tell me what is the reason?"
>
> "Mr. Dana," said Sheridan, "I long ago made up my mind that it was not a good plan to fight battles with paper orders—that is, for the commander to stand on a hill in the rear and send his aides-de-camp with written orders to the different commanders. My practice has always been to fight in the front rank."
>
> "Well, General," said Dana, "that is more dangerous; in the front rank a man is much more liable to be killed than he is in the rear."
>
> "I know that there is a certain risk in it," Sheridan replied, "but, in my judgment, the advantage is much greater than the risk, and I have come to the conclusion that that is the right thing to do. That is the reason the men like me. They know that when the hard pinch comes I am exposed just as much as any of them."

Throughout the winter of 1865 Dana was busy in Washington. On Jan. 5th he wrote in a letter to Wilson: "I came near leaving here about a fortnight ago to take the place of Adjutant General of the State of New York. The inducements were complete control of all military appointments among the troops of that State, the opportunity of great political usefulness, and an amount of pay on which I could live. But Mr. Stanton would not consent. . . ."

With the surrender of Richmond Dana was sent to that city to gather up such papers of the Confederacy as had been allowed to remain there. Richmond, partly burned and pretty thoroughly starved, needed more than anything else sustaining food and sympathetic direction. The tendency to abandon all further thought of rebellion and return to the old allegiance could be encouraged or the contrary, and Dana was sympathetic with the appeasing methods of General Weitzel, who was in command. In the midst of his work he met Andrew Johnson, the new Vice-President, and was surprised to find him opposed to any policy of consideration.

> He took me aside [Dana recorded] and spoke with great earnestness about the necessity of not taking the Confederates back without some conditions or without some punishment. He insisted that their sins had been enormous, and that if they were let back into the Union without any punishment the effect would be very bad. He said they might be very dangerous in the future. The Vice-President talked to me in this strain for fully twenty minutes, I should think. It was an impassioned earnest speech. . . . Finally, when he paused and I got a chance to reply, I said: "Why, Mr. Johnson, I have no power in this case. Your remarks are very striking, very impressive, and certainly worthy of the most serious consideration, but it does not seem to me necessary that they should be addressed to me. They ought to be addressed to the President and to the members of Congress, to those who have authority in the case, and who will finally have to decide the question which you raise." "Mr. Dana," said he, "I feel it to be my duty to say these things to every man I meet,

whom I know to have any influence. Any man whose thoughts are considered by others, or whose judgment is going to weigh in the case, I must speak to, so that the weight of opinion in favor of the view of this question which I offer may possibly become preponderating and decisive." That was in April. When Mr. Johnson became President, not long after, he soon came to take entirely the view which he condemned so earnestly in this conversation with me.

Dana also set down for the future historian a resumé of a conversation with Grant after the surrender of Lee. Grant told him that Lee had said he would devote all his efforts to pacifying the country and bringing the people back into the Union.

"He had always been for the Union in his own heart, and could find no justification for the politicians who had brought on the war, the origin of which he believed to have been in the folly of the extremists on both sides."

XVI. PORTRAITS OF LINCOLN AND HIS CABINET —THE BARGAIN THAT MADE NEVADA A STATE—A PRESIDENT WITHOUT ILLUSIONS—LINCOLN ON THE WISDOM OF HOLDING ON TO A BOLTING ELEPHANT'S HIND LEG.

DANA had not failed to set down his impressions of Lincoln and his chief advisers. The first man in the cabinet was William H. Seward, Secretary of State, who had been Lincoln's most formidable opponent for the Presidential nomination. The most powerful weapon used against him in the struggle for the coveted honor was that he was from New York, and the New York branch of the Republican party was controlled by a "boss". Even then there was a prejudice against bosses, one which Dana frankly did not share. People, he declared, seemed to think that a party should direct itself.

"Exactly what that means," he added, "I have not been able to understand. An army without a general is of no use, and a ship without a captain doesn't get navigated safely. I notice, too, that the class of politicians who are most strenuous against bosses are those who are not able to control for themselves the boss who happens to be in power in their district or their State."

Seward was of optimistic temperament and "had the most cultivated and comprehensive intellect in the administration. He was a man who all his life was in controversies, yet he was singular in this, that, though forever in fights he had almost no personal enemies." With great ability as a writer he combined what Dana declared was rare in a lawyer, a politician or a statesman—imagination. An impressive though unpretentious speaker, his manner was that of one engaged in conversation, of one deliberating "out loud", which gave added emphasis to his words. He was fixed in the opinion that all North America should be in the Union.

Chase, Secretary of the Treasury, was "a very able, noble and spotless statesman, a man who would have been worthy of the best days of the old Roman republic". Also a candidate for the nomination, "the opposition that had been raised against Mr. Seward would not have availed, because, while Mr. Seward had a friend who was the boss of the Republican party in New York, Mr. Chase bossed it himself in Ohio." He was tall, impressive, a portly man with a very large, handsome head. Generally genial, he was also tenacious of his views and would sometimes criticize the President, which Seward was never heard to do.

These two and Stanton were the most impressive of the Cabinet. The Attorney General, Edward Bates, had been Greeley's candidate, who was credited with having dictated his selection. He was an eloquent speaker but did not impress Dana as a lawyer or a personality—"an amiable and a gifted man, entirely creditable and satisfactory, without possessing any extraordinary genius or any unusual force of character."

Gideon Welles, head of the Navy, "was a curious-looking man. He wore a wig which was parted in the middle, the hair falling down on each side; and it was from his peculiar appearance, I have always thought, that the idea that he was an old fogy originated." Governor Andrew of Massachusetts came into Dana's office one day asking for "that old Mormon deacon, the Secretary of the Navy". Yet he was a very wise, strong man. Nothing "decorative about him, there was no noise in the street when he went along", but he understood his job and did it well.

Caleb Smith, Secretary of the Interior, and Montgomery Blair, Postmaster General, did not get much attention from Dana. They were both efficient and eminent, and Blair was sharp, keen "and perhaps a little cranky". Dana got along with him very well, but not everybody was equally successful, Stanton among others, so that when Blair wanted anything in the War Department he came to Dana.

However it was a decidedly harmonious Cabinet, and above all on excellent terms with its chief. Now and then a mumble of pettishness here and there, perhaps, for they were after all human beings and probably more decided in their individuality than most, but really very seldom was the spirit of cordiality absent in the relations of any of them with the President.

And the latter was always master of them as he was of himself. Never putting on any airs and never uttering a harsh words to any one. Always calm, equable and uncomplaining, never impatient or in a hurry or trying to hurry anybody else, yet everybody knew that no question of consequence was settled until he had given his decision. In any discussion of important matters whatever he said showed the deepest thought, even when it was expressed in the form of a joke. No one could fail to be impressed with his authority or with the fact that there was always a strong force in reserve.

Dana, always impelled by his nature to be alert for the feet of clay, found his god well-nigh impeccable. Impressive even physically, and not at all awkward or ungainly, as some would have it. When he rode out on horseback, a tall hat topping his six feet four inches, he looked a giant. Strong and muscular, with neither excess nor waste of material. Very quick in his movements, when he chose to be, and of extraordinary physical endurance. Working late and hard night after night, he appeared the next morning fresh and vigorous. The thought of his fine physical condition was in Dana's mind at their last meeting. It was the day he was shot and Dana had come to the White House to see him. He was in a small side room, washing his hands, his coat off and his sleeves rolled up, and Dana noticed particularly the absence of fat in his long arms and how well developed and flexible his muscles seemed to be.

His smile was captivating. "I have never seen a woman's

smile that approached it in its engaging quality; nor have I seen another face which would light up as Lincoln's did when something touched his heart or amused him. . . . There was such a charm and beauty about his expression, such good humor and friendly spirit looking from his eyes, that when you were near him you never thought whether he was awkward or graceful; you thought of nothing except, 'What a kindly character this man has!' Then, too, there was such shrewdness in his kindly features that one did not care to criticize him. His manner was always dignified, and even if he had done an awkward thing the dignity of his character and manner would have made it seem graceful and becoming.

"The great quality of his appearance was benevolence and benignity: the wish to do somebody good if he could; and yet there was no flabby philanthropy about Abraham Lincoln. He was all solid, hard, keen intelligence combined with goodness. Indeed, the expression of his face and of his bearing which impressed one most, after his benevolence and benignity, was his intelligent understanding. You felt that here was a man who saw through things, who understood, and you respected him accordingly."

That understanding, especially of human nature, was what Dana believed to be the basis of his extraordinary skill as a politician. A demonstration of it came when he had decided the time had come to amend the Constitution so as to prohibit slavery. Apart from its ethical side it was regarded as a military measure, affecting not only those who abhorred slavery but also those who were seeking to uphold it. It was conceived to be equivalent to new armies in the field, because it would paralyze the enemy. But when it came to counting up the votes in Congress to accomplish his purpose—it had to be approved by three-fourths of the States—Lincoln saw he would probably not have enough. Another state was necessary. Nevada was organized for that purpose. Dana remarked once that when he heard people say Nevada was superfluous, not big enough to be a state, he could hear Lincoln answering that criticism with, "It is easier to admit Nevada than to raise another million soldiers."

One afternoon in March of 1864, while the question was being fought out in the House of Representatives, Lincoln came to Dana's office. He came in and shut the door.

"Dana," said he, "I am very anxious about this vote. It has got to be taken next week. The time is very short. It is going to be a great deal closer than I wish it was."

"There are plenty of Democrats who will vote for it," Dana assured him. "There is James E. English, of Connecticut. I think he is sure, isn't he?"

"Oh, yes; he is sure on the merits of the question."

Dana mentioned "Sunset" Cox, of Ohio. Lincoln agreed he could be depended on. But there were some others—in fact, there were three he thought Dana could deal with better than anybody else. One was from New Jersey and the other two were from New York. Dana asked what inducement they would be likely to demand.

"I don't know," said Lincoln; "it makes no difference, though, what they want. Here is the alternative: that we carry this vote, or be compelled to raise another million, and I don't know how many more, men, and fight no one knows how long. It is a question of three votes or new armies."

"Well, sir," said Dana, "what shall I say to these gentlemen?"

"I don't know," said Lincoln, "but whatever promise you make to them I will perform."

Dana sent for the three Congressmen, one after another, and got their pledges to vote for the admission of Nevada. It took some dickering. Two were easily disposed of. All they wanted was some internal revenue collectorships. The third was after a bigger game, an appointment in the New York Custom House worth twenty thousand a year.

"I understand, of course," said this one, when Dana

promised the appointment, "that you are not saying this on your own authority."

"No," said Dana frankly, "I am saying it on the authority of the President."

They voted as agreed and Nevada became a State. It was one of the States which voted to ratify the Thirteenth Amendment, and both Lincoln and Dana felt that the executive authority had been employed judiciously.

Parenthetically it should be said that the promise as to the Custom House appointment was not kept. It was to go into effect when the term of the man holding the job ran out, but Lincoln had been assassinated before that time and Andrew Johnson was President. Dana was in the West when he received a telegram from Roscoe Conkling, summoning him to Washington. When he arrived Conkling said to him:

"I want you to go and see President Johnson, and tell him that the appointment of this man to the Custom House is a sacred promise of Mr. Lincoln's, and that it must be kept."

Dana did as requested, explaining fully all the preliminaries leading up to the promise he had made in Lincoln's name, and wound up with:

"I trust, Mr. President, that you will see your way clear to execute this promise."

"Well, Mr. Dana," Johnson replied, "I don't say that I won't; but I have observed in the course of my experience that such bargains tend to immorality."

In relating this Dana made no comment, beyond saying that the disappointed Congressman did not hold him to blame when the appointment was not made, but his very reticence showed how he regarded Johnson's unctuous parade of political virtue. Later on, when he had regained the power of the editorial pen, he paid the reckoning with interest.

Another of Lincoln's political deals tickled Dana's sense of humor to the point that he could not refrain from giving it to the world. This one was with his old friend, Horace Greeley. Greeley had been a severe and constant critic of the President's conduct of the war, exhibiting increasing irritation as this dragged on with peace ever deferred. In the summer of 1864 Greeley received a letter from one who claimed to be an agent of the Confederacy which invited him to meet two alleged "Ambassadors" of Jefferson Davis, who had full powers to negotiate peace. These were now in Canada, but would cross the border if he secured from President Lincoln the promise of protection. In the meantime the writer asked for a personal interview at Niagara Falls. The day after the letter reached Greeley he received a telegram reading: "Will you come here? Parties have full power."

With his usual impetuosity Greeley wrote the President, pointing out that here lay the opportunity to make the peace so long delayed by the ineptitude of the Government. Critical and acrimonious even, the letter concluded with the opinion that no time should be lost in appointing an ambassador, or at least a diplomatic agent, to meet the agents of Mr. Davis. By return post Greeley received from Lincoln a request that he himself be the Government's representative and proceed at once to Niagara Falls.

> If you can find any person anywhere [Lincoln wrote] professing to have any proposition of Jefferson Davis, in writing, for peace, embracing the restoration of the Union, and abandonment of slavery, whatever else it embraces, say to him he may come to me with you, and that if he really brings such proposition he shall at the least have safe conduct with the paper (and without publicity, if he chooses) to the point where you shall have met him. The same, if there be two or more persons.

Poor Greeley! With all his great ability and years of experience he remained to the end the type people select as the butt of practical joking.

Meeting Dana shortly after the dispatch of the letter, Lincoln remarked, with one of his infectious twinkles:

"I sent Brother Greeley a commission. I guess I am about even with him now."

Something else in Lincoln impressed Dana greatly. It was his instinct for timeliness, which was so wonderful as to be awe-inspiring. "He never stepped too soon, and he never stepped too late," was Dana's way of expressing it. With what seemed to be the whole country clamoring for a proclamation to abolish slavery, Lincoln remained unmoved. Deputations trod upon each other's heels. There was one such, mostly clergymen from Massachusetts, all in black coats, and filled with ardor. Still he was adamant. The time was not ripe. Even in the North there were still many who believed in compromise and who might resent the closing of the door to all future dicker with the slaveholders. Dana was of the opinion that if Lincoln had given way to the clamor of the Abolitionists at the outset the war would have been lost. Coming when it did the proclamation satisfied everybody. Even the Confederates expected it.

And Lincoln was a great general, in fact the greatest general of the war. This was Dana's solemn assertion, born from his many contacts with the President during the war. Lincoln had known very little about military matters at the beginning, but before the close even "von Moltke was not a better general, or an abler planner or expounder of a campaign". A better general than Grant or Thomas, and Dana appealed to the records of the war as conclusive evidence of the soundness of his judgment.

One day Dana came into Stanton's office and found the Secretary looking over some manuscript. "Edward Everett has made a speech," he remarked, "that will make three columns in the newspapers." He was referring to the speech at Gettysburg. "And Mr. Lincoln," he added, "has made a speech of perhaps forty or fifty lines. Everett's is the speech of a scholar, polished to the last possibility. It is elegant. and it is learned; but Lincoln's speech will be read by a

thousand men where one reads Everett's, and will be remembered as long as anybody's speeches are remembered
who speaks in the English language."

And yet, observed Dana, Lincoln was not what one called
educated. The only college he had attended was that of the
man who "gets up at daylight to hoe the corn, and sits up at
night by the side of a burning pine-knot to read the best
book he can find".

Dana was greatly impressed by what Lincoln had made
of his scanty opportunities. All his life the former had
believed in the necessity of formal education to develop the
capacities of any man. He believed in college education as
essential. He continued to believe in it, and many years later
he made public declaration of his conviction. Just as he was
convinced of the fundamental importance of languages, in
complete agreement with the poet who wrote, "He who
knows no other tongue can know but little of his own."
Then how explain the gripping eloquence and masterly
understanding of the most perplexing problems by this son
of the soil?

"He was a man of genius," Dana said simply, "and,
contrasted with men of education, genius will always carry
the day."

One weakness he had, and it was well known. One day
General Augur, commander of the forces around Washington, came to Dana with the request that he sign the death
warrant for a spy. The man had been tried fairly and found
guilty. Spies caused a lot of trouble, and it was essential
that there be an example made of them now and then to
protect the army, but the President could not be brought to
see this. So Augur was taking advantage of the fact that
he was not in Washington that day to get the necessary
authority from someone else. He had been to Stanton, who
had ducked, probably salving his conscience with the reflection that Dana had charge of the secret service, which
included spying. Dana, satisfied that the General was right,
and scornful of the moral cowardice which shirks a duty

because it is unpleasant, signed the paper. It turned out to be wasted effort. The next morning Augur told him Lincoln had returned in the early hours and stopped the execution.

And yet he found Lincoln singularly free of all illusions. Things were so or they were not so. His mind refused the may-be's and might-be's of those who seek to avoid the actual, and worked only on facts, of which it could invariably grasp the essence. It never got things twisted. It never went beyond what was clearly in evidence, refusing any indulgence in guesswork. Dana never heard him intimate definite consequences to stated conditions without those consequences following. He was the man of wisdom, and wisdom, being superior to talent and to education, showed again his genius.

Ten years after Lincoln's death Dana told the world how highly he esteemed him in an editorial entitled "A Presumptuous Undertaking". It was inspired by a report that Lincoln's secretaries, John G. Nicolay and John Hay, were about to attempt a biography of their former chief, and Dana was hot at what he conceived to be sheer effrontery.

> Mr. Lincoln has already suffered more bitter treatment at the hands of his biographers [wrote Dana] than he did from the bullet of Wilkes Booth.

Now came these two "mere writers of jeux d'esprit, dealers in the effervescent or pretty literary work which the gossips of literature delight in", and the result was likely to be even greater injustice to Lincoln than had been done him by those who had already "daubed his impressive figure on the contracted canvas of their limited sight".

"The time has hardly come for the writing of an adequate life of Mr. Lincoln," he declared, "nor does one who surveys the field of our living authorship readily discover the fit person to attempt it. Assuredly it is not a task for dilettanti, nor for those who occupy themselves with the superficial and sentimental foam of literature."

Sometimes Stanton, among whose talents humor was not

conspicuous, was annoyed at what he thought was Lincoln's tendency to trifle at moments that called for seriousness. On the night of the election which was to determine whether Lincoln was to carry on for another term, the members of the Cabinet and a few others were closeted with the President in Stanton's office, the returns being received at the War Department. As the telegrams arrived Stanton would read them, and then everybody would listen attentively to the President's comments. Certainly a serious occasion and the atmosphere tense with suspense that was almost painful. Had the people realized the difficulties met and conquered? Had they appreciated what was at stake and what it would mean not to sustain the existing Administration at this crucial time in the war? Lincoln's was the only face which did not show the strain of such thoughts. Presently, when there was a lull in the returns, he called to Dana:

"Have you ever read any of the writings of Petroleum V. Nasby?"

Dana replied that he had glanced at some of them and had found them quite funny.

"Let me read you a specimen," said Lincoln serenely, and, pulling a yellow-covered pamphlet from the breast pocket of his coat, he began to read aloud from the humorist.

Dana could see Stanton fidgeting with annoyance, of which Lincoln pretended at least to be entirely unconscious. He would read, stop to listen to a telegram, and then resume. Presently Stanton got up and went into the next room, beckoning to Dana as he did so. The only purpose was to vent his indignation, which he could smother no longer, to someone. With the safety of the Republic at issue, this man, the leader and most deeply concerned, could give up his mind to this balderdash, could laugh at frivolous jests and forget that history was in the making. It was disgusting, damnable! The fire of Stanton's wrath was scorching.

"He could not understand," said Dana, "that it was by the relief which these jests afforded to the strain of mind under which Lincoln had so long been living, and to the natural gloom of a melancholy and desponding temperament—this was Mr. Lincoln's prevailing characteristic—that the safety and sanity of his intelligence were maintained and preserved."

Once again, in April, 1865, Stanton was offended. Word had been received that Thompson, the Confederate agent already mentioned, was on his way from Canada to England, and would take ship at Portland, Maine. "Arrest him!" was the Secretary's order immediately the news was brought to him, but as Dana was leaving the room he reconsidered. Better consult the President. Dana found the latter in a little room adjoining his office washing his hands, the business of the day being finished and everybody else gone.

"Hello, Dana," he said, "what's up?"

Dana read him the telegram from Portland.

"What does Stanton say?" he asked.

"He says arrest him, but that I should refer the question to you."

Slowly wiping his hands, Lincoln said:

"No, I rather think not. When you have got an elephant by the hind leg and he's trying to run away, it's best to let him run."

When Dana returned to the War Department he found Stanton waiting for him.

"What does he say?" he asked.

"He says," replied Dana, "that when you have got an elephant by the hind leg, and he is trying to run away, it's best to let him run."

"Oh, stuff!" said Stanton.

One can see Dana struggling hard to maintain his composure and doubling up with laughter the moment he had withdrawn from the presence of his august superior. In all the world there was not another who would enjoy more keenly just such a situation.

But there was a tragic ending to the incident. That same night Dana was awakened from a sound sleep by a messenger from Stanton telling the news of the President's assassination. He rushed over to the house in Tenth Street where the President lay unconscious, though breathing heavily, on a bed in a small side room, while all the members of the Cabinet, and the Chief Justice of the Supreme Court, were gathered in the adjoining parlor. The surgeons had declared there was no hope, and the wise men were almost as incapable as their suffering chief. Stanton alone was in his full stride of mental and physical energy.

His coolness and clear-headedness, foreseeing every possible complication which might ensue from the tragedy, were manifest in every letter and telegram which Dana wrote down at his dictation. No one knew then what ramifications might be behind the assassination, nor how far they threatened the existence of the Government. There was the safety of Washington to look after, the possibility of manifestations around the country. There must be official notification to the people. The conspirators must be found. Thirty years later Dana expressed the conviction that no clearer brief account of the tragedy existed than that contained in Stanton's telegram addressed to General Dix, military commander at New York, and dictated within three hours of its occurrence.

They worked together until three in the morning. Lincoln was still alive and breathing regularly, though heavily, and quite unconscious, when Dana left. At eight o'clock he was again awakened by a messenger from the War Department.

"The President is dead," said the messenger, "and Mr. Stanton directs you to arrest Jacob Thompson."

But Thompson was never arrested. He had taken another route, avoiding the United States.

XVII. DANA BUYS THE *Sun*—HIS THEORIES ON RUNNING A NEWSPAPER—CHARACTER OF THE *Sun* UP TO THEN, AND CONDITIONS IN THE COUNTRY'S METROPOLIS.

DANA was now forty-six years old and had certainly been through more unusual experiences than most men of his age. Yet he was really only at the threshold of the most eventful part of his life. All that had gone before had only been preparatory to what was now to begin. Curiously enough, he manifested a disinclination for the job in which he was to achieve his really great success. Perhaps it was the influence of Washington, of the work in the War Department, making contracts and observing how riches poured into the laps of some men with a faculty for business enterprise. Money, after all, meant a lot to a man with a family and more than the average knowledge of what money can procure. In a country teeming with opportunities for the making of wealth why should he not follow the most direct path to that end? In fact, he must have money. He had come out of the war poorer than he went in, for his small salary had not begun to pay for the maintenance of his family. To his friend Wilson he wrote:

"As you are aware, it has not been my wish to return to my old profession on retiring from office, but to find some sphere of practical or industrial activity." But Fate sometimes compels for our own good. The Arabs have it that men are propelled into Paradise against their will. So Dana's seekings for business opportunities fortunately did not disclose an easy road to fortune and he was forced back into journalism.

Almost a year was given to a venture in Chicago. Senator Trumbull of Illinois and other prominent men induced him to take the editorship of the *Daily Republican*, organized with a nominal capital of half a million. But the money failed to materialize and, after a prolonged effort to make bricks without straw, he cut loose and returned to New York. Chicago left an ugly taste in his mouth ever after. The failure of those leading citizens to redeem their promises was not forgotten.

Nearly twenty-five years later space was found in the *Sun* for an article covering a whole page, signed by Archibald Gordon, allegedly descriptive of the Western metropolis, which was not so far removed from Dante's lurid picture of the Inferno. Many a reader must have blanched at the horror of it. A city of physical as well as mental torments, where one's nostrils were filled with blood-laden odors from the slaughter houses, and over which, as if to warn the traveler against its infection, hung suspended at all times a forbidding cloud of foul miasma.

Taunting phrases and paragraphs of ridicule recurred frequently. A man fell off a bridge over the Chicago River and broke his leg on its solid contents of city refuse. When the great Fair was projected a cable from Rome told of an alleged offer of Chicago capitalists to buy the Coliseum and have it re-erected on the Fair grounds. There was no let-up. Malice tempered with humor always, but with sincerity behind it. He never ceased to believe that the bluff and deception from which he had suffered were typical.

Yet that failure had been fortunate. There was only one city in the United States—probably in the whole world—which could be the real home of his peculiar genius, and that was New York. Paris, if he had been a Frenchman, would have been equally fitting, for that, too, has always offered a glad hand to the probe of satire and the unafraid critic of sham and pretence. But New York fitted him perfectly, and New York awoke to that fact soon after he was able to demonstrate his capacity.

Originally the purpose of the men who joined with him had been to found a new paper for him to conduct after his own theories, and a title—*The Evening Telegraph*—had actually been decided upon, but eventually they purchased the *Sun*, established some thirty-five years earlier as a penny newspaper to inform, instruct and entertain the common people. It was a distinguished group that supported this later venture—Roscoe Conkling, United States Senator; Edwin D. Morgan, also a Senator and former Governor of New York; Alonzo B. Cornell, Governor-to-be; William M. Evarts, reputed the ablest lawyer of his generation; Cyrus W. Field, of Atlantic cable fame; William H. Webb, big shipbuilder; Amos R. Eno, banker and owner of the Fifth Avenue Hotel; Thomas Hitchcock, financier and scholar, and a score of others of almost equal prominence.

They must have had faith in the ability of the editor, for there could hardly have been any great urge for these men of wealth and position to support the kind of paper the *Sun* then was or promised to be. It was not and would not be a party organ, therefore no promoter of political ambitions; it was not and probably would not be read in the homes of fashion, therefore not influential in club or social life. All that could be expected of it was that it would "present its daily photograph of the whole world's doings in the most luminous and lively manner". That was all that was promised in the declaration of policy and principles signed by Charles A. Dana, Manager and Editor. That and this further illumination, which proved to be perhaps most important of all:

"It will not take as long to read the *Sun* as to read the *London Times* or *Webster's Dictionary.*"

In the first issue under Dana's direction—January 27, 1868—at the end of a sketch describing the Tammany Hall on Printing House Square, which was to be the future home of the *Sun*, appeared the following:

No new Halleck can sing:
"There's a barrel of porter at Tammany Hall,
And the Bucktails are enjoying it all the night long;
In the time of my boyhood it was pleasant to call
For a seat and cigar 'mid the jovial throng."

So far as the corner of Nassau and Frankfort Streets are concerned, *L'Empire est paix*. The Sun shines for all; and on the site of old Tammany's troubles and tribulations we turn back the leaves of the past, dispel the clouds of discord, and shed our beams far and near over the Regenerated Land.

Dana was fully prepared for his task. Those years with Greeley had not only taught him all there was to know about the technique of newspaper making, but it had revealed the don'ts as well as the do's, which the editor must cling to if he would push out from the ruck and win a following. Greeley had done it in spite of definite drawbacks, and even a less observant man than Dana could see why he had achieved his success. His powerful pen, obvious sincerity and original personality were bound to attract attention. But Greeley was ludicrous at times. People laughed at him even while they respected his opinions. That sort of thing would never do for a Dana. He wanted his readers to laugh —with him; not at him.

No doubt of his having given many hours to a close study of the problems of chieftainship during the days on the *Tribune*, for he was not the man to be content with anything but first place, and they must have recurred to him on many a lonely night in camp, when the exploding bombs and roaring guns made sleep impossible.

One fact had impressed him particularly. The man at the top must walk alone. While he might listen to counsel and the judgments of others he must abide by his own and be immovable in the face of pleading or of opposition. He must have his own principles, create his own program, meet each problem and emergency in his own way. Not unlike the general laying out his campaign. In the end success would come to him who had definite ideas and definite vision and never wobbled. Wobbling would wreck the most brilliant plan. It would likewise destroy the most sparkling journalist. In fact, the first axiom of the editor must be to be not only himself, first, last and all the time, but to stay put.

He must impress his personality upon his readers, must give them a definite conception of what he was like. Not a true portrait in every respect necessarily, but true in the main. Once that was established in the popular mind it would ensure a following as long as he lived up to it. If he was a Puritan, and shouted for blue laws, other Puritans would cling to him as long as he preached the faith; if he stood for personal liberty and the less laws the better, that must be his attitude through thick and thin. As theatre-goers get to like a favorite actor in a certain type of rôle and resent his coming before them in any other, so the readers of a newspaper come to picture its editor as a certain character, and will have him as that or not at all. Old Bennett might be horsewhipped in the public streets by his rival, but so long as he had the courage to reveal the fact to his readers, telling the story in his own brazen way, he would not suffer in their esteem. Undignified, to be sure, but he had never made any pretense of dignity, and they did not expect it of him. Enterprising, outspoken, iconoclastic, vulgar, buffeting the nobs with a bladder and never quite sincere—but always in character. That was the way they wanted him.

In those days, at least, when people spoke of the editor quite as often as they did of his paper, success implied the possession of some of the qualities which make a good actor and a good politician. That is, an understanding of human nature in the raw. Dana knew that and was confident he had the required gifts. In the test he proved he was not mistaken.

He must have searched himself very thoroughly before he arrived at the plan upon which he proceeded, dragging into the light all the qualities which might be of use and submitting them to critical assessment. Possessed of many and varied gifts he must needs decide which should be made most prominent to the public eye. With his storehouse of knowledge and his unusual and varied experience, combined with the gifts of the propagandist, as shown in the early days when he preached the cause of association, he might have stood forth as the champion of one of the causes which he believed in—unswerving Americanism and the strengthening of the Union by annexation of whatever lands would add to its strength and security, for instance. That would have had a certain popularity and could have been shaped so as to produce a following. Or he might have appealed to the cultivated in the community, pointing the way to its development in taste.

What grew out of his self-analysis was the determination to make a universal appeal. The patriot, the esthete, the fifty thousand mechanics and small merchants who constituted the existing circulation, the man in the study and the man in the street, all who could appreciate a thoroughgoing newspaper, well written, well printed, intelligently directed, would be catered to. It was a big undertaking, but that only whetted his appetite. Until now, with the exception of the abortive experiment in Chicago, he had always been only second in command. Now he was out to prove his right to first rank, to show the world that a new Daniel had come up for judgment.

Certain definite theories became the foundations of the plan which he followed from the day he took his chair in the room on the third floor of the old Tammany Hall, facing City Hall Park, to the end of his career. They may be summarized thus:

> There is good and bad in all men, there being none all saint or all sinner. If saints did not sin they not infrequently made fools of themselves, which might be equally pernicious in the results.
>
> There is quite a lot of humbuggery in the world invisible to the innocent and the ignorant, which puts upon the wise and clear-sighted the obvious duty of unmasking these pretenders.
>
> Life's panorama is constantly revealing new and interesting phenomena, which it is the province of the understanding editor to bring under the searchlight.

Finally, and be sure he clung to that as the miser to his nest egg ever since he had coined the phrase in his letter to Pike, the first duty of the editor is "to stir up the animals". Had his soul been put upon the dissecting table it would have revealed nothing more truly and intimately Danaesque than that.

There were other ideas and theories, and some of them came to public attention when he stood at the pinnacle, and men listened to him as the Greeks to the Oracle. They will be presented here in due course, but without the affirmations as to their verity which go with the foregoing. Postprandial discourse, and even averments from the solemn lecture platform do not always draw from the speaker his most intimate conclusions. Without intentional insincerity his reticences or actual suppressions distort the picture.

The paper Dana now controlled had at least nothing to live down. If its history had been uneventful, and its editors had left both the heights and the depths undisturbed, they had at least kept clean and untarnished its reputation for honesty and independence, not so slight a matter in the days when many an editor was no better than a pirate, flaunting the Jolly Roger and overriding with bold defiance the restraints which bound decent men. It had tried to avoid being dull by giving prominence to the unusual in the city's life, minimizing such serious matters as politics and finance. It had even shown flashes of humor, as when in one of its earliest issues it made this jocular comment:

> Dull times, these, for us newspapermakers. We wish the President or Mayor Downing or some other distinguished individual would happen along again and afford us material for a daily article. Or even if the sea-serpent would be so kind as to pay us a visit.

Nor had it been lacking in courage, challenging a certain Mr. Boudinot who had set a crowd to beating and abusing a Negro in Wall Street, to carry out his threat to sue for libel. The editorial spoke of him thus:

The man who will do this will do anything; he would dance on his mother's grave; he would invade the sacred precincts of the tomb and rob a corpse of its winding sheet; he has no SOUL.

There was personal risk for the editor who made himself offensive in those days. Dueling, if forbidden by law, still existed in practice. It was not uncommon for editors to be beaten up in the streets, even as Mr. Bennett had been. Yet the editor of the *Sun* boldly denounced the fiery J. Watson Webb, editor of the *Courier and Enquirer*, Bennett's assailant and the hero of a dozen duels, telling him in so many words if he was looking for fight he, the spokesman of the *Sun*, was at his service. Even the poet-editor of the *Evening Post*, William Cullen Bryant, waylaid a rival whip in hand. Street brawls were no longer in fashion in the late 'Sixties, but the editors still showed their claws and spat ink at each other.

When Benjamin H. Day, the founder of the *Sun*, heard of Dana's purchase, he remarked confidently:

"He'll make a newspaper of it."

Day had sold out years before, and this prediction may have been to some extent a slur at his successor, but he was sincere nevertheless. He had known Dana as the managing editor of the *Tribune*, and he was voicing the judgment of the newspaper world. There was quite a little excitement in Printing House Square.

The New York of today was still in the making. Its component parts, Manhattan and the Bronx, of which the latter was little more than fields and woods, with an occasional farmhouse, contained only a million inhabitants. There were Belgian blocks on Fifth Avenue and cobblestones elsewhere where the traffic was heaviest, and macadamized roads in the residence districts. The complaints heard nowadays about the difficulty of getting about issue from the throats of a population spoiled by luxurious living. In the cars and busses of that day one was jounced and bounced from beginning to end of the journey. Traffic jams lasted hours on Broadway and the other main arteries, while the air was blue with the oaths of cursing, quarreling drivers.

In other respects travel was made odious. Men spat everywhere without restraint, on the sidewalks—those romantic sidewalks of Little Old New York, which were only a shade less filthy than the gutters—and on the floors of car and omnibus, even those, and they were many, who chewed tobacco. Prostitutes ranged every thoroughfare and crowded every public resort. Whole districts were given over to houses of ill fame. The clergy thundered from the pulpits and denounced the police, and reformers vented their indignation in meetings and letters to the papers, but the average citizen accepted philosophically conditions which would be thought impossible today.

The conviction was practically universal that in a city so large, and with so many different racial strains in its inhabitants, matters could not be otherwise. Politicians must be expected to be corrupt and in league with law breakers, with the police their creatures and bullies into the bargain. Certain sections were still unsafe for the decent citizen to venture in. Gangs held possession of the East Side and the saloons and brothels had improved not at all. The normal inclination to lawlessness characteristic of Americans had not been lessened by the end of the war and the return to civil life of the soldiers. Withal New York was provincial in tone and taste. Even the rich and educated were untraveled and lacking in the culture which comes from contacts with varied customs and different reactions to life. Where could an editor like Dana find a richer field to cultivate?

XVIII. WHAT THE READERS THOUGHT OF DANA'S PAPER—NOT POPULAR WITH THE POLITICIANS—"STIRRING UP THE ANIMALS"— SUNBEAMS AND FORKED LIGHTNING.

AMERICAN periodical literature has seen various publications rise from the ruck from time to time through the genius of editorial direction. Such was *Puck* in the days of Kepler and Bunner, when a single cartoon or caption might fire or convulse the entire country. *McClure's Magazine*, using the methods of yellow journalism, purged of vulgarity and misstatement, to catch and fasten the attention, was another. Among the newspapers the Springfield *Republican*, the Louisville *Courier-Journal*, the Chicago *News*, the Detroit *Free Press* and the Kansas City *Star* were among those which achieved national reputation either through their editors or some feature of individual flavor, whether of wit, humor, penetration or plain common sense. But the *Sun*, the *Sun* of Dana's making, stood alone. It was the national Iconoclast, and, more than any other journal, was continually doing the unexpected. As well attempt to hold down the pestiferous flea as try to forecast its attitude on any given question. That was what Dana had meant to do from the outset, that was what justified the utterance of a later period:

> The Sun has held it to be a duty and a joy to assist to the best of its ability in the discouragement of anything like lethargy in the menagerie.

To accomplish this, Edward Page Mitchell wrote in his preface to Frank M. O'Brien's *The Story of The Sun*, "Sometimes he borrowed Titania's wand; sometimes he used a red-hot poker". In the popular judgment that man Dana was just a mischievous sprite—a sort of mixture of

Mephistopheles and Peck's bad boy, and not a few laid their two cents on the newsstand every morning, less to read the news of the past twenty-four hours than to discover something new to shock, dazzle or amuse. It was equal to going to the play. It became a habit, like taking a cocktail, and for many was even more stimulating. The effects of the cocktail wore off; the *Sun's* fillip would be remembered until bedtime, at least, would be repeated to friend and acquaintance with the relish men feel when they believe themselves true connoisseurs of the printed word. And what *Sun* reader did not so hold himself? Had he not become initiate through his very reading of it?

That was another of Dana's accomplishments. In some subtle, indefinable way he brought it about that every confirmed reader of the *Sun* was convinced that he alone could interpret its real spirit. Others might take the printed word for its dictionary meaning, but he knew that seldom did Dana's editorials connote what this simple interpretation would imply. Dana was a wit, a satirist, sly and the prince of *doubles entendres*. Then why take him seriously?

Of course, there were times—plain enough those—when he hit out with the force of a battering-ram; but the usual thing, that made the uninitiated wrinkle their brows and wonder what he was driving at, doubled up with laughter those who felt they were in the secret of the writer's inner meanings. Many a straightforward statement would be wrenched and twisted by these wiseacres to conform to their convictions. No solution of a word puzzle ever brought the thrill of joy that came to that type of reader when he felt he had penetrated the Machiavellian dexterities of the editor and laid bare his real purpose. Not a man on the staff but heard many a time from some chance acquaintance, "That man Dana has a way of twisting his knife in the other fellow's insides"—and the grin would broaden with the irrepressible relish of the speaker.

There must have been thousands of old fellows around the country whose chucklings at the breakfast table, or under the evening lamp—your real *Sun* reader never finished with his paper before bedtime—were primarily due to unshakable belief that Dana could not be otherwise than subtly ironic when he was not openly amusing.

Some even carried this interpretation to the news columns. Like master like man. The *Sun* reporter too must be a devil of a fellow, and was received by many with a grin that was really a compliment to his implied wit and cunning. Sometimes it was embarrassing to those who felt it misplaced.

On one occasion all New York was agog over a romantic marriage in the higher circles. A wealthy bachelor, member of the best clubs, prominent at the most exclusive functions, had fallen in love with a poor girl, daughter of a mere employe in a mercantile shop. To be sure, she was a great beauty—professional beauty, was the term used then—and the protegé of a social leader. Still, it was an unusual happening and the *Sun* gave a column to the wedding. The day this appeared the reporter met an acquaintance, who hailed him with delight.

"Congratulations, old man," he said. "That story was a corker. You've managed to acquire the *Sun* style all right."

"Glad you think so," said the reporter, both flattered and astonished at the other's effusiveness.

"Gee!" the latter went on, with an admiring grin, "the way you put it over that the marriage had to be. I laughed myself sick over it. It must be in the office air."

"I don't know what you mean," the reporter confessed frankly.

"Ah, go on," scoffed the wise one, "anybody could see from what you wrote that she was *enceinte*."

"Good Lord!" exclaimed the reporter, and turned away. No use trying to undeceive. It would only enhance his reputation for slyness.

To many of those who were seeking to control the affairs of the country Dana was far from entertaining or amusing. They found him simply cantankerous, unreliable, almost certain to upset the apple-cart. Admittedly the most brilliant of all the editors—and for that reason the most dangerous. One to watch and avoid.

Journalists are rarely welcome in political circles, being regarded as Ishmaelites, and of untrustworthy disposition. And here was one who simply could not be made to walk in line through any external influence. He marched with the powers that were when he felt so inclined, but was apt to take to by-paths or even to move in the opposite direction whenever the mood seized him. Your bedfellow tonight and poking you out from under the covers in the morning. One of those exasperating fellows with no sense of allegiance to boss or coterie.

Efforts to apply the brake to him always proved infernally expensive. His diabolical talent for phrase making could wreck seemingly invincible combinations. Like magic those Mephistophelian groupings of innocent words would sweep the country, invading the remotest hamlet, and everybody would be gleefully repeating the damnable refrains, chortling with joy at the discomfiture of their masters of yesterday. "Turn the rascals out," one of many of them, brought troubled dreams to thousands of office-holders, good reliable party men, and reaped a harvest of official heads.

Yet he could be such a valuable ally! Could insert the knife into the vitals of the opposition with a dexterity unmatched by any of his rivals. And, when so disposed, exhibited a catholic forbearance in judging the minor peccadillos of "the boys". How useful to the leaders, looking for the opportunity to displace the "ins" and turn their jobs over to the "outs", was that other phrase of his: "To the victor belongs the spoils!" Invaluable, the cuss, when he chose to play the game. But it must be said that most of the time he was a festering thorn in the side of the politician.

In a country where the liberty of the press has always been a fetish, far more solidly intrenched as a bulwark of human rights than the liberty of the individual, the editor of a newspaper has ever had extraordinary power and opportunities to impose his will, and at this time they were even less restricted than they are today. Here and there some indignant individual might rise to ask why the presentation of the news carried with it authority to pass judgment upon the behavior and performance of citizens in general and public officials in particular, but nobody gave ear long enough to vouchsafe an answer. Nor did the protester get any better audience when he shrieked that unconscionable editors were converting liberty of the press into license. The editors, fight as they might among themselves, presented a solid barrier to every effort to put teeth into the lax libel laws. Such laws as have existed in England time out of mind for the protection of the individual from invidious newspaper comment have never found welcome in this country. The average American enjoys the lampooning of the other fellow sufficiently to be willing to take a chance on being a target himself. It must be admitted that Dana did not permit his opportunities to take on rust for lack of use. Many of the unfortunates incorporated in the *Sun's* portrait gallery squirmed and writhed. Some took it good-naturedly. At least, they were being pilloried by a master who rarely used the bludgeon and was adept in handling the rapier.

To make his paper interesting, to make people talk about it, was his first object. But so it has been with every editor since the Fourth Estate became an influence in the social life. Most of them copied each other, eager to find any new feature which gave promise of holding the public's attention even for a little while, and restrained by no sense of shame in imitation. Only a few have been real pathfinders, because only a few had the understanding of human nature and the instinct to recognize what moved its emotions and appealed to its curiosity.

The fifty thousand mechanics and small merchants must have stirred a bit uneasily when part of the four pages of their *Sun* suddenly was given over to "Poems Worth Reading" and book reviews. To be sure, some of the poetry had fun in it and some of the reviews had spicy accents, but they were new and part of what some must have felt to be a general upheaval. "I have revolutionized the character of the paper, and as a matter of course increased expenses and lost readers in the process," Dana wrote to Huntington. But he had no doubts. When the circulation reached seventy-five thousand, of which he was confident, it would be well established on a profitable basis.

To help towards that goal no opportunity to "stir the animals" was overlooked. The Irish agitation against English domination was promptly seized upon. It was the beginning of a considerable following among the Irish in America, and New York alone had a lot of them. Perhaps he was sincere—he had always been critical of English politics; but whether or no, his editorial instinct could never have foregone this splendid opportunity to stir up a rumpus and keep it going.

Personally too wise and broad-minded to be bound by racial prejudices, he was nevertheless aware that nothing stirred the blood more deeply. To make appeal to them would have been beneath him, but to utilize them after his subtler fashion could not be condemned, even though it aroused sleeping dogs and filled the air with their barking.

Thus the Jews were brought into the limelight. Remarkable people, declared the *Sun* solemnly, and excellent citizens. But were they not avoiding their opportunity to settle the age-old question of racial antipathies by refusing intermarriage? In countries where they were oppressed and subjected to indignities that could be understood. Justifiable pride would intervene and keep them apart from their oppressors. But America had created no barriers and shown no favoritism. Jew and Christian were on an equality in the land of the free. And if they mingled their blood streams it would be to the advantage of the new race slowly developing from the mixture of many different strains, each of which contributed something of value to the making of a better humanity.

Nothing could be more complimentary, more kindly in tone, more obviously inspired by a desire to be helpful than were these editorials, reiterated at reasonable intervals to keep the pot boiling. One could almost see the kindly philosopher laboring to make manifest his purpose to solve a problem which had drenched the world with blood and tears for nigh onto two thousand years. Nothing ever appeared in them to shock their racial pride. No suggestion of conversion or abandonment of Judaism. Just intermarriage. The problem of two different faiths existing in the same household, and what should be done with the children, was not touched upon. That the object sought was accomplished cannot be doubted. Those Jews who were drifting from the faith and habits of their forefathers may have been encouraged to take the further step. In any event they would be pleased and become constant readers. The great mass would shrug their shoulders, as had their ancestors to similar well-meant efforts to eradicate the so-called Jewish problem, but they could not resent what was manifestly so well-intentioned, and the compliments would be remembered after the counsel had been forgotten. They too helped swell the growing circulation.

That was before the Russian pogroms had sent millions from the Russian ghettos to the protection of Uncle Sam. In the midst of that mighty immigration the same Archibald Gordon who had satirized Chicago came on the scene with a letter protesting against the wholesale adoption of his time-honored Scotch cognomen by these aliens. Thousands of *skys* were being made over into Gordons, he complained, without sloughing any of their old characteristics or taking on those which properly belonged to their new appellative. The ghetto of New York's East Side swarmed with the signs of "Gordons" who dealt in old clothes, delicatessen and other commodities to which the proud name of Gordon had never before been attached. Did the law offer no protection to the legitimate owner of such a name?

Dana came out to the city room with this letter, his big

blue eyes twinkling as might those of a boy who had found a new way of tying a tin can to the tail of a mutt.

"Now we are going to have some fun," said he. "There will be a lot of letters denouncing Archie and just about as many praising him. Let's give each side a fair show."

They descended in an avalanche and it took weeks to print only the most violent in the column on the editorial page reserved for them.

It was a small paper—only four pages, with no Sunday issue—and the advertising was growing with the circulation. So the space for reading matter was extremely limited and much of it had to be condensed and set in small type. A lot of information, especially curious lore, appeared under "Sunbeams", on the editorial page. It was a repository of all sorts of odd incidents and observations gathered by outside contributors as well as members of the staff, usually limited to three or four lines, such as:

"There is a dyer in Hartford whose sign reads: 'We live to dye and dye to live'."

Dana's dream was to keep the paper small and achieve a circulation which would be profitable enough to enable him to dispense entirely with advertising.

> There are two tendencies in our newspapers [he declared], one toward the purely intellectual side of journalism, making the newspaper a medium of opinions and intelligence; the other toward the merely commercial side, making it a convenience for the publication of advertisements. . . . It is evident that this tendency to convert influential journals into immense advertising sheets cannot go on forever. . . . The public will grow weary of turning over a dozen pages of advertisements in order to get at two or three pages of reading matter. Who will start a newspaper from which advertisements are excluded? It will come some day, and then there will be journals for advertising alone, and others devoted to information and political and general discussions and not to advertisements; and these will probably be esteemed the true models of journalism.

The theory that advertisements in themselves drew readers did not commend itself to him. "Make the paper interesting" was his invariable motto.

Dana did not spare himself in the effort. Every morning found him at his desk, where he remained, with an interlude for luncheon, until late in the afternoon. Practically every line that went into the editorial page passed under his critical eye, and not a few bore the mark of his blue pencil, though he never interfered arbitrarily with any man's form of expression. Individuality he held in high esteem and protected against any invasion, but now and then even the good man might be bettered. And all the time he was impressing his own personality on the paper, not alone through his writing but through that subtle, indefinable influence which makes even the office boy in a newspaper of distinctive character realize its aims, its policies, its individual slant on what counts, in a newspaper sense, among the happenings of each day.

Here, clearly enough, was a wise man, traveled, informed, of broad scholarship and artistic instincts in all matters of taste and culture, competent to instruct and to guide, and gifted with rare powers of expression. Using the weapons of the laughing philosopher, he was able to chide, correct and destroy many illusions. The eternal enemy of sham and pretence, he was forever engaged in exposing the hypocrisies derived from decadent Puritanism or pure self-seeking; unmasking the holier-than-thou and the self-styled reformers of mankind. If he played the imp occasionally, he did it with a skill and cleverness that compelled the admiration of the judicious even though it might also make them grieve. And then there were times enough when the seer appeared, inspirational and beyond all criticism.

Was it necessary to tell the workers how they should perform to emulate his example and give roundness and homogeneity to the whole product? Certainly not those worth while, and none other survived for long. There was never a rule promulgated by him, nor even a dictum to guide his collaborators. There was never a council of editors, as became the practice in other offices. He alone contrived the policies and sketched the way to put them into effect. Yet there was no working at cross purposes. Everybody divined and followed. It was almost miraculous.

But the guidance in essentials was clear enough. Had he not made it clear that commonplace would not do? That tradition and convention were to be respected only where they carried in themselves indubitable truth? That the weapons of controversy were wit and humor, and even a humbug must not be assailed with a meat axe?

Then there were single sentences which were as guide books to the initiate:

Men must be at liberty to say in print whatever they have a mind to say in print, provided it wrongs no one.

"The right of silence is every bit as sacred as the right of speech."

Not always carried into practice, yet the following put on guard and on the defensive the ubiquitous reporter:

The practice of publishing private conversations without special permission should be regarded as a vulgar and reprehensible encroachment upon the right of every man to have his sentiments communicated to the public only by his own volition.

It was expressions like the above which gave to the paper, despite its frolicsome side, an air of dignity which none could deny. But then it never descended to vulgarity, never approached humor through the channel of cheapness. Like its master, it was ever the aristocrat, ever perched above the crowd, even when seeming to be communing with it.

The news columns as well as the editorials were different from those in any other paper, and men in the profession came to give a definite meaning to the phrase, "A *Sun* story". As illustration here are some excerpts from an article entitled, "Pleasures of the South", telling about a ball given by a colored regiment of the National Guard of South Carolina at the capital of that State.

"Will this be a recherché affair?" the *Sun* reporter asked Governor Scott.

"Oh, yes," said the Governor, "the crême de la crême of our Colored Society will be there, and if you go you will have a pleasant time."

"Shall you and Mrs. Scott attend?"

"Well, hardly. You see," said the Governor, and here his eye twinkled, "I haven't been very well of late, and anything like violent exercise, such as dancing, for instance, throws me off my feet. Mrs. Scott and I have sent regrets."

But the Mayor was there and the City Clerk and the Board of Aldermen.

> Mayor Smythe is a white gentleman and danced very frequently. He was not accompanied by ladies, but found no scarcity of partners on the floor, as the young colored ladies esteemed it an especial honor to dance with His Honor, the Mayor. The Mayor seemed partial to the waltz, and the delicacy with which he clasped his partner in that enchanting dance was the admiration of all present. . . . By ten o'clock the ball room was crowded with the youth and beauty of Columbia's colored society. There was also a fair sprinkling of whites, but not enough to mar the pleasure of the company.

A number of Tammany Hall politicians went on a junket to California in a special car. They were members of the Blossom Club, "probably the most intellectual association of gentlemen in New York City".

> The car was fitted with a cellar underneath, in which the traps of the party were stowed away. These traps consisted of 100 baskets of Americus Club champagne (for the party); 50 dozen of brandy (for the party); a large jar of chow chow (for the heathen Chinese); 75 boxes of whiskey (for the party); a small Stilton

cheese (for Dr. Andrews, who does not drink); 50 flasks of gin (for cocktails); 10,000 cigars (also for the party); 42 revolvers (for the Indians on the railroad); 4 gallons of Sixth Ward firewater (for the Tammany Indians); 1000 smoked tongues (for the speechmakers); 750 boiled hams, well salted (for the purpose of keeping thirsty); 75 decks of steamboats, well sanded (for the Pacific slopers); 1000 ivory chips (for the same); one English twist-double-barrelled-breach-loading-steel-mounted-treble-back-action-pivotal-range-spring-lock extra superfine sporting gun (for to kill Indians and prairie lobsters) . . . and crockery, silver and glassware enough to stock Tweed's hotel. . . . Under each seat were placed two baskets of champagne, and boxes of other liquors were piled up in the staterooms.

It is no easy task to attempt to define this unique product of a real genius. Dana's *Sun* was for him what a violin is to a Kreisler, except that the former had to fashion his instrument. Being an esthete as well as a virtuoso, he made the equivalent of a Stradivarius, by means of which he could express all the many shadings and subtleties of his varied and complex nature. And, like any true artist, he brooked no interference with his own interpretations. Cost what it might, his was the only way.

There are great newspapers today, more comprehensive than ever they were in the past, reflecting the larger world and the greater complexities of our time, but where is the great editor pursuing his personal bent regardless of friend or foe, of the counting room, the circulation and advertising departments, heedless of even his own readers when it is a question of abandoning his views or offending theirs? If not wiser, they are certainly shrewder than Dana was.

XIX. MEN WHO HELPED DANA MAKE "THE NEWSPAPER MAN'S NEWSPAPER"—AMOS CUMMINGS, WHOM GREELEY DISCHARGED FOR PERSISTENT PROFANITY—DOC WOOD, THE GREAT CONDENSER—ALL SORTS GO TO MAKE A NEWSPAPER—OR DID THEN—EVEN ROGUES.

THE confirmed Sunite, that old fellow who chuckled himself to sleep over its deviltry, knew perfectly well that Old Man Dana was personally responsible for it all. Of course he wrote it all himself. Not those things which contained the illuminating phrase, "the reporter of The Sun" learned, heard, saw, was told, and so on; but the entire contents of the editorial page, where most of the mischief centered. No use to tell him that a dozen choice brains were at work there. You couldn't fool him. He knew the hands of Esau and no goat skin disguise could deceive him.

The professional newspaperman, fully aware of the facts, was nevertheless at a loss to tell what was truly Dana's handiwork and what that of his assistants. In a book of pleasant reminiscences published fifty years after the fact, Edward Page Mitchell, Dana's chief aid for many years and later on his successor in editorial direction, relates how mystified he was. As with many another of the journalistic tribe Mitchell would forget the work to be done on the paper which employed him—the Lewiston *Journal*—when the postman brought in the slim wrapper containing the four-page *Sun*. Spreading it out, he would proceed to analyze the contents of the editorial page, ever pursued by the tormenting question: "Which is Dana's?"

"Three salient and very distinct styles of editorial English" challenged his judgment.

The first style was the modernized Addisonian of the Spectator essays, infused with well-bred humor, sometimes gentle, sometimes sly, occasionally even mordant, but with a bite that never deposited venom. It was employed on a wide range of subjects—the minor moralities, the social amenities and transgressions, the inexhaustible questions of non-polemic theology, of sentiment particularly in Cupid's domain, of conscience, of common-sense principles in the every-day affairs of life.

Surely that must be the veritable Dana! But then he noted a second and was plunged in doubt.

This was as different from the first as a Daquiri cocktail is from champagne cider. Here was gorgeous rhetoric blazing with superlative adjectives and adverbs, scintillating with figures of speech of every variety, lush with quotations and historical allusions, overrich, overbrilliant, perhaps, but for the vigor of thought that propelled the astonishing vocabulary. It was a throat so muscular that it could afford to display an incandescent necktie.

One significant fact seemed to make the authorship of this secure. It showed an intimacy of acquaintance with the characters and the inside history of the recent war which no other journalist could be expected to possess. This was indubitably Dana. But there was the third style to make the eager investigator waver: "Here was an editorial pen from which flowed very little of Addison, quite a sufficiency of Dean Swift, and very much of John Bunyan and Benjamin Franklin." Masterpieces of "stenographic English, direct, powerful, containing no useless word, employing no long word when a short Saxon word was at hand, no pretentious word when a homely word did the business". The final decision favored this last.

Later, when he was himself a member of the staff and initiated into the mysteries of the office, Mitchell discovered that none of these was the product of Dana's pen. The first had been written by Frank Church, forever famous in the history of American journalism through his immortal answer to a child who had written the editor to inquire into the verity of Santa Claus. General Fitz Henry Warren, the man who created the Tribune's slogan, "Forward to Richmond", was responsible for the second style. William O. Bartlett, the master of the third, the trenchant form, will appear again in these pages.

No, Mitchell, keen as he was, had not found Dana in his paper. But there seeped into his consciousness, after he had discovered the truth, that the great editor's greatness lay no less in his ability to summon and coördinate other talents than in his own power of expression.

Even as Mitchell yearned to become part of the paper which challenged his professional admiration, so did many other brilliant minds, and never did they find Dana lukewarm in reception. In fact, the building of the staff and finding of recruits to hold the pace, was from the beginning one of his chief interests. The reader of the exchanges was ever on notice to let no striking workmanship escape his attention. Brought to Dana's notice, stray paragraphs even, if they contained the rare original note, the mark of unusual talent, would inspire a correspondence with the author which often ended in an invitation to come on and be one of the merry buccaneers.

It was an odd as well as able group that the editor had assembled at the outset. Owing to their irregular hours of work, as well as to their peculiar vocation, most workers on a morning newspaper lived a life apart from other men. Working when others played, sleeping when others worked, they, like the people of the stage, were apt to drift into peculiar habits. It took strong will and firm purpose to keep to the narrow path of sobriety, for one thing. It was all very well for the editorial writers and those others who had day jobs, and could live like other folks, to keep their balance, but for the great majority, emerging after long arduous labors into dark, deserted streets, perhaps into the rigors of bitter winter weather, there was almost irresistible lure in the friendly lights of the ever-open saloon and the cup that cheers. Besides, most newspapermen of that time were strays in the social sense, for whom the irregular habits imposed by their calling were not its least attraction. Not a few of them had drifted into journalism from other vocations for the very reason that they could not tolerate the conventional life. In that early *Sun* staff there were among others a number of graduates of the composing room, and printers have been ever irremediable bohemians.

Such was Amos Cummings, one of the most brilliant of them all, and one who had much to do with making what came to be known as the *Sun* style of writing for other pages than the editorial. A roughneck, if ever there was one, and the last man one would have expected to see associated with the fastidious and elegant Dana. Greeley, who had discovered his talents while Cummings was a printer on the *Tribune*, and had made him its city editor, finally could not put up with his roughness and profanity, and by his dismissal gave Dana the opportunity to add to his staff one born with the instinct for selecting from the passing events those which would have greatest appeal to the largest number. He became managing editor, and the town soon was talking of the humorous characters he dragged from the passing crowd, and laughing at the funny sides of life none other had been able to discover. Not that he was omitting the important happenings, but humor was his specialty, the fun to be squeezed out of life all that made it worth while. Presently the eagerness to find it drove him out of the executive chair to make his own researches. More valuable to the paper than ever as super-reporter, his sketches, interviews, satires and interpretations, brought a host of new readers and endless publicity.

Dana, Cummings, Wood were the three who gave the *Sun* its special character. The writers mentioned by Mitchell were of great value. So was Mitchell, and many others. But the builders of the features which were of fundamental importance in distinguishing it from all other newspapers then or since, and to which it owed its unique reputation, the features which made it the darling of all newspapermen the country over, and earned for it the title of "the newspaperman's newspaper", were the three named. That Dana alone would have made it witty, brilliant and wise, is certain; but the other two were outstanding as associate builders.

Doctor John B. Wood, known throughout the profession as "Doc" Wood, brought a unique talent for removing surplus words. The Great Condenser, as he has been called by every writer about the *Sun*, was its night editor. That is, assistant to the managing editor, but his value to the paper was his establishing the rule, never to be abandoned during Dana's life, that no unnecessary word must be permitted to enter the columns of the paper. From his day on the blue pencil was the mightiest of editors, and Mitchell described his way of working thus:

> Every few minutes boys came up to him on the run, bringing sheaves of yellow paper. These manuscripts he seized and scrutinized from beneath his green blinder, and disposed of them with a speed nigh incredible. To one batch he would scarcely give a glance before tossing it contemptuously into the basket at his feet. Another batch he would subject to merciless mutilation, seemingly sparing neither the dignity of the stateliest paragraph nor the innocence of the most modest part of speech as his terrible blue pencil tore through the pages leaving havoc in its wake. . . . His only pause was to "project a violent stream of tobacco juice in the direction of a distant cuspidor".

Thomas Hitchcock, stockholder, treasurer of the company, and the wisest and most profound writer on finance that ever wrote for a newspaper, was as different from those two as he was unlike Dana. An angry-looking man, with a beard which was rarely well-trimmed despite the fact that he enjoyed the ministrations of Pujol, the celebrated French barber, he boasted that his clothes cost less than those of any other man in the office.

"See this suit?" Hitchcock asked Dana once, holding out

The Ulysses Grant Who Was Anathema to Dana.
The Bulldog on the Right is the *Sun.*

(*After a Cartoon by Thomas Nast in Harper's
Weekly.*)

an arm to display the yellow tweeds he wore, "cost me six dollars."

"H'm," said Dana, "that must be less than you paid for your butler's."

A sore subject, as Dana well knew, and Hitchcock's face fell.

"Yes," he muttered, "I paid a hundred and forty dollars for his."

The truth was he was not a miser, by any means, but he had an inveterate dislike of paying more than the lowest market price for anything. With a keen scent for developments in Wall Street, he would appear in ecstatic humor on days of panic and, rubbing his hands gleefully, would exclaim, "Bargain day! bargain day!" then disappear in the direction of his broker's offices. Long before the words "multimillionaire" had become familiar he was believed to have accumulated more than ten millions.

Prominent in society, he was the watch dog of all the society news and comment, and the column of social items which appeared on the editorial page when the Sunday edition came into being was under his critical guidance. He had a big house in town and another at Newport and paid without a murmur the big bills of his two sons, famous polo players, yet he was a regular patron of Dennett's dairy restaurant, and it was a familiar sight to find him threading his way through crowded Nassau Street, with a sandwich and a piece of pie balanced on a glass of milk, to the *Sun* office. After Dana's time, when the *Sun* was under less skilful guidance, Hitchcock sold his stock.

"How is that, Mr. Hitchcock?" a friend asked him. "Did you not tell me that it paid you handsomely?"

"As high as one hundred and ten per cent. some years," Hitchcock replied. "Lately it has been paying thirty."

"But you cannot earn thirty per cent. with every stock," the friend observed.

"Oh, no," Hitchcock returned, "but I am conserving my capital."

The next year the paper omitted its dividends altogether, and they were not resumed for five years.

The Monday *Sun* for many years had the largest circulation of any daily issue, and this was traced directly to the "Matthew Marshall" article which appeared on that day. People subscribed for that issue from all over the country, and all Wall Street waited to see what it would say. Unlike any other financial article it plunged deep into the fundamentals. Neither a tipster, nor an I-told-you-so, "Matthew Marshall" laid bare the basic causes of market movements. He was a financial scholar, philosopher and seer. No one has ever approached his penetration or his wisdom, and the attempt to replace him proved abortive.

John Bogart belonged to the early days. Like Cummings he had been a soldier in the Civil War. A kindly, lovable soul, who, in the latter part of his tenure of office, at least, gave the impression of immolating himself daily upon the altar of duty. Toiling unremittingly all day, when six o'clock arrived, the hour for transferring his job to the night city editor, his eyes had a far-away look and the perspiration streamed down his cheeks. Whereby hung a tale, rarely repeated, of his earliest days, when perhaps the irregularities developed in his war experience had not yet disappeared.

The story went that he appeared in the city room one morning the worse for wear, and in a mood entirely foreign to his nature. Well-meant efforts to induce him to go home were waved away belligerently, and when somebody volunteered that the chief might appear any moment, and that he would be annoyed to find him in his existing condition, Bogart thrust out his fist and yelled defiantly:

"You can tell Charles A. Dana to ———"

It is curious how even the best of men will revert to the language of the gutter at such times. When he had finished even he was affected by the ominous silence which had fallen upon his listeners. Looking around he saw Dana standing in the doorway. The latter had come in suddenly and had heard it all. No need to tell the offender. Dana, incensed, was not likely to be misunderstood even by one unduly exhilarated. For an instant thunder and lightning centered in those eloquent blue eyes. But dignity conquered. Sternly but quietly he said:

"John, you had better go home."

Those present said Bogart turned stone sober in an instant. And he never touched liquor again. From that day on he was a slave to duty. He was the first to arrive at the office, and he had then already gone through a number of papers, marking the items which called for investigation. At noon he went out to lunch at a restaurant across Nassau Street, where there was a standing order to have half a dozen oysters and a glass of milk ready for his arrival. He seemed hardly to have slid on to his stool at the lunch counter before he was off again and on his way back to the office. Repeated timing by curious observers fixed his absence at exactly six minutes.

There were ruffians in those days who would take advantage of such a martyr. The *Sun* for far too long carried three such on the reportorial staff. A burly fellow named Cochran was the leader. He had been an assistant librarian at Cooper Union, and may have been worth his oats once upon a time, but that was far gone when the scene about to be described had become a daily occurrence. His most famous exploit had been the carrying of a parcel around to the East Side police stations, which he was assigned to visit at night to inquire for late news. Slamming this down on the counter before the officer in charge, he said:

"Sergeant, I've brought ye 'round a bit o' dynamite."

True or false, he contrived to clear the police out of most of the stations.

The procedure with poor Bogart was invariably the same. Cochran and his co-conspirators would watch until the worn-out man was in the act of leaving his chair, when they would proceed in unison, blocking his way, and swaying before him in drunken rhythm while Cochran would exclaim, in a tearful voice:

"Haven't you one kind word for a poor old man?"

Then there was Clarke—Selah M.—who suggested his given name in appearance but not in conduct. Tall, thin, with the looks of a New England divinity student. Seated at the night city desk, spouting short, rapid puffs of smoke from his clay pipe in rhythm with his breathing as he worked, engrossed and excited, over some reporter's manuscript, or created one of those magical heads which would catch the eye and fire the imagination, he through many years was the inspiration of the night force. More admired and damned than any other executive, a genius whose fame spread to all the newspaper offices of the country. Full of fun and deviltry in the idle hours, a slave driver in the heat of labor.

The body of a woman had been found buried under the furnace ashes in a basement once occupied by a Chinese laundry. Was it the Celestial's white slave, or a chance customer trapped in his den? It was the kind of yarn that in those early days of New York, still confined and provincial in outlook, received three columns in a four-page paper. Its mystery and horror would haunt the average household for many a day and no woman would venture alone into a Chinaman's shop for months to come. Half the *Sun's* staff were at work on it and every possible avenue of investigation had seemingly been covered, when Clarke called one of the young reporters.

"Feel all the bones, they may have been broken," he directed. "And look carefully at the teeth for gold fillings."

The body had been buried a long time and looked like a mummy, with the ashes clinging like a cere-cloth. The mouth was firmly closed, the lips tight against the teeth. Even the police pitied the poor reporter, whose gorge rose against his undertaking. But the man was not born who dared return and face Clarke with his duty unperformed.

A late report on a wintry night announced a wreck off the shore of Staten Island, and the reporter on night duty— the long wait, it was called—was directed to find a tug and proceed to the scene. The reporter had reached the door when he was called back:

"Just remember," Clarke reminded him coldly, "you are a reporter of the *Sun* getting the news, and not a life-saving expedition."

One of Dana's important services to the *Tribune* had been the organization of a literary department, in which had appeared the best book reviews then written. Naturally, one of his first moves was to engage the best man obtainable to write reviews of books for the *Sun*. The little merchants and the mechanics might not appreciate J. C. Heywood's discerning analyses of the works of Anthony Trollope and the youthful Henry James, nor the later scholarly expositions of worth-while books by Mayo W. Hazeltine, but there were new readers who not only did but talked about them until the *Sun* took first place in the esteem of writers and publishers. In time Hazeltine's page review of a single book in the Sunday *Sun* became almost obligatory reading for those who wished to keep abreast of the most significant books appearing. Nor was the reader interested in literature likely to omit the exquisite and witty review taking up a column or so of Saturday's paper, the product of perhaps the most graceful and charming writer on the staff, the delightful Erasmus Darwin Beach.

There were many others with outstanding talents on the staff, besides contributors whose fame in the profession was well established. Pike of the *Tribune* days, who had been successful in politics, transferred his journalistic allegiance; the ecstatic Oliver Dyer, founder of the "Answers to Correspondents" column on Bonner's *Ledger*, in which he advised forlorn lovers and anxious mothers among the endless inquirers on all imaginable subjects, wrote in a scholarly vein for the *Sun*.

Dana knew how, or had the natural instinct, to develop enthusiasm in these collaborators and their successors, as in the lesser satellites, to make a homogeneous working body of individuals of the most varied and even opposing characteristics.

"If I were in the article of death," Sam Wilkeson wrote the editor in charge, "I would straighten up in bed and write on the call of the *Sun*."

That was no verbal boast. There wasn't a man on the staff that would not march unflinching into any danger at the word of command. And yet, in those days, even more than now, it took all sorts to make a newspaper, even downright vagabonds. The perfect type was the adventurer with a gift for unusual expression, men like Cummings or the later prince of reporters, Julian Ralph—Ralph of the *Sun*, as he was known to statesmen, captains of industry and the entire writing profession the world over; in South Africa or London as well as Washington or New York—men who in the old days would have been soldiers in foreign legions, and in the early times of this country would ever have been pioneers on the frontier, though rarely settlers.

In rival shops the *Sun* staff was known as the "happy family", a phrase invented by a reporter for the *Herald*, where the prevailing conditions were far from ideal. Dana was absolute master through no assertion of authority, but by the common consent of his followers. With that spirit, and its sympathetic and inspired direction, the *Sun* could not do otherwise than go over the top. Being all the time, as one of the crowd wrote of it, "beloved, I believe, like a creature of flesh and blood and living intelligence and human virtues and failings". The darling of the profession, its master both a prince and his court jester.

XX. PERSONAL JOURNALISM—DANA'S DEFINITION—SOME ILLUSTRATIONS OF ITS OPERATION—THE TRULY GOOD DEACON AND THE "HEBETUDINOUS CRANK".

IN THOSE DAYS men had quite a little to say about what they called Personal Journalism. Most of what they said was critical or slurring. Even intelligent men have been loth to recognize the truth expressed by Job Hedges that while "theoretically the press is an impersonal instrument, actually it reflects the opinions and wishes of the individual who owns it". There has always been a lot of Pollyanna sentiment about the press, and it has always evoked grins in the editorial sanctum.

The public could not blame the papers for its misconceptions. Most of them were showing in black type what they thought of each other. Times innumerable they had called Greeley a free lover, a poltroon and an incendiary. He had retorted in kind. William Cullen Bryant got this: "You lie, you villain, you sinfully, wickedly, basely lie." Bennett the elder received the pleasant nickname of Jack Ketch; Raymond of the *Times* was The Little Villain. Everybody knew this and yet almost everybody expected the papers to be above suspicion in all matters affecting the public weal, regardless of the interests, the inclinations and the prejudices of their owners.

The leading editors were much better known then than they are today to the man in the street. It was customary to use their names rather than those of the papers in quoting. "Greeley says"—not the *Tribune*. So with all of them. Their names were household words. And they were synonymous with power. That was where the criticism came in. The critics did not care what the editors called each other. It was what they did to the outsider who had climbed high enough to be a conspicuous target. They had it in for Dana especially, to whom no cranium was sacred, and this is what he retorted:

> A great deal of twaddle is uttered by some country newspapers just now over what they call personal journalism. They say now that Mr. Bennett, Mr. Raymond and Mr. Greeley are dead, the day for personal journalism is gone by, and that impersonal journalism will take its place. That appears to mean a sort of journalism in which nobody will ask who is the editor of a paper or the writer of any class of article, and nobody will care.
>
> Whenever, in the newspaper profession, a man rises up who is original, strong, and bold enough to make his opinions a matter of consequence to the public, there will be personal journalism; and whenever newspapers are conducted only by commonplace individuals whose views are of no consequence to anybody, there will be nothing but impersonal journalism.
>
> And this is the essence of the whole question.

This appeared some years later, for of course Bennett, Greeley and Raymond were still very much alive while Dana was making the *Sun*. In fact, Dana was going to say some very nice things about Greeley and going to heap coals of fire upon his head by his efforts to do him good turns, though it must be said that here again word and motive were suspect in some quarters, and in none more than Greeley's. Oliver Dyer's comparison with the Greek God keeps recurring, and with it the recollection that while Greek gods were wonderful they were also rather human.

Did the *Sun* print the temperance speeches delivered by Greeley during his campaign for the Presidency because they were news or especially interesting—or because they were sure to make ructions among the whiskey-drinking Democrats? Greeley's own view may be gathered from his conversation with the reporter who attended all the meetings:

"Who sent you?" asked Greeley. "Was it Amos Cummings or old Dana?"

The reporter truthfully replied that he had received his orders from the city editor.

Greeley could not suppress his suspicions.

"Well, it must be old Dana told him to," he said.

There was no spirit of vengeance in the poking of fun at Greeley. What else could a Dana do with this tempestuous reformer, whose personal ambition, vanities, egotism and childlike naïveté in many matters made him an irresistible target, even though his high virtues and great abilities could not be denied?

Greeley had given occasion enough for reprisal. Even though his cavalier treatment of long ago might be forgotten, there was more recent performance to consider. Would Colonel Mix of Greeley's staff have gotten out his pamphlet, *The Biter Bit, or the Robert Macaire of Journalism*, if Greeley had not approved? Not at all likely, for while it aimed directly at William O. Bartlett it hit Dana *en route*.

Personal Journalism was at its most vitriolic here, as it always was in anything which involved this man Bartlett. One of the ablest editorial writers this country has known, he was likewise a mystery. He had been associated with the *Tribune*, the *Herald* and the *Evening Post* before he had been taken in by Dana, but nowhere had he played any such rôle as he did on the *Sun*. To this day there has been no explanation of the extraordinary influence he exercised there, or of his personal relations with Dana.

Mix was only repeating the back-stairs gossip of the *Sun* office about Bartlett. The latter was a lawyer first, and a writer incidentally, but his ability and reputation as the former did not compare with his achievements with the pen. Yet, to all appearance, he was using his journalistic talents to a large degree, at least, to further his progress in the law.

He spends most of his time [declared Mix] writing puffs for all the judges who throw at him and his son Willard, also a lawyer, the fat bones of the courts, such as references, receiverships and street openings, from which Bartlett & Co. have already amassed a fortune.

But that was only a peccadillo compared to the major offense with which he was charged. Judges who were in his disfavor were attacked with a virulence which would be inconceivable in our day. Here is a comparatively mild illustration:

> Judge Woodruff is new upon the United States bench. He is new in criminal cases. We believe the Fullerton case was the first indictment that he ever tried. *That case ought to be a warning* to him. He undertook then to reverse and overrule the long-established practice of the court in an offensive and arbitrary manner. In the end it proved that one of the greatest defaulters and villains of modern times had been engaged in a conspiracy to sacrifice the defendant . . . a distinguished lawyer and judge. Does Judge Woodruff feel that he himself is exempt from the assaults of some such scoundrel? Judge Woodruff undoubtedly looks forward to a long career in some court of the United States. If he perseveres in the way he has begun, *it will be a rough one, and, we apprehend, will soon worry him to death or madness.* The lawyers, much as they sometimes abuse each other, are a noble and generous band of brothers. They will stand by any court that treats them properly; *but,* on the other hand, the history of tyrant-judges, is it not already written?

Dana replied to Mix in a signed editorial beginning:

> James B. Mix, blackmailer; A. M. Soteldo, Jr., self-acknowledged scoundrel; Horace Greeley, philanthropist; and John Russell Young, convicted sneak news thief, are responsible for an anonymous pamphlet of sixty-nine pages, the product of a malicious but feeble disposition to injure The Sun.

It concluded with:

> Mr. Greeley is a Universalist, and believes that nobody will ever go to Hell, or he could not have been

tempted to stand godfather to the anonymous libel of two scoundrels and one thief.

In between these two paragraphs Dana demolished the charge that he had accepted a bribe to suppress an article attacking Fisk and Gould.

Mitchell called Bartlett "not only the peer of any of the contemporary group of writing journalists in New York, but the master of most of them and the teacher of all of them" and of hundreds of their successors. Even as he waxed enthusiastic over his sane judgment, effective humor and knack of original phrase making, so must Dana, ever an admirer of skill and forcefulness in writing, have done so. Evidently, too, admiration warmed into personal liking. Bartlett & Co. came to have their office in the *Sun* building, and Dana concerned himself with the interests of the Bartletts even to the second generation. The firm became counsel for the *Sun*. Willard Bartlett, later an honored judge of the Supreme Court of the State of New York, rising to the chief judgeship of the Court of Appeals, wrote the *Sun's* editorials on legal matters when his father was no more.

It was an expensive friendship too, destined to cost the *Sun* more than half its circulation, together with a large share of the profits, not to mention a lot of bitterness centered upon Dana personally, for which William Bartlett was responsible.

But Dana never reckoned the cost of doing what he wished. Nor was there any limit to his friendship—except where friends took exception to his acts. He did not inquire too closely into their performance and harbored no suspicions. These were some of the luxuries which Personal Journalism permitted to the editor who was also controller of his paper.

The staff, too, was covered with the ample mantle of protection, in some instances where that could hardly have been expected. Cummings, for instance, got into trouble one night, and found it advisable to leave the city while Dana exerted his influence with the authorities. Though he scorned to ask any favors for himself he would do that for a friend or a member of his staff.

Extraordinary his patience and indulgence with those whose work pleased him. One of them was caught robbing the paper. He was being paid for his work at so much a column and had charged for work done by another who received a salary, and therefore did not turn in to the managing editor the clippings of what he had contributed. So the scheme went undiscovered for some time. The managing editor was for discharging him, at least, if not prosecuting him. Dana pondered the matter for some moments, then negatived the suggestion. It took all sorts to make a newspaper, he said, and the fellow was undeniably clever.

"Tell him not to do it again," he concluded.

There was another, an accomplished writer for the editorial page who would drink too much now and again. Usually he was harmless enough, but on one occasion Mitchell caught a paragraph he had sent to the composing room when it was returned in proof. It was a monstrous attack on the Pope! Dangerous to have around, that type, for there might not always be on hand a Mitchell to intervene at the right moment. Of course, Dana heard of it, but nothing happened.

There was a different instance of this standing-by one Sunday when I happened to be in charge at the city desk. Rarely did Dana come to the office on Sunday but he happened to be there then. In the middle of the morning my telephone rang and a man of prominence, one of the Fifth Avenue art dealers, was at the other end. I could guess what he wanted for there was a review of some of his pictures in the paper that day, and the art critic had attacked them without mercy, declaring flatly that the pictures exhibited as old masters were not what they were alleged to be.

"I am sending you down a letter," said this man, "and

I ask that it be printed. I know Mr. Dana personally, and I am sure he will allow me to defend myself."

When the letter arrived I saw that the writer had not only controverted the assertions of the critic, but charged the latter with ignorance and personal animus. I showed it to Dana.

"Tell him," said he, "I advise him not to print it."

By the time I got back to my desk the dealer was again on the telephone. He wanted to be sure his letter had arrived. I gave him Dana's message.

"Tell Mr. Dana," he replied, "that I insist. Please let me know what he says."

I went back to Dana.

"Very well," he said quietly, "tell him we will print it."

I could hear the dealer's grunt of satisfaction. The next morning the letter appeared prominently on the editorial page. Not a word had been softened or omitted, but the heading covered all:

MR. BLANK WRITES A FOOLISH LETTER

Men ground their teeth and choked with rage over things like that, but those had reason to be sorriest who encountered the editor in his playful mood. Perhaps it would be more correct to say when he assumed the playful mood, for often this was but the mask worn in honest-to-goodness fighting. Incidentally, it was at such times that were invented those words and phrases which lodged in men's minds, some of them to become definitely incorporated in our language.

It was the unfortunate Mr. Cowles of the *Cleveland Leader* who inspired the word "hebetudinous", being described as "the most hebetudinous crank anywhere within the bounds of latitude and longitude". Was he ever allowed to forget it? Not much. There were plenty of journalists around the country to keep it going.

H. C. Bunner, the brilliant editor of *Puck*, burst into verse over this:

> Oh, put me away in a graveyard cool,
> Amid verdure damp and dank;
> For I am the man whom Dana called
> A Hebetudinous crank.
>
> I should like to call *him* an isotherm,
> And a fulminiferous plug;
> And bring the blush of binomial shame
> To his antiphlogistic mug.
>
> But I know that I never, no never on earth,
> Can rival that awful word—
> The meanest and newest and cussedest cuss
> That mortal ever has heard.

There were thirteen stanzas in all.

Then there was Richard Smith of the *Cincinnati Gazette*. He appeared in the *Sun's* portrait gallery as Deacon Richard Smith, a truly good man, desirous above all things to make his newspaper a mirror of the virtues, yet continually thwarted by his wicked partners, particularly one named Romeo Reed. Did Smith ever look into the eyes of his friends—it is not necessary even to consider his enemies—without suspecting that they were grinning over the way he was being held to the gridiron? For the *Sun* was remorseless, continuing to reveal the good deacon's hopeless struggles, with new and ingenious variations to pique the interest and whip up the laughter, month after month and year after year.

> The *Albany Evening Journal* desires to be informed why Deacon Richard Smith of Cincinnati is truly good. If the question is to be understood as implying doubt respecting the purity of Deacon Richard Smith's motives, we repudiate it and refuse to respond. His reason for being truly good is doubtless because he loves it, knows that it is the part of wisdom, and has culti-

vated his moral nature up to that point; and we will not in any way seem to admit that his conduct proceeds from any lower impulse. But if the questioner merely wishes to ask why it is that we pronounce Deacon Richard Smith truly good, we answer with pleasure. It is because we have watched his course for years, and have become convinced that such is the manly beauty of his character. He is truthful, modest, honest, kind, brave, reverential, temperate, sincere, magnanimous, forbearing, generous, friendly, faithful, patient, dutiful, unselfish, a fine orator with a strong voice and impressive utterance, a lecturer in behalf of good causes, a voting citizen, an industrious editor, an attentive deacon, patriotic, straightforward, noble in his phrenological developments yet not vain, seeking no reduction in his taxes, and laboring with marvelous perseverances, affecting courage and unflinching self-sacrifice for the reformation and restoration to integrity of his wicked partners. Such is the man; and though the profligate and scornful may jeer at his red beard and the curvilinear shortness of his legs and a certain swift flush of passionate temper belonging to his complexion, we hold all such peculiarities as trifling accidents, and admire and honor him because he is a truly good man; and if the *Evening Journal* disputes the justness of this judgment, we will deplore its dissent but none the less adhere to Deacon Richard Smith. And the public at large, in all portions of this great country, appear to be of the same opinion.

Men have lost their health or gone mad under milder persecution.

George W. Childs, the wealthy and highly respected owner of the Philadelphia *Public Ledger*, paid dearly for an attempted rebuke to the *Sun*. Thenceforth he was always George Washington Childs, a scholar who should have received the degree of Master of Arts, and one of the truly great poets of his time, the evidence of which lay in the verse appearing in the *Ledger's* death notices, a special feature of the *Ledger*, all of which, the *Sun* asserted solemnly, were the great poet's personal inspiration and written with his own hand. Childs established many drinking fountains and gave many stained glass windows, and these the *Sun* credited to the memory of different great poets of the past, Shakespeare, Milton and the like, the magnanimous tribute of a great genius to his rivals. That Childs was able to go on with his philanthropies was evidence of strong nerves.

Other victims were named for diplomatic posts or consulships at unheard of places, whose very names, often invented, incited grins and laughter. Of course, this was a game which was successful only where the manipulator was a true artist in the use of wit and words, adept at moving the risibles without provoking counter emotions. In Bartlett, and later Mitchell and Edward M. Kingsbury, especially the last-named, the *Sun* had three who never stumbled. Nor did Dana, for that matter.

Not everybody enjoyed or approved these scintillations. The *Sun* of Dana was still in its early youth when Governor Nelson Dingley, Jr., of Maine, one of the proprietors of the *Lewiston Journal*, said to Mitchell, whom he saw absorbed in the *Sun*:

"Dana's a good teacher for condensation and for saying what you want to say, but as to what he generally wants to say!"

That was the repressed judgment of a mild-mannered and cautious critic. There were plenty who did not control their emotions. Especially later on, in the heat of the Grant and Hayes and Cleveland controversies. A gentle, well-bred old gentleman, who was sent from the business office to see about some advertising, returned with the report that he had no sooner mentioned the name of the paper than the man he was addressing seemed to go out of his mind. Raging like a wild cat, spitting and sputtering, he broke out with:

"That—sheet! Go back and tell your man Dana I wouldn't use his rag to ——"

Never mind the rest. It is not unusual for men who lose

their self-control to find a safety valve in obscenity. A Freud might find a fruitful field of investigation in the problem of how many such have escaped apoplexy and heart disease through this vent to overwrought emotion.

The irritating element lay in that man Dana's disregard for other men's judgments, more particularly their valuations of public men. Such an utter lack of reverence too for causes and conventions held sacred by thousands. His path was strewn with the fragments of idols and the tattered remains of holy writs. One never knew what might come next. Even in his own office, as Mitchell confessed, one never could tell whether it would be Republican or Democrat. But one thing was certain. There was no list in the *Sun* office, as there was in many others, of favorites to be protected. Somebody once asked Dana what clubs he belonged to.

"None," he replied. "In every club in New York there are enough scoundrels whom I have had to expose to furnish sufficient blackballs to keep me out. So I have never allowed my name to be put up."

In fact, for years the paper was not to be found in the libraries of any of the so-called leading clubs. Not even in that of the Century, preëminently the club of writers in that period.

Office gossip had it that disapproval extended to the wife of a close relative; that when he disappeared from the breakfast table she would take up the paper with the fire tongs and deposit it in the grate.

It is quite possible that the vehemence of the opposition intensified the transgressions. From the point of view of circulation, of keeping the menagerie in agitation, there could be no better editorial tactics. Iteration and reiteration are magical words in the editorial lexicon—or were in the days of Personal Journalism. Rubbing into the wounds kept the animals from forgetting who inflicted them.

No man ever thrived more under criticism. It was not the growing circulation or profits that brought the merry twinkle to his eyes and the marked buoyancy to his step. His performance sometimes interfered with the material rewards. It was the game that counted. And the conviction that he was doing a good work in puncturing the bladders and swollen reputations. Of course, he went too far sometimes. The ethics of journalism as expounded by him in later days were not always respected. In the heat of the fray the blows were not always fair, perhaps. But, what will you? He was human, a man of red blood and high zest for the fight.

Dana inspired and developed the best in the large group of men who came under his influence in the thirty years he dominated the *Sun*. He unmasked hundreds of frauds and conspirators against high morals and good taste. If a few heads were cracked unfairly, he at least sent a lot of rascals packing, and in the meantime inspired many a good laugh. Not the type to please the hero worshiper who will not allow his idol to have any failings, but well suited to the rest of us.

"There will never be an end to the personality of journalism," wrote Colonel Henry Watterson, himself a brilliant illustration of his dictum, in the early 'Seventies. That was in the course of a piece on journalism as practiced in New York, wherein he had this about Dana:

"He, of all his fellow-creditors of the great metropolis, has passed the period of middle age; though—years apart —he is as blithe and nimble as the youngest of them, and has performed, with the *Sun*, a feat in modern newspaper practice that entitles him to the stag-horns laid down at his death by James Gordon Bennett. Mr. Dana is no less a writer and scholar than an editor. . . . In a word, Mr. Dana at fifty-three is as vigorous, sinewy, and as live as a young buck of thirty-five or forty."

Why shouldn't he have been? He was having the time of his life, and the goose hung high in the office of the *Sun*.

XXI. DANA TURNS ON GRANT—A TIME WHEN A TWO-FISTED EDITOR HAD PLENTY OF FIGHTING ON HIS HANDS—BOSS SHEPHERD TRIES TO "RAILROAD" HIM TO A WASHINGTON JAIL—A PHILADELPHIA CROOK MAKES A SIMILAR ATTEMPT—FUN WITH GREELEY.

ALTHOUGH he had proclaimed the *Sun's* independence of party affiliation in his announcement of ownership, Dana bound himself for the ensuing national campaign. He would support Grant for the Presidency. Regardless of his views of the fitness of the soldier for command in civil life, Dana felt it was most important to fasten down the fact that the country was determined to clinch the results of the war. There must not be anywhere any recrudescence of the idea that slavery was not dead or secession not done for, and Grant stood as a symbol for the new order.

There may have been some doubt in Grant's mind as to Dana's attitude. In a letter received from Wilson while Dana was still in Chicago there was an intimation that Grant had come to believe he was no longer friendly. Dana had replied promptly, asserting that only a fool could believe such a thing. To be sure, he had found it necessary to oppose the bill in Congress to make Grant General-in-Chief, but only because he thought it a dreadful mistake, exhibiting as it did a desire for rank and money which could only detract from his greatness. That same letter contained a phrase which was to explain Dana's attitude in many a personal clash of the future. "There seem to be some gentlemen," it said, "who don't realize the difference between a friend and a lackey."

But Dana had acquitted Grant of being responsible for the proposed legislation. "I have never been more afflicted by any public measure than by that bill," Dana declared, and laid it to unwise counselors and ingratiating politicians. Wilson intimated in his book that persons inimical to Dana were close to Grant at this time, though they had not yet been able to influence the latter.

It is not likely that Dana was ignorant of Grant's weaknesses. Both by nature and by training he was accustomed to judge men objectively. General Wilson declared that even when Dana had supported Grant for military command he had never asserted that he was a great organizer or tactician, but championed him because he was in his opinion the best material in sight. The same seemed to be true now. Grant was sure to make mistakes, but he was honest and he had a reserve of common sense. Finally, he was modest and not above listening to good advice—and there was always Rawlins. Rawlins could be relied upon to undeceive when politicians and other self-seekers sought to delude his master with their cunning. Even Dana could not foresee that Fate would remove Rawlins and leave Grant the prey to his own incapacity to deal with scoundrels.

Dana's genuine interest in Grant's election is further evidenced by his undertaking to get out a life of the hero at a time when he must have been fully occupied with his new venture. While the actual writing of the greater part of it was left to Wilson, Dana scanned and edited with his customary precision and wrote three chapters himself. Only the fact that it was expected to help in the campaign induced him to undertake this.

It was a bitter campaign, with all the mud slinging common to that epoch. Even Grant's military services were assailed mercilessly. The opposition journals, notably the *New York World*, held up to bereaved parents the terrific slaughter in the fighting against Lee. Thousands had been sent to their graves or returned maimed and useless to their homes, the victims of incompetent leadership. The word "murderous" was used to describe the tactics employed.

That kind of attack must have had tremendous influence, and Dana stood above all the other defenders in meeting it.

He had been an eye-witness, knew all the details, and understood military matters as no other editor could. His comparative tables, showing Grant's losses to be materially less in winning the contest than had been those of all the generals who had preceded him in losing it, besides being accomplished in only a fraction of the time consumed by them, could not but affect all reasoning voters.

So Grant was elected, and his backer assured his readers that the evils which had characterized the administration under President Johnson would cease from the day of the installation of the new President. He could be relied upon to practice rigid economy in the employment of the public funds, would enforce the laws impartially in every part of the country, would hold all office-holders to their proper functions, besides keeping the Government out of enterprises with which it had no legitimate concern.

All these were factors for which the *Sun* stood under its new leadership. To decentralize the Government as much as possible, to keep it from encroaching upon the liberties of the people, was fundamental. Quite a few changes had come into the views of the editor since the days when he had subscribed to the theories of Fourier and coquetted with those of Proudhon. No Socialism, no government venture into undertakings which could be conducted to better advantage by individuals. The Dana of the *New York Sun* was an individualist.

The parting of the ways came shortly after Grant's induction into office. There was plenty of reason for an editor of a newspaper which had loudly proclaimed its independence politically, and had at the same time made known its views on the subjects mentioned, to be in opposition. Grant's very Cabinet was an offence to any high-minded citizen. Two of the appointees were not only absolutely new to the political world and to the administration of public affairs, but it was clear that they owed their appointments to the single fact that they had contributed to a fund for the purchase of a house for Grant. A. T. Stewart, famous as the

first among the drygoods merchants of the country, had thus
been named for the Secretaryship of the Treasury. It was
a flat violation of the law, for he was a large importer of
foreign wares. Adolph E. Borie, the other recipient of
Grant's gratitude, had been named Secretary of the Navy.
He was a genial, kindly nobody, standing for nothing but
good intentions, and admittedly ignorant not only of naval
affairs but of the functions of government in general. Grant
had to let both these out, but he did it unwillingly, even
going so far, in Stewart's case, as to ask that the law be
changed. Worse things came later, and many of them came
again through his good-will to those who had brought him
gifts.

Dana's newspaper rivals, who happened also to be supporters of Grant, laid his criticisms to personal disappointment. He became Grant's enemy, they asserted, because
Grant had failed to appoint him Collector of the Port of
New York. Therein lay a story of over-zealous friendship
and the danger of mixing into other people's business.

Wilson and Rawlins were responsible, and the former
admitted it frankly. After the election the two had agreed
that Grant ought to show his appreciation of the great
service rendered him by appointing Dana to some post which
would be both a distinction and remunerative. They decided
between them that the Collectorship fitted both requirements.
Dana would still be able to attend to the more pressing
needs of his paper, and the salary would be appreciated.
Dana was not consulted—Wilson made this positive declaration. The two friends separated and when they met
again a few days later Rawlins told Wilson that Dana would
receive the appointment and asked him to tell him so. Wilson did not say whether he conveyed the message, and there
is no evidence on that point. To Wilson's great amazement
the office went to another.

It is likely enough that Dana did know of Rawlins's
promise and, like Wilson, took it for granted that it had
been authorized by the President. Consequently, there is

every reason to believe that he was seriously offended. Nor was it likely that the smart was lessened by the formal offer of the subordinate post of Appraiser, carrying less distinction, less power and patronage and a lesser salary. Grant seemed to have acquired a talent for doing the wrong thing so far as Dana was concerned.

Boutwell, the new Secretary of the Treasury, was a personal friend of Dana, and his letter showed clearly enough that he did not expect Dana to accept the Appraisership. "You will have heard of your nomination as appraiser—an office for which probably you have neither taste nor inclination," he wrote, "and which, regarding your own claims only, should not have been tendered you, and yet I hope you will not decline it." It was an appeal to Dana's patriotism and willingness to sacrifice to serve the country. Dana did not fail to take advantage of the splendid opportunity.

> Having been educated to commercial pursuits [he wrote], the office is not repugnant to my tastes; and as for serving the Government at some sacrifice of my own interests and convenience, I trust that during the past few years I have sufficiently proved my readiness to do it. But I already hold an office of responsibility as the conductor of an independent newspaper, and I am persuaded that to abandon it or neglect it for the functions you offer me would be to leave a superior duty for one of much less importance. Nor is it certain that I cannot do more to help you in the pure and efficient administration of the Treasury Department by remaining here and denouncing and exposing political immorality ——

For those who knew Dana, or could read between the lines, there was plenty to excite curiosity as to the future performance of the *Sun* in those concluding words.

A well-known editor of a London newspaper, to whom it was suggested that he ought to round out his career by entering Parliament, answered cynically: "Why should I? I need only whistle and I can have five members of Parliament on their knees in my private office." Certainly the uncontrolled editor of a powerful newspaper in any country holds a prouder position and wider influence than any office-holder, and the collectorship of the Port of New York sounds like mighty small potatoes for the scalp-raising Dana. Yet his rivals persisted in charging his condemnation of Grant's shortcomings to disappointment in that affair, which led to the following editorial:

> The idea that the editor of the *Sun*, which shines for all, could consent to become collector of the port of New York is extravagant and inadmissible. It would be stepping down and out with a vengeance. . . . The office of the collector is respectable enough, but it is not one that the editor of the *Sun* could desire to take without deserving to have his conduct investigated by a proceeding *de lunatico*.

It took courage to persist in the fight on Grant. He was the hero of the nation. Of greater moment to Dana was the fact that he continued to hold the support of many of Dana's own friends, including a number of those who had joined in helping him to secure control of the *Sun*. For the first time in his life Dana saw friends falling away. They first used every argument and personal influence to dissuade him, but found him adamant.

"A few years from now," he was quoted as saying, "I shall be willing to accept whatever judgment the nation passes on my course of action; but now I must do as I think right."

He could not have done otherwise, with the information that came to him, and have been true to himself. Maybe he did at times hit pretty near the belt, but it was a fight to a finish, with no evidence that the other side would be mealy-mouthed as to methods.

Twice they tried to get him personally, and once it was a tight squeeze. It was a young man named Elihu Root who fought off the conspirators. That same young man was writing dramatic criticisms for the paper in spare hours from the law, when he was not learning Icelandic from Professor Dana in the latter's home.

Boss Shepherd of Washington was trying to lay the editor by the heels. Alexander Shepherd, Vice President of the Board of Public Works, was the Tweed of Washington. Not a member of the Grant administration, but of the same stripe and working in harmony with the rascals who brought that administration into disrepute. The *Sun* laid bare the conspiracy by which Shepherd and Henry D. Cooke, Governor of the District of Columbia, were turning over paving contracts to a company in which they were interested, and they fought back.

In New York Bill Tweed, while assuming a bold front against his accusers, secretly strove with all the influence of money and personal intercession to placate the newspapers. A member of the *Sun's* editorial staff, seeking a reference book in the inner editorial room one night just before the Tweed scandal was exposed, found the big boss on his knees, slobbering like a spanked boy and holding forth wringing, pleading hands to Amos Cummings. Amos wore a smile which proclaimed the most intense enjoyment. This little tragi-comedy did not do Tweed any good, but it showed his disposition towards the press.

Shepherd tried to have Dana indicted for criminal libel in Washington, whereat Dana had this to say in his paper:

> There is not the slightest possible occasion for Mr. Shepherd or any one else to indict *The Sun*. If he knows anything good about himself, let him send it to us. We will not only print it, but we will pay him liberally for it. A newspaper depends for its success mainly on the news; and this would not only be news, but surprising—and if we may use an unloved phrase—sensational news.

The Grand Jury before which Shepherd's district attorney brought his charges refused to act on them, whereupon Shepherd got a subservient magistrate of a Washington police court to issue a warrant for Dana's arrest, and another of the boss's tools, an assistant district attorney of the District of Columbia, came on to New York and procured an order of arrest on the strength of this warrant from the United States Commissioner.

The purpose was plain enough. If Dana could be dragged to Washington he would be tried by Shepherd's magistrate, without a jury, and the result was forecast. Even with the cards stacked in their favor, they must have been almost naïve in their folly. Such a decision would have lasted only as long as it would take to bring the victim of the conspiracy before a higher court in habeas corpus proceedings. Unless the scamps felt they could influence the higher courts too. It was a time when even the courts were not always the haven of the persecuted.

However, the United States Judges then sitting in the New York district would have none of the nonsense. Judge Samuel Blatchford, to whom an appeal was taken from the Commissioner's decision, vacated the order of arrest with the common-sense observation that "the Constitution says that all trials shall be by jury, and the accused is entitled, not to be first convicted by a court and then to be convicted by a jury, but to be convicted or acquitted in the first instance by a jury."

"Those who sought to murder liberty, where they looked for a second Jeffreys, found a second Mansfield," said Dana in his paper, and for once newspapers throughout the country were with him. The attempt to drag an editor to Washington could not be supported even by rivals or partisan opponents. Incidentally, it was generally recognized that the decision protected the rights of the individual, regardless of vocation or position. The conspirators made another try, this time before Judge Addison Brown, seeking from him a different decision, and it was in the argument before him that Elihu Root appeared as counsel for his friend and teacher, and secured an affirmation of the principle laid down by Judge Blatchford.

There had been a previous attempt to get Dana within

the jurisdiction of a foreign and therefore possibly unfriendly court. That was in the affair of W. H. Kemble, State Treasurer of Pennsylvania, which must have given Dana unalloyed joy for many a day.

The *Sun* had uncovered a letter written by Kemble to Titian J. Coffey (that name alone must have delighted the editorial slaughterers) introducing "his particular friend, Mr. George O. Evans". Mr. Coffey was a government official, with certain powers in passing upon claims against the United States, and Mr. Evans had such a claim—"of some magnitude". Kemble omitted to add that his friend was a defaulter, but perhaps that was unnecessary in the light of his closing sentence:

"He understands Addition, Division and Silence."

How Dana must have chortled when his eyes fell upon that! Depend upon it, his appetite was excellent that day and he slept like a babe that night. Had some oriental jinnee been invoked to make a situation suited to his purposes he could not have framed it better.

The country rang with that phrase from "Dan to Beersheba". It became one of Dana's choicest illustrations of the damning power of reiteration. And it told the country what kind of officials were in power under Grant, when one of them could be addressed in such cynical terms.

Kemble had the effrontery to try to bluff it out. His words had no such meaning as Dana had imparted to them, he declared, and when the former was passing through Philadelphia he was arrested for criminal libel and put under bonds of fifteen thousand dollars. A futile gesture of a foolish rogue, of course. Eight years later—in 1880—he was convicted of attempting to bribe members of the Pennsylvania legislature, and spent a year in the penitentiary.

What a welter of official debauchery overwhelmed the whole country at this time, beginning at the fountainhead of government and extending even into the hamlets! Tammany at its worst, and the politicians elsewhere no less willing to make the most of their opportunities, if not so skilful. The country needed a Dana, one who had not only the talent to detect and the courage to denounce, but who pursued the game with such unwearied zest. Never did he serve the country better than at this time.

In a leading editorial dated January second, 1871, which began with a survey of conditions in Europe—the overthrow of the French Empire, the consolidation of the German states, the unification of Italy and the unfortunate condition of the working-men everywhere—Dana switched to a discussion of affairs at home as follows:

> The personal government proclivities exhibited by General Grant in his Dominican proceedings [the reference is to Grant's desire to annex San Domingo], and in his appointments and resentments, tend not only to undermine the Republican party, but also to shake one's faith in the stability of free institutions, and to belittle the American Republic abroad as well as at home. . . . He has opened the doors to hypocrisy and corruption by disregarding fitness and propriety in his appointments, and regarding only the claims which persons related to his family, or who make him presents, or who assist him in his personal schemes may have upon his recognition.

Grant himself was no plunderer, nor did Dana ever suggest that he was. On one occasion, when an exposed scoundrel offered to prove the contrary for sufficient reward, declaring flatly that the gang with which he was identified had sent many boxes of cigars to the President, with one-thousand-dollar notes snugly placed between the layers, Dana expressed his conviction that the fellow was lying, and Mitchell was sent across the country to confirm this. But the "corrupting and demoralizing" influence upon the lesser officials of Grant's acceptance of gifts from rich individuals Dana did not hesitate to point out in his own way from the outset.

Dexterously the challenger smote the monsters and defended the innocent. A lesser editor might have charged everything, belittling the good performance as well as denouncing the bad. Dana was clever enough to make his praise sound just as loud as his denunciations. That was what made the assaults so effective. Very likely those assailed were in doubt of the sincerity behind the occasional approval, but that might have been because of bad consciences. And then, it must be admitted, Dana's good-will to his enemies was apt to be short-lived. Thus he had no sooner defended Grant against the charge of being involved with Gould and his fellow-conspirators in the effort to corner the gold of the country, commending his attitude with the utmost heartiness, than he was declaring that the successor to the Assistant Secretary of the Treasury who had been dismissed for complicity could not be any one who had "made donations of money, houses, horses, or anything else to General Grant". What a peculiar standard of ethics must have prevailed at this time to make such a declaration worth the printing!

The assault became more vitriolic when the time came around for nominating candidates for the Presidency. In July this appeared on the editorial page:

THE PRESIDENCY
OFFICE HOLDERS' CANDIDATE

For President:
USELESS S. GRANT
THE PRESENT-TAKER

Relations of Useless S. Grant whom the other Office Holders want to Renominate along with Him:

There followed a list of thirty-four relatives of Grant and Mrs. Grant, beginning with the President's father, Jesse Root Grant, postmaster at Covington, Kentucky, and concluding with James S. Wadsworth, "son of the sister of the mother of the President's wife", nominated for Marshal at New York, "but rejected by the Senate on account of his bad character".

In November satire was temporarily dropped for straight assault under the heading,

THE ONLY ISSUE

All other questions that have hitherto divided the American people disappear before this one: Can public corruption be stopped? Can public robbery be put down? Can bribery and present-taking be banished from political affairs?

Ten years ago the great question was slavery. It was settled through the war of the rebellion, with its immense losses of life and treasure and its gigantic heritage of public debt. Since then other questions growing out of the war have arisen. Fortunately, they are now all ended and cleared away; and there is no other subject to distract the attention of the people from the supreme issue: Can robbers, thieves, bribe-givers, bribe-takers and official blackmailers be driven from power and honest men put in their places?

Dana was like a sleight-of-hand performer before the public, keeping all the issues going, and allowing none to drop out of sight. In a thundering editorial of February, 1872, he listed them all:

The carpet-bag governments of the Southern states, stifling efforts to restore stable government and bring back order, because the plunderers were not yet satisfied with their booty.

The sale of arms by the War Department to France, obviously for use in the war with Germany, out of which it was openly charged high officials and individuals close to the Government had made millions.

A deficit of six millions in the stamps of the Internal Revenue Department, investigation of which, like those proposed inquiries into Custom House frauds and the causes of the terrible panic called Black Friday, had been choked off.

The frauds of the Washington bosses, surpassing in greed and boldness even those of Tweed and his cohorts.

The Postmaster General's participation in claims against his own department, and in the whiskey frauds against the internal revenue.

The Navy Department a sink of corruption, its officials involved in crooked contracts.

How, thundered Dana, had all these villainies dared to be, and pointed the finger of denunciation at the President himself, holding him primarily responsible. It was he who had destroyed "in the public mind all distinction between right and wrong", and had made it appear that the "great object of life and the chief purpose of official authority is to acquire riches, and that it makes no difference by what means this end is attained".

The attacks aroused the public and secured coöperation from some of the leading newspapers of the country, among which the Chicago *Tribune* and the Springfield *Republican* served most effectively. At the close of Grant's first term many leading Republicans were disaffected. It looked as though the seed sown by Dana might produce a real harvest. He was the outstanding leader of the revolt, and it became clearer day by day that this could be translated into action. What then induced him to name Greeley as the standard bearer against Grant?

"The nomination of Greeley for the Presidency made the *Sun's* staff smile," wrote Chester S. Lord, then a reporter and later managing editor, in some reminiscences printed by *The Saturday Evening Post*. "Somebody laughingly asked Dana which candidate he would support, and he replied with a twinkle of eye that he thought we were likely to have a little fun."

There had been no fooling in the fight hitherto, and there was plenty of straight hitting from the shoulder even now, so the only reasonable explanation of his bringing forward the "Philosopher of the *Tribune*" at the crucial moment would be his inner conviction that Grant could not be defeated. That being so, what better lamb to bring to the sacrificial altar? Dana was always possessed by an irresistible inclination to let the world know the profound depths of Greeley's innocence. That appeared in the sending of the reporter to Greeley's talks on temperance, already mentioned, as it did in Cummings's rushing over to the *Tribune* office to snatch an interview from Greeley the moment the news of his nomination had reached New York and while he was still hot with elation.

Most of what he wrote was devoted to a description of Greeley's sanctum and his personal appearance.

From the street Dr. Greeley can be seen at almost any hour between 4 and 9 P.M. preparing his editorial articles. The room is carpeted. Yesterday it contained 3 chairs, 2 desks and a high stool. Two of the chairs were cane-bottomed, and one of them had a broken arm. . . . There was an old sofa in the room, where the Great Reformer rests after the visits of importunate visitors. . . . The Great Editor's desk was littered with newspaper clippings and manuscripts. Some of these looked as though they had slept on the desk since the time that Henry Clay had run for President. . . . A ricketty pair of scissors also swung from a chain. Dr. Greeley's hat lay inside-up among the papers on the desk. The small drawers of the desk were half drawn out. Postage stamps, envelopes, letter paper and old pamphlets seemed ready to creep out of the drawers. A box of common red wafers was half upset on the left, while an old-fashioned sand box was standing guard near the scene of the accident. He had laid seven Virginia worm fences in ink, and then had bitten them off in the middle of a word. . . . The Doctor's desk is either very high or his chair is very low; for when he writes his desk is on a level with his chin. He is near-sighted. His chair is a high, cane-backed affair, rigged on a swivel. It squeaks when it turns.

The Great Economist was dressed in a black suit throughout. He wore a steel pen coat. His pantaloons were drawn over his bootlegs, and his cravat was not out of place. He wore no jewelry. Plain china shirt buttons glistened on his bosom, and a black silk watch-guard ran about his neck.

For some months Dana had run Greeley's name at the head of the editorial page, but there could have been little gratification for Greeley in the way he did it. Here are some of Dana's variations on his theme:

Proposed Nomination for President:
The Farmers' Candidate
The Great And Good
Horace Greeley of Texas

The Farmers' And Mechanics' Candidate
Useful H. Greeley
Of Texas And New York

Now and then it would be Dr. Horace Greeley of Chappaqua, formerly of Oregon. Again his name was followed by the quotation, in italics:

"And that old friend, so sage and bland,
Our later Franklin"—Whittier.

There were repeated outbursts in doggerel:

Hurrah For The Old Tree-Chopper!

———

Hurrah for Horace Greeley,
The Tree Chopper, honest and true!
Hurrah for him with a will and a vim,
With your votes, and with victory, too;
For when he springs into the combat
With his battle-axe heavy and broad,
He will level the tree of rank robbery
And chop off the head of Fraud.
Hurrah for H. G.!

There was a lot of the terrible stuff. Dana was having his fun all right.

At that it looked for a time as though the country was so thoroughly incensed over the crookedness exposed that it might turn against its soldier idol. But the spasm did not last. Greeley's endorsement by the Democrats made the North pause. Greeley would have to listen to the same secessionists who had made the war, would have to put them in the places of power where they could renew their efforts and revive their doctrines. There were too many bereaved families, as well as doubts of the sincerity of the new faith asserted by the recent sinners, to make possible a wholesale flocking to their standard bearer. And it could not be denied that with all his fundamental goodness, and his many abilities, he was lopsided. In fact, fantastic. Better trust Grant to see the light and clean his own house than experiment with explosives.

Some of the rascalities exposed during Grant's second term read as though they had been plotted by the most sensational authors of the then highly popular "dime novels". Who else could have conceived the scheme to burglarize the office of the Washington District Attorney, seize books of account belonging to an accused contractor, plant the same in the home of the wealthy and highly respectable accuser of that contractor and then arrest this accuser on the charge of being responsible for the burglary? Yet that was what the *Sun* showed were the facts in the famous Washington Safe Burglary Case. Plotted by the District Attorney himself and carried out by professional burglars hired for the purpose! The safe is dynamited while the police see there is no interference. But Providence is kind. Columbus Alexander, the intended victim, and his family sleep so well that night that no one answers the conspirators' ring of the doorbell and the planting of the loot in his home cannot be accomplished. Still the conspirators are not at the end of their resources. One of the three burglars is arrested and induced to sign an alleged confession, charging Alexander with having hired him to commit the crime. Involved in this melodramatic conspiracy were the President's private secretary, General Babcock, the Solicitor of the Treasury, the chief of the Secret Service Division, the heads of the local police, a number of Congressmen and a host of contractors, all of whom had been robbing the Government.

The Whiskey Ring seems almost too commonplace after that. But it brought a better harvest to the exposers. The other fellows were indicted, but packed the jury to bring about a disagreement. When the whiskey looters were finally disposed of the Government had recovered quite a lot of money and valuable liquor, indicted one hundred and fifty-two outside the government service and eighty-six within, of whom many were convicted. More convictions might have been obtained had not the President interfered.

Then there was the Credit Mobilier, organized in Grant's first term to finance the building of the Union Pacific Railroad, and corrupting Senators, Representatives and endless officials with gifts of stock. How tame read the Harding oil scandals compared with this one, which tarnished the reputations of many distinguished "statesmen", including the existing Vice-President and a future President!

On Jan. 8, 1873, appeared this editorial, with the caption,

> Definitions Wanted:
> What a dreadful slander that was in *The Sun* last summer about *Oakes Ames* and the Credit Mobilier. The entire Republican party, including the most religious of its journals, stood aghast, not at the crime of *Oakes Ames* and the dishonesty of the members implicated, but at the audacity of *The Sun* in telling such a dreadful tale about such good people. Well, we cannot always be entirely right. It seems we were in error. Not as to the distribution of the stock, which was so vehemently denied; not as to the names of the recipients, most of whom burned up their diaries and swore great round oaths, with great staring, indignant eyes, that they never heard of the Credit Mobilier and had

only a slight acquaintance with *Mr. Oakes Ames*; not as to *Mr. Oakes Ames's* placing the stock "where it would do most good," for it seems he did that—but we have to confess we were in error as to the motive of that estimable man.

We supposed that when he distributed this stock where it would do most good, it was in the nature of a corrupt approach. We hasten to make amends for the wrong done him. In his letter to Col. McComb of Feb. 22, 1868, concerning this distribution, *Mr. Ames* does, indeed, give as his reason for distributing stock to members that "we want more friends in this Congress"; and a superficial reader, or one who was not acquainted with *Mr. Ames's* character for righteous-- ness, might think this had the look of buying votes— such a statement from any other man we should say might be open to that objection—but *Mr. Ames* hastens to add, what explains the drift of his mind with great beauty and simplicity, "If a man will look into the law, and it is difficult to get them to do it unless they have an interest to do so, he cannot help being convinced that we should not be interfered with." And so what might to the carnal mind seem bribery is explained in the most satisfactory manner. All that *Mr. Oakes Ames* desired—and we apologize for misconstruing his mo- tives—was to get members of Congress to look into the law.

It is manifest enough, of course, that they would not look into the law unless they had an interest to do so. And here, by the way, it occurs to us there is a very common mistake in the popular apprehension of the duties of Congressmen. The impression that we send men to Congress and pay them $5,000 a year and mileage to care for public interests and look into the merits of all measures upon which they act is entirely erroneous; and *Mr. Oakes Ames*, who is a representa- tive man of the good old Puritan Commonwealth of Massachusetts, and who, being a member of Congress, knows precisely how it is himself, has done the public great service in enlightening it upon this point. . . .

Nobody knows how sorry we are at having done these good people injustice. We do hope the investigating committee which has this matter in hand will make some provision against such misunderstandings in the future. The committee will not of course reflect upon the eminent gentlemen whose names have been brought into this business; but it can at least give us some definitions whereby hereafter we can distinguish between bribery and making it for a man's interest to look into the law. At present they are rather mixed.

Exposure had more effect than in Grant's first term, and some of the rascals were really being forced out, but others of them were clever enough to find a new way to protection. The third term idea had lodged in Grant's mind and all that was necessary to secure his intervention against any honest effort to suppress corruption was to insinuate that these behind it were with the opponents to his renomination.

Dana started in to scotch that without delay. This editorial, written by the redoubtable William O. Bartlett, appeared on Washington's Birthday:

One man tried to destroy George Washington and came very near destroying him, as well as the glorious cause of liberty which Washington represented. This man was American born. He was, in military affairs, a man of remarkable parts. He was a daring, a dauntless soldier, a warrior of genius. His own veins had been opened, some of his own blood had been shed, in defence of his country. Yet he was very different from Washington. He was selfish and base. His name survives and stinks: Benedict Arnold.

A man has recently arisen among us who is trying to destroy the example of Washington, or to impair its force. He, too, is a man of military renown. As a soldier he has rendered services to his country of unsurpassed and incalculable value. And yet, if he were to succeed in what he has now undertaken—in breaking the force and violating the sanctity of Washington's example—he might do as great an injury to his country as that which Benedict Arnold attempted in vain!

Dana was not sparing Grant in any way, and the one-time friends who had departed because of his attitude found plenty in the *Sun* to offend them. In the Grant-Greeley campaign there was printed a proposed platform for the opposition which called for summary punishment for the acceptance of gifts as well as bribes, and denied to the President the right to appoint to public office either his own relatives or those of his wife. Then came a linking of Grant's name with John Barleycorn and finally, in the course of attacks upon Grant's policy in the Southern states, appeared the picture of a tombstone, with this inscription:

Sacred
To the Memory of
American Liberty
Born
July 4, 1776
Died
At Columbia, S. C.,
By Order of
Ulysses I
November 28, 1876
Age 100 years, 4 months, 24 days

And yet this implacable opponent would not permit false accusations to lie unchallenged. Mitchell tells how somebody was pretending to quote Grant in remarks thickly inter-larded with oaths, whereupon Dana broke in with:

"Stuff and nonsense! Don't tell me you ever heard a word of profanity from Grant's lips. You didn't!"

XXII.
SLOGANS OF THE *Sun*, POLITICAL AND PHILOSOPHICAL—THE BEECHER SCANDAL—CRIES OF "MALICE" AND "VINDICTIVENESS"—WAR ON HAYES, THE "FRAUDULENT PRESIDENT"—UNFORTUNATE HANCOCK.

"NO FORCE BILL; no Negro Domination!" was one of the first of the slogans which other newspapers helped to carry across the country and which kept people everywhere talking of that man Dana. Not that he always invented them, but they appeared in the *Sun*, and the two continued to be interchangeable in the minds of all except the few in the know. Dana tried to enlighten the public. While testifying before a committee of Congress some years later he was asked the authorship of some editorials and replied promptly:

"They were not written by me. I wish they were; I wish I had the faculty to write such things."

Dana was always friendly to the Negro; he was always opposed to any recrudescence of his exploitation or oppression in any form. But he could not tolerate the methods of the carpetbaggers, through which the Negroes, regardless of their unfitness, were placed in political power over the whites. That for political motives Grant should tolerate the humiliation of cultivated men and women stirred Dana to the depths. The inextinguishable aristocrat in him cried out against such performance.

In the Greeley campaign appeared for the first time another of these catch phrases, one mentioned earlier—"Turn the Rascals Out". Hundreds of thousands of marching men must have repeated it in the great torchlight processions which were inevitable in all elections of those days. It was repeated endlessly in the editorial columns of the *Sun*, often appearing at the close of some article in no way associated with the subject.

At the same time that the fight with Grant was going on pellmell, the battle with Tammany and Tweedism was also on the carpet. It must have been the most satisfying period of Dana's life. Here was the never-ending test of courage, of nerve, of his brains and resourcefulness against some of the keenest in the land. And he and his little band were lustiest when the blows were thickest.

Only that spirit can explain the extraordinary slogan which came out in the local campaign:

"No king, no clown, to rule this town!"

Imagine that being plumped down upon the desk of the responsible editor in the heat of a fierce campaign against predatory politicians whose effrontery, when exposed, was equal to Tweed's notorious retort: "What are you going to do about it?" Analyze the thing. What relevancy was there in this talk of kings and clowns? What was the man in the street who, after all, was the one the editor was after, to make of it? It is all very well, in the light of results, to exhaust the superlatives of praise, but how many editors would have realized that here was a stroke of genius, one of the undefinable, unexplainable phrases that pulsate with a rhythm to which all intellects and all intelligences respond, as though they were the offspring of magic?

Dana had no doubt about it, for he played it up from the start, and kept it going. And soon the whole town was throbbing with it. All the meetings of protest and indignation echoed with it. The marchers chanted it. Even the urchins in the street were shouting it. Newspapers everywhere were quoting it and printing long articles from correspondents who were frankly amazed at the reception given it in all circles of metropolitan life. Nowhere had it struck deeper than in Tammany itself, and Tweed had lost his bravado. Score again for William O. Bartlett!

The impudent and colossal robberies committed by the Tweed raiders belong to the history of the development of

Grover Cleveland as Seen by Dana in the Days
of "Rum, Romanism and Rebellion."

(*From F. T. Richards' Cartoon in Life.*)

the greatest of all capitals. To the *Times* went the glory of exposing them. Curiously enough, the *Sun* had the first chance and missed it! It came during an unfortunate absence of the pilot, and Hitchcock, as chance would have it, was the one to whom came this splendid opportunity. The most conservative man on the staff, being the richest, with a considerable personal stake in the fortunes of the paper, he would not take the risk of a suit for libel before courts notoriously packed by Tammany. There was all the evidence, brought in by a disgruntled associate of the thieves—not a mere underling, who could be brushed aside, but one high up in the inner council, the Sheriff of the County of New York. Dana must have writhed when he got back and saw the triumph of his rival.

The fiasco is the more inexplicable because he had been laying the foundations for such an exposé. Jimmy O'Brien, the informer, felt that, or he would not have turned to the *Sun* in the first instance.

At no time did the paper illustrate better its inimitable manner of getting after a man than in the tale of Tweed's barn, published on March 4th, 1870. Even today its eloquent exaggeration and satire maintain their cogency:

> The Hon. William M. Tweed, more familiarly known as Tweedy, is a candidate for the chairmanship of the Democratic National Committee, now held by the Hon. August Belmont. The latter gentleman has been too aristocratic in his tastes and feelings to handle the helm of the great Democratic ship. The fighting Democracy have been casting about for another pilot, and many of the clubs have advocated the selection of the Hon. Big 6 [referring to the volunteer fire company through which Tweed first got into politics]. In former years, when foreman of the greatest fire engine company in the world, Mr. Tweed was an unpretentious, hard-working representative of the Democracy. But with wealth came aristocratic tastes and feelings, until now, in point of luxurious magnificence, he outstrips even the regal style of the gorgeous Belmont. A

reporter, who has recently visited Mr. Tweed's stable in Fortieth street, estimates as follows, the sumptuous paraphernalia of that institution:

A list of seventy-three items, with the reporter's valuation for each, sets forth with all the solemnity of an auctioneer's appraisal every detail of furniture and furnishing, and those of the small merchants and mechanics who were still reading the paper must have gasped not only at the magnificence but equally at the alleged expensiveness of seemingly commonplace items.

Satin-lined clarence	$2,800.00
Two-horse caleche	1,500.00
Black walnut harness cases (very fine)	15,000.00
Gold-plated harness	1,500.00
Set of silver-plated harness	1,000.00
Silver speaking trumpet with which the Hon. Big Six gives orders to the coachman	750.00
Bronze lion heads with rings in their noses	600.00
Iron wash basins and drinking trough	150.00
Coupe with fine claret cloth trimmings	2,000.00
Lady's pony wagon	2,800.00
A large family sleigh	1,200.00
Stove for Tweed's room	100.00
Walnut bookcase, without books	200.00
Furniture in the groom's room	1,000.00
Furniture in the retiring room	250.00
Two black walnut carriage doors	500.00
Figured ground glass for doors	1,000.00
Silver pitcher and goblets	500.00
Two diamond-handled whips	300.00
Cut glass whiskey jugs and glasses	150.00
Silver-plated champagne coolers	100.00
Photograph of P. B. S. [Peter B. Sweeney, Tweed's pal]	4.00
Photograph of the Hon. Big Six	15.00
Four packs of cards	4.00
Ivory poker chips	24.00

The total, including land and building, and seven family horses, amounted to $132,438. One must not forget that millions were not so plentiful in 1870, nor that the dollar bought a lot more of the things mentioned than they would today. Neither should one abandon altogether the suspicion that the reporter may never have gone beyond his office chair in making up his summary. At the close of this appeared this promise to the reader: "Mr. Tweed owns another stable, similarly furnished, in the country, which a *Sun* reporter proposes to visit at an early day." How the Hon. Big Six must have shivered when he read it! It all reads suspiciously like Amos Cummings.

There was still one slogan which was dear to the *Sun* worshiper, and which ran through the years intermittently, bobbing up unexpectedly at the end of all sorts of editorial articles, or standing forth in the glamor of its own illumination. Attributed to an anonymous Chinese philosopher through the agency of Edward M. Kingsbury, one of the most brilliant of Dana's collaborators, and discoverer of many geniuses like the author of

Alas for the South! Her books have grown fewer—
She was never much given to literature,

this assertion of invincible optimism must always have had a place in Dana's mind, as it must have lifted the gloom from many a reader's:

We may be happy yet,
You bet.

In the heat of the political fights Dana was not neglecting other topics. The sensational killing of Jim Fisk, associate of Jay Gould in unconscionable finance, by Ed Stokes, which upset the equanimity of the entire American continent, left Dana in a mood of musing philosophy. Not a few virtuous citizens, confident of their own impeccability, must have been affronted by this assertion of common human weakness:

Col. Fisk was regarded by many with detestation; by many with admiration; by all with interest. He was a man of prodigious vitality. His energy, his audacity, his love of display, his wit, his adventures, his ready generosity, his freedom from religious or moral scruples, all combined to make him a conspicuous figure. . . .

There are doubtless those who will look upon this tragedy, beginning in the dispute for the possession of an abandoned woman and ending in murder, with a sense of spiritual superiority, as the Pharisee of old thanked God that he was not like the sinners he saw around him. What an insane delusion! Fisk and Stokes are not different from other men. Their nature, their passions, their desires were the same as belong to all the rest of us; their acts were such as other men might commit.

The effort to impose prohibition upon the country was active even then, and came to a test in New York State in an election in the spring of 1874. This was Dana's comment after the voters had expressed themselves:

Recent elections disclose the wholesome fact that the masses of the people are convinced that no man has the right to analyze the contents of another man's stomach while the man who owns the stomach is alive and voting. . . . In the countries where wines are pure, cheap and plentiful, there seems to be no necessity for the interference of Church or State. Such a country we should make of this. Lift the burdens from the producers of innocent wines and beer; enact rigid laws against adulteration; allow pure wines to be sold with as much freedom as bread; and a very brief trial will show that the royal road to temperance, as perfect as human nature is capable of, has been found at last.

Dana's attitude in the Beecher scandal showed again how ready he was to attack the idol of the public when he believed the facts warranted it. Henry Ward Beecher had become a household word for righteousness throughout the country. With unrivaled eloquence he had preached the word of God and the brotherhood of man, standing always for love and tolerance as well as the accepted virtues. It went against the grain of the average man to believe he could be guilty of the disloyalty to friendship, not to mention the more heinous sin involved in Theodore Tilton's charge of seduction and adultery.

It is quite possible that the scandal might have been smothered after the church investigation which exonerated Beecher had not the *Sun* kept on his trail. On Dec. 12, 1874, this appeared:

> In the Beecher case there is one thing that the public will neither fail to understand while it is going on nor forget after it is over: *Any compromise and arrangement or settlement, except through a trial in court, is a confession that Henry Ward Beecher is a guilty man.*

Although the *Sun* had only four pages to devote to all the news of the world, plus the editorials and advertisements, it did not hesitate to give full space to this issue. Tilton's charges occupied six columns; Beecher's defence eleven columns. Francis D. Moulton, one of the principal witnesses, took up seventeen columns in one issue and sixteen in another.

"I don't read the *Sun*," Beecher told a reporter, "and don't allow anybody to read it to me. What's the good of a man sticking pins into himself?"

To which Dana replied:

> Everybody reads the *Sun*—the good, that they may be stimulated to do better; the bad, in fear and trembling lest their wickedness shall meet its deserts.

Having finally forced a trial in the secular courts of Tilton's accusations, Dana took a pot shot whenever the occasion offered at anybody and everybody who stood for the preacher. As the trial lasted six months there were plenty of such opportunities. Perhaps no better illustration of

Dana's manner of attack ever appeared than the following from the editorial page of the *Sun* of April 13, 1875:

> We are sorry to be obliged to say that lawyers as a class are not noted for their piety. Why this melancholy fact is, we cannot now undertake to show; but we think it will not be denied by those who have experience among them, that the most marked characteristic of lawyers is not, as a rule, their piety. This may be due to the circumstance that the lawyers have frequently to deal with very wicked men; and it is said that the contact with pitch defiles. But, however this may be—and it unquestionably is open to argument— if we had particular occasion for a pious lawyer we should not go out and select one at random from among the legal profession. . . .
>
> Fortunately, however, there is no need for such a search, in New York, at least. The bar here contains an example of piety so conspicuous, and so unmistakable, that the attention of the world is fixed on him. Though he is in fact a very short man, yet, metaphorically speaking, his piety is so tall that everybody must look up to him. Physically he is of low stature; piously he looms up to gigantic dimensions. The picture we are drawing is, of course, that of Brother Shearman. Why this brother has kept so highly pious in a profession which so often makes men at least tolerant of wickedness, is a question easily answered. It is because he has a feeling heart. Tears are his daily food and his nightly potion. . . .
>
> When Mr. Beecher got into trouble, therefore, nothing was more natural than that Brother Shearman should be retained to work up his case for him. He was a flower of the Plymouth garden, a tender plant, nourished by the showers of weeping, and, besides, an attorney as sharp as a thorn. There was no legal trick that he did not know, for he had been the attorney of James Fisk, Jr., who might never have been so successful as he was in his projects for the development of our railway system if it had not been for the piety of Brother Shearman. . . .

The presence of Brother Shearman in the Beecher case is the one bright fact in the night of doubt which broods over that shocking affair. We know he would not be there if his soul was not satisfied that the spiritual welfare of mankind required that he should use his piety and legal methods to defend his pastor. His previous experiences taught us that. He then learned to avoid wickedness, pursue virtue, and maintain his piety under circumstances which made beholders tremble with apprehension. The lawyer who could assist Fisk in developing the railway system of the country without his piety changing in the least, must have fitted himself thereby to defend his pastor against a charge of adultery as he could have done in no other way. It shows that piety is a good thing, whatever the wicked may say to the contrary.

Brother Shearman prays with all his old fervency, and may frequently be heard at the Friday evening meeting, the tones of his pious voice made more telling by the upward gush of his abundant tears. We shall never desert this brother, for a highly pious man always fastens himself to the feeling heart as with hooks of steel; and who is such, if not Brother Shearman!

The trial ended in a disagreement of the jury, nine favoring Beecher and three his accuser, but Dana never wavered nor missed an opportunity to proclaim his conviction of Beecher's guilt. Twelve years later, when the preacher died, the *Sun* printed an eight column review of his career in which nothing was omitted, and the next day appeared an editorial containing the following:

Genius associated with frailty is undoubtedly attractive to the mass of men. Frailty is sometimes even more attractive than genius. The confession of Francesca da Rimini touched the heart of men and women more than all the great intellect and burning thought of Dante. But Mr. Beecher made no other confession than that found in his letters.

The anti-Beecher campaign cost the *Sun* quite a lot of circulation, and Beecher's friends rent the heavens with shouts of "Malice" and "Vindictiveness", which undoubtedly spurred Dana to further assaults. In those days, at least, it was worth while in the long run to be known as a tireless fighter.

Out of the fight against Tweed and Tammany came Dana's personal friendship for Samuel J. Tilden and his support of the latter's candidacy for the Presidency. Tilden had shown himself just the man to put into effect Dana's cry to "Turn the Rascals Out". He had been elected Governor on the strength of his record, and the fact that he had supported most of Lincoln's policies and had previously been an anti-slavery Democrat gave him strength in the North, where even then the average Democrat stood under suspicion of being no better than lukewarm in loyalty.

Tilden came to visit Dana during the campaign a number of times and is described in Mitchell's *Memoirs* as follows:

> The characteristic attitude in conference of that great political philosopher and past master of political detail was not such as to indicate either the dimensions of his intellect or its really human and even humorous perceptions. He would sit on the edge of his chair, leaning forward slightly, and whisper communications that might refer to literature or art or the wine cellar or the dogs at Greystone but sometimes seemed to an unhearing onlooker as if they must be sinister suggestions for the overthrow of the Republic. . . . He was slow of movement, unimpressive of utterance, deliberate in his judgment, unexcitable of temperament, capable of absolute personal detachment even from a situation that greatly concerned himself, capable likewise of momentous decision, though his characteristic phrase when such matters were put up to him was the half audible "I'll see you later." . . . In the uncertainties following that memorable election day hundreds of thousands of Democrats came to think of Tilden, first of all, as a whisperer and a procrastinator.

There must have been times when he could not have failed to irritate Dana. The great campaigner against corruption in city and state must have appeared to the militant editor timid and irresolute in the contest growing out of the disputed Presidential election. The latter left no one in doubt as to where he stood. Tilden was elected, and all the political trickery and legal manipulations, could not alter that fact. If Tilden chose to be cheated out of his rights nobody could force him to do otherwise, but the man who sat in the presidential chair was not there by the voice of the people but through downright dishonesty on the part of election officials, supported if not inspired by higher-ups, among whom the occupant of that chair was *particeps criminis*. So Dana yelled "Fraud" not alone at Republican managers, but at Hayes himself, whom he never designated by any other title than that of "Fraudulent President". To fasten down his judgment of him, so that even the most casual reader could not miss it, he printed an outline portrait of Hayes with the word "Fraud" running across the forehead.

All who joined with Hayes were included in his guilt. There was Carl Schurz, the most distinguished German to adopt American citizenship. He had fought bravely and with success in the Civil War, achieving a major-generalship, and later became United States Senator. When he accepted the post of Secretary of the Interior in Hayes's Cabinet this was what was handed to him:

A Birthday In Dishonor

Mr. Schurz is a man of talent, but when he sold himself to Hayes he left nothing unpurchased of which his adopted country can be proud. It is impossible to felicitate a man on the occurrence of his fiftieth birthday when that anniversary finds him involved in a situation of shame and dishonor.

Schurz continued to be a target for many years, but once Dana happened to be present when Schurz exhibited his remarkable talent for oratory, and it was like the temperamental editor to relent long enough to indulge his appreciation in a paragraph which ended thus:

> Few persons know that this red-bearded Teuton has the eloquence of Demosthenes and the fire of Kossuth.

In newspaper and political circles it was known that John C. Reid was responsible for the decision. Not a pleasant or popular person, John. His red, bloated features warned of his hot temper, his angry little eyes of a disposition to tyrannize, all of which was borne out by the stories which came from ithe unfortunate reporters subject to his whims. As managing editor of the *Times* he was able to bring wretchedness and misery to many a poor devil who could not afford to resign. One of his pleasant habits was to cut down the amounts earned by the reporters arbitrarily, cursing out any who dared to protest and even proceeding to physical violence if they persisted.

The story of how Reid inspired the Republican campaign officials to claim the votes of South Carolina, Florida and Louisiana, bulwarks of Democracy, after reading late despatches from the Republican managers of those states, has been printed before. It was for that service to his party that Tom Platt gave him a sinecure place when he was finally dismissed from the *Times*. Daniel F. Kellogg, at one time city editor of the *Sun*, used to tell with glee this tale of Reid:

"Mr. Reid," said Kellogg, entering the latter's office in the Fifth Avenue Hotel, "I just heard a man say outside in the lobby that in his opinion it was impossible for a Democrat to be a gentleman. What do you think about it?"

Looking up with glowering eyes, and pounding the desk with his mighty fist, Reid roared:

"By God! I know it!"

Dana never let up on Hayes, thereby saddening those former friends who deplored what they called his vindictiveness, but it was after all only an incident in his editorial career. If that had been needed, it merely went to emphasize his persistence in supporting the causes he once championed, and similarly his devotion to the individual who had won his allegiance.

After Hayes came Garfield. The latter was one of the members of Congress smirched in the Credit Mobilier affair. The *Sun* told all about that when he was nominated, and added for good measure the charge that he was also involved in a lot more of the misconduct which had given bad odor to Grant's administration. Unfortunately for Dana's cause, whatever effect these allegations may have had was more than neutralized by the playfulness of William O. Bartlett. When the latter remarked casually in the course of an article about General Hancock, the Democratic nominee, that he was "a good man, weighing two hundred and fifty pounds", the merits of that gentleman were forgotten. A candidate for the Presidency may survive many things but not the ridicule which passes from mouth to mouth.

Years before, during Dana's term as Assistant Secretary of War, he had spoken highly of Hancock's generalship in the battles around Spottsylvania Court-House, his impetuous and successful assault of the enemy's works, and nothing had arisen since then to alter his good opinion, but the cream was spilt with that editorial. In fact, there was little of the daring and impetuous soldier in Hancock's utterances. His letter of acceptance, in the opinion of the *Sun*, was "as broad and comprehensive as the continent, as elastic as India-rubber, and as sweet as honey".

Mitchell reports that Bartlett's reference to the candidate's avoirdupois was unknown to Dana until it appeared in print, and he also asserts that Dana was loyal in his support of Hancock, even though he would have preferred Senator Bayard or Samuel J. Randall. The *Memoirs* state:

> That gallant soldier and honest gentleman received nowhere sincerer tribute than *The Sun's* for his purity, his patriotism, and his ability; and after this 250-

pound utterance the efforts of the paper were redoubled to help carry New York for the Democratic ticket.

The one word in that quotation which may be open to doubt is "ability". It does not accord well with this extract from a *Sun* editorial following the election, which showed that while Garfield had a large majority in the Electoral College his popular vote was only about seven thousand more than that for Hancock:

> What the Democratic party needs is leaders who are not knaves and not fools. It has votes enough.

It would have been difficult to make people believe that Dana really wanted Hancock elected.

XXIII.
A COSTLY FIGHT ON CLEVELAND—ITS ORIGIN AND THE BITTERNESS IT AROUSED—BIRTH OF THE OFFICE CAT.

IT HAS BEEN SAID that the first private telegraph wire ever installed in a newspaper office appeared in the editorial rooms of the *Sun* in the summer of 1884. Nominally it connected the newspaper with its correspondents at the Democratic convention; actually it connected them with Dana, whose eagerness to get the news inspired this improved method of communication. Never was there a better illustration of how human he was.

A young reporter was seated at his desk, awaiting orders from the city editor, the day the nomination was made. Only a few feet away was the telegraph instrument, with its operator busily taking the messages. The only other occupants of the long city room were the city editor and his assistant, and the office boys at the entrance gate.

Suddenly Dana came from the inner editorial quarters, crossing the room with his usual long, vigorous stride, and stopped to read the telegrams. He must have read quite a few when he turned abruptly and started back to his private office, the picture of absolute concentration. The persons present were not visible to the eyes obsessed by an inner vision; he was not aware that he was speaking his thoughts aloud. Driving a clenched fist into the palm of the other hand, he said vehemently:

"It isn't Cleveland. It can't be Cleveland. It shan't be Cleveland!"

Again he was in a muss because of the Bartletts. This time it was Franklin, one-time colonel of a regiment of militia, and expecting to be made adjutant general on the staff of Governor Grover Cleveland. But Cleveland would have none of it.

Why he refused is a mystery. Whatever might be said of his father, Franklin stood before the world without a blemish. He was agreeable in manner and pleasantly outspoken. Nice old ladies in society employed him to look after their estates and investments. He was counsel for the *Sun*. Secretary for years of that home of New York's aristocracy, the Union Club, and yet not haughty to common men. Although his feet were ungraceful—they must have been flat or turned in—he was always a leader of the cotillion at the most exclusive dances. Once he let the *Sun* in for heavy damages in a suit brought by a printer through harping before a jury on "the rights of the master". But really quite harmless in a political sense—and Dana so rarely asked for anything. Cleveland should have granted this little favor. What did the adjutant-generalship amount to, anyhow? His refusal came near costing him the Presidency. If it had not been for a stupid, fanatical preacher named Burchard, and his ranting about "Rum, Romanism and Rebellion" from the platform of a Republican meeting a few days before the election, when the injury could not be made good, Dana would have defeated Cleveland.

That was a strange and exciting time in the *Sun* office. It tried the allegiance of many loyal workers—and it must have tried Dana's soul too. It took an unusual spirit of patience and tolerance on the part of the omnipotent chief to see his men flaunting buttons bearing the portrait of the hated Cleveland under his very eyes. There might be excuse for objection by stockholders, for obviously this campaign was going to be expensive, but these underlings were certainly taking a chance.

Dana knew well enough how costly it would be. He had had a talk with his managing editor on a similar situation only a few weeks earlier. The *Times* had bolted the Republican nomination because of its opposition to Blaine, and Dana predicted it would lose half its circulation. Men would not tolerate attacks upon their politics or their religion, he said. The *Times* had always been a Republican newspaper and its refusal to support the Republican nominee would mean that a lot of readers would throw it over. He quoted instances in which his theory had been tested—the bolt from the Democratic nominee by the *World* in 1868; the bolts from Grant to Greeley by the *Tribune,* the Cincinnati *Commercial* and the Chicago *Tribune* in 1872.

"Watch," he told Lord. "You will see the *Times* circulation take a tumble."

To be sure, the *Sun* was not a partisan newspaper, but Dana knew by his own experience what it cost to attack popular idols. He had seen the circulation drop with each attack upon Grant and Henry Ward Beecher, the size of it commensurate with the vigor of the assault.

There was no mistaking the fact that Cleveland had become such an idol. The bolters from the Republican party were especially hot for him. It was for them that Dana perverted the meaning of the Indian word "mugquomp", signifying chief, into mugwump, intending it to be a term of reproach, of disloyalty and instability, of conceit and swollen-headedness. But that did not affect the intensity of these revolters, who could always retort that Dana himself had vowed to cease writing and burn his pen before he would support James G. Blaine.

After that first emotional outburst over the despatches Dana became the objective editor again. Opposition and denunciation moved him not at all, unless it was to indulgent smiles. The morning after Cleveland's nomination the *Sun* contained this:

> This is going to be a mighty interesting canvass. It has begun in surprises, and we dare say it will be surprising all along. . . . We shall make it more than ever our business to report these events, and to cast the light of philosophic insight and the cheerfulness of good humor and patriotism upon them all. It will be great entertainment, with heaps of instruction, for those who want to learn.

There was a little scene one day in the publication office when he met two stockholders before the cashier's wicket. Both wore large Cleveland buttons in their coat lapels, and there was that in their manner of exchanging greetings with him which implied both criticism and resentment. His smile, showing through the white beard and giving added luminosity to the splendid eyes, could not have been more suave or kindly.

"Well, gentlemen," he said pleasantly, "I see that we differ politically."

"Yes, Mr. Dana," replied one of them, with marked truculence, "and our side is going to win."

Still smiling, Dana inclined his head politely.

"The world would be less interesting if we all agreed," said he.

The fact that the situation provided an unusual dilemma only spurred him on. Being against both candidates it was necessary to create a third, and whom should he pick on but General Benjamin F. Butler—Ben Butler—of somewhat dubious reputation. Perhaps it is unnecessary to point out that Dana, like other great ones, gave little heed to the requirements of consistency, but here was an instance where he had declared himself in terms difficult to explain away. Just ten years earlier there had appeared an editorial referring to Butler in which was packed all the venom his sharpest critics could have supplied. The accusation, later disproved, that while in command at New Orleans Butler had confiscated for himself the silverware belonging to wealthy families, was not overlooked; his drooping eye and general lack of pulchritude were held up to scorn. Altogether he was made to appear despicable. It was brutal denunciation, with less than the *Sun's* usual wit and more than its usual viciousness. Dana did not write it—the author was Fitz Henry Warren—but Dana made himself responsible by giving it space on the editorial page. This is an extract:

Girdled as he was with reeking scalps, and triumphant on every hand, Butler the argentiferous, is yet unhappy. 'Tis a pity and we grieve to record it; but it verifies the remark of the preacher that all—at least all that Butler ever achieved—is vanity, and that of the meanest kind. . . . Butler is not fair to look upon, and being neither sweet nor pure he is seldom the cause of pleasure in others; but he has always seemed, like Quilp, to enjoy himself. He is usually a noticeable figure, merely because the extravagance of his antics demands attention. He would be still more conspicuous if he were painted red under the cockeye, or carried a kit of silver plate on his back.

There had been other attacks during the Grant administration, although Butler's condemnation of the verdict of the Electoral Commission and his publicly expressed view that Tilden had been elected—which was not made, however, before it was too late to have any effect—may have had real influence in changing Dana's views about him. The fact that the *Sun* had suggested him as the strongest candidate the Democrats could nominate some months before the convention met cannot be taken as incontrovertible evidence of Dana's real judgment. It may well have been no more than the prevision of an astute editor, foreseeing the threat of Cleveland and seeking to prevent it.

Certainly Butler's political career up to that time could not have appealed to him. Originally a pro-slavery Democrat, whose being on the Union side in the War was doubtless due entirely to his being a Brigadier General in the militia of Massachusetts and ordered to the front by its Governor; then a radical Republican, calling for the payment of the obligations of the United States in depreciated greenbacks, he had been erratic and undependable throughout. To the man in the street he was either anathema or a joke. Still he was the only tool at hand to use against Cleveland, for he had been nominated by the Greenback and the Anti-Monopolist parties, and was therefore in a position to draw votes from the other candidates, with the chances favoring his getting more from the Democrats than the Republicans.

Only Dana's cynical humor could have made possible even the appearance of a serious campaign in favor of this candidate of doubtful repute standing on "a platform of administrative reform with greenback-labor declarations which Dana would scarcely touch with tongs", as Mitchell put it.

Very likely Dana did not expect too much from Butler, although he called solemnly upon all the Republicans who could not stomach the political misdeeds of Blaine, and all the Democrats who for any reason were disinclined to vote for Cleveland, to register their protests by casting ballots for Butler. At all events, he felt himself free to indulge every whim and vagary in waging his war. Some aroused intense feeling, some moved to deep laughter, but it must be admitted that the former was more pronounced.

It was not the masses who were stirred to the depths nearly so much as the cultivated and better informed. The type that often takes a holiday on Election Day, and prefers a book by the fireside to registering its political judgment by standing in line with *hoi polloi* in an election booth, was on its toes, marching in torchlight processions and screeching its wrath at the defamers of Grover Cleveland. Many of them were readers of Dana's paper and straining at the leash. If he had not been entirely blind to his own interests he would have put brakes on the abuse of their hero. But it was not in him to hold back once he was in the fray. Everything which anybody might consider depreciatory was hurled at the Democratic candidate, while the Republican was treated almost with consideration. It had become a fight on Cleveland altogether. In the end the mud hurled splashed back. The circulation had begun to fall with the opening guns on Cleveland. It went on a toboggan slide with the printing of the Buffalo hangman stories.

For once the prejudices of the aristocrat warped the judgment of the editor. Dana could not visualize a gentleman in the role of hangman, even when actuated by a high sense of public duty. The thought of personally yanking the rope which would send the condemned to death was so repulsive that he jumped to the conclusion that it would bring about a revulsion of feeling in the mugwumps. Could any man of sensibility want to see the public hangman in the White House?

Sound enough argument in ordinary contingencies. But this was not such. Men were aflame with indignation—against the tyranny of the politicians and their corruption. They had found what they believed to be the Incorruptible, adamant in following his sense of right, absolute in independence against every attempt to move him from his chosen path of duty. Not a genius, not the flower of refined culture, but of indomitable courage, clear vision, straight thinking, sturdy as an oak, like the prophets of old. No better evidence of that than his taking the rope when he read the law to mean that the sheriff must do that in person. No doubt he had found it unpleasant too, but when taste and duty clashed the former must be squelched. So thought the readers of the *Sun* who were for Cleveland, but had still clung to their favorite newspaper, closing their eyes and minds to its anti-Cleveland articles, which they expected to end with the triumphant election of their candidate.

With the publication of those articles intended to make Cleveland appear an insensate brute they exploded. At least that was so in New York, where the floors of the street cars and elevated trains were strewn with copies of the *Sun* flung there and trampled by men bound for Wall Street and the marts of trade on the morning of the first publication. Other passengers unaware of the incitement, must have looked on amazed when these men of usually calm demeanor suddenly became vessels of wrath, swore, sputtered and appeared on the verge of apoplexy. Dana's name must have been taken in vain many thousand times that day in his own home town.

At the beginning of the Cleveland campaign the *Sun's* circulation was one hundred and fifty-eight thousand. At its close it was seventy-eight thousand. Most of the difference went by the board in that single day. It had been able to boast that it had the largest number of buyers as well as readers; it lost that proud position in twenty-four hours.

Did that fearful loss halt the editor? Not for a moment. The hangman articles continued. So did the denunciatory editorials. Then came the election. The great campaign for Butler had ended with his polling 175,300 votes, practically all of which had been cast by the two parties he represented. It is doubtful whether a baker's dozen were influenced by the *Sun*.

Just one ameliorating circumstance emerged from the wreckage. When all the other newspapers were of the opinion that Cleveland had been defeated and Blaine elected, the bulletin board of the *Sun* bore the announcement that Cleveland had won. Dana's insistence that the news columns must give the facts, regardless of the editorial policy, was adhered to in this time of stress. While the mugwumps were marching in a solid body to the home of Jay Gould on Fifth avenue, with the avowed determination to do violence to that magnate, because rumor had it that he had directed the Western Union Telegraph Company, which he was supposed to control, to hold out for the election of Blaine, with the suggestion that there might be another manipulation of returns, as in the Hayes-Tilden election, word came that the *Sun* conceded Cleveland's election. With that announcement from Cleveland's bitterest opponent the marchers dispersed. Many of the other papers continued to maintain that Blaine was the winner. With only a few thousands lead in New York, the pivotal state, it took several days to make sure. But the *Sun*, whose election experts were always infallible, never wavered, and it received credit for its fairness as well as correctness even from the disgruntled.

Dana was the least cast-down of all the editors of the *Sun* the morning after. The prestige of the paper had been rudely shaken. It had given Joseph Pulitzer a splendid opportunity to profit by its attitude. Obviously the *Sun* would have to struggle to get back anything like the circulation it had lost. But Dana was convinced it could be done. As he told his managing editor, it all depended on making the paper interesting.

He was not through with Cleveland. Far from it. As with Grant, there was not lacking abundant praise when the new President did what appealed to Dana as worth the doing. As, for instance, the reconstruction of the Navy by Secretary Whitney. But ridicule lurked off-stage, always alert for use when the opportunity arrived. The President's maiden sister, Rose Elizabeth Cleveland, offered one excellent opportunity. The publishers of what Eugene Field characterized as "that delectable mush bucket", *Literary Life*, thought they might acquire a circulation by having her on the editorial staff, though it was soon made clear that she had not the slightest aptitude for the job. A great many columns of valuable *Sun* space were given to Machiavellian efforts to make her appear a geyser of profundities and, incidentally, the inspiration of her brother. There was no malice in this, just reasonable satire, which would have been justified in any event as part of the process of exposing an effort of an unconscionable publisher to capitalize the relationship of a somewhat simple, guileless woman to the President.

Cleveland's ponderous way of expressing homely truths made him a perfect target for the *Sun's* sharpshooters. Even after Dana had forgiven him, moved thereto—by his own admission—through the conviction that Cleveland had really given the country a good administration, they could not resist taking a shot at him now and again. The temptation was at times irresistible.

In December, 1894—that is, during his second term—while making an inspection of lighthouses and shooting ducks with Admiral Bob Evans, Cleveland indulged in some remarks on Southern hospitality and patriotism while the guest of a club at a small place in South Carolina. "I have always esteemed Southern hospitality the more," he said, "because I have felt it was the underlying principle of American citizenship." Quoting this, the *Sun* went on to comment:

> No wonder the gentlemen of the Winyah Indigo Society applauded the sentiment. No other American statesman ever sounded so deep as that in the depths of our political philosophy.
>
> "It is well for the occupant of this high office," continued the President of the United States, "to honor and meet with the people of our country, for it is only thus that the close bond of sympathy can be obtained which will enable the Chief Executive to mete out equal justice to high and low, rich and poor, as he is called upon to do." The language and the view taken of the constitutional functions of the executive are alike confusing at first glance, but they become clear as crystal when we remember Haroun-al-Raschid and likewise bear in mind the underlying principle of Southern hospitality.
>
> Thus splendidly ends the voyage of the *Wistaria* for the inspection of lighthouses and underlying principles. The honest, ruddy face of Fighting Bob must have glowed with genuine pleasure as he assisted his precious charge down the steps of the Winyah Indigo Hall at Georgetown and back to the buffet car.

Once in Cleveland's first term Dana hit hard, seeming to have lost his temper, but it must be admitted he had real provocation. An interview with the President appeared in another New York newspaper, in which he was quoted as saying that the *Sun* had gone so far in malignancy as to attack Mrs. Cleveland. The accuracy of the reporter was challenged later, and certainly the charge had not been justified. There had never appeared in the *Sun* anything relating to that estimable lady which did not accord with the general chorus of admiration expressed all over the country. But the incident resulted in the coining of an epithet which caught the fancy of all but the idolators, even though not restricted to the person aimed at. The Stuffed Prophet came to be applied to almost anybody who took himself seriously.

It was during Cleveland's first administration that there came into being the *Sun's* Office Cat. Most famous animal that ever lodged in a newspaper office, it was the creature of accident. One day the *Sun* was "beaten" by practically every newspaper in the country. It did not contain a message from the President, the kind of news no newspaper has the right to omit. Coming at the time when the *Sun* was missing no opportunity to get in a dig at Cleveland, it looked as though the omission was intentional, an act of inexcusable journalism of which Dana never could be guilty. Yet the true explanation would sound very lame—would, in fact, be regarded as a weak prevarication.

"It was hot in the office last night," Dana told Judge Bartlett, who happened in that morning, "and the windows were open. A breeze must have picked up the Washington despatch and blown it away before it was read. Papers all over the country will make a lot of it."

"Oh, say the office cat ate it," suggested Bartlett.

That was the kind of inspiration Dana knew how to use. The *Sun's* remarkable cat, endowed with a sixth sense which enabled it to find unerringly in the deluge of copy arriving at the *Sun* office those items whose dullness rendered them unfit for publication, but for which it had a voracious appetite, was introduced to the world in the next issue. It reappeared from time to time, was accepted by the other newspapers and made the subject of comment for years thereafter.

XXIV. VIEWS ON BRYAN—A CONNOISSEUR OF ART, OF MUSIC, OF GASTRONOMY AND OF ARBORICULTURE, DANA'S INTELLECTUAL CURIOSITY LEADS HIM TO SOME STRANGE CONTACTS—GERZONI, WHO FOOLED ALL THE NEWSPAPERS.

THOUGH Dana had held to his original proclamation of political independence, circumstances had led to his leaning to the Democrats repeatedly, usually because he was opposed to the Republican candidate. It was the nomination of William Jennings Bryan that drove him into the Republican camp.

"I am unable to reconcile with any ideal of integrity," he declared, "a change in the law which will permit a man who has borrowed a hundred dollars to pay his debt with a hundred dollars each one of which is worth only half as much as each dollar he received from the lender."

Curiously enough, he had favored the silver standard for a time years before when the decreasing output of gold was worrying some of the economists, as it does at present. His reason for dropping silver then had been the realization that the countries using the gold standard would dump their silver surplus on the United States.

There was reason enough for activity on the part of the editor opposed to Bryan in that first campaign. Joseph Pulitzer, one of the shrewdest judges of political campaigns in the country, told the writer, when he visited him at his Bar Harbor home in the early summer of 1896, that if the election were held then Bryan would win. It was Mark Hanna's cleverness later on that turned the tide. Dana did his share, but he was now seventy-seven years of age, and there was no personal element involved.

In the beautiful home he had built at Madison Avenue and Sixtieth Street, largely from his own designs, was a wonderful collection of rare art objects which demanded attention. Especially the Chinese porcelains, which were among the choicest specimens to be found anywhere in the world. A famous connoisseur asserted that not even in France, Germany or England was there a collection which would illustrate as did this one the history of Chinese porcelain. Not only did it contain prized examples of peach blow and *sang de boeuf, clair de lune* and other choice monochromes, as well as decorated pieces, but the collector had worked with a definite purpose and had accomplished what he had set out to do. Here were specimens which had been dug up at Madagascar and Ceylon, on the coast of Malabar or an island of the Malay Archipelago, illustrating the wanderings of these rare art objects as they were carried from China to the nearer Orient by Arab traders and other travelers.

Immersed in the contemplation of these treasures, fondling the surfaces of bits of egg-shell which seemed almost to yield to his interpretative fingers, studying and deciphering signatures and inscriptions, arranging and rearranging with the connoisseur's delight in solving problems in legitimate juxtaposition, or gratifying the critical eye for proportion and gradation of color, Dana found new occupation for his talents. Visitors who were interested in such matters found that here was one collector who not only understood all about his treasures but could talk about them so clearly and entertainingly that the veriest tyro was interested as well as enlightened. After one of the famous Sunday night dinners, at which it was rare not to find some guests of unusual distinction in music, literature and the arts, he would frequently wander off to the handsome room containing his porcelains with a group of interested listeners.

Benjamin Altman, himself a distinguished collector of art objects, which are now among the chief glories of the Metropolitan Museum of Art, once said that the American collector was born at the Philadelphia Centennial Exhibition. Americans, even those of great wealth, had not been given to extensive travel up to then, and few had been interested more than superficially in art. To be sure, the Metropolitan Museum had been organized seven years before, but it was only an infant even then and hardly known outside the small organization that had founded it. At Philadelphia, according to Altman, the type that could be developed into a collector first saw under one roof a great assemblage of art objects, gathered from all parts of the civilized world, and showing the works of the masters. The effect upon the millionaires was startling. Here was a new outlet for surplus wealth, one that could be made a permanent source of distinction as well as pleasure. Hitherto city mansions and country estates, blooded horses and costly yachts had been the luxuries which differentiated the possessor of great wealth from lesser mortals. What were any of these compared to ownership of picture galleries and tapestries and Persian rugs, enamels and porcelains, the product of artistic genius throughout the centuries! Incidentally, there had come to America with these superb exhibits those master salesmen of Paris and London who were not slow to point out to the interested magnates and captains of industry the fascinations of the new sport.

Whether Dana fell under this influence or whether he had become interested during his visits to Europe, the fact remains that he was already initiated when he arrived at the state of affluence which enabled him to indulge his taste and use his knowledge.

In the days at Brook Farm he had evinced an interest in the dining room and the kitchen. Wanderings in Paris and Berlin in the revolutionary period, and visits to various parts of the world thereafter were not without their influence in developing this early tendency. In a little book called *Eastern Journeys* he wrote:

> Why is it that Turkish coffee is so much better than all others? It is a potentialistic and transcendental preparation that other lands do not know and very poorly imitate.

In Russia this same instinct for appreciation of the refinements of gastronomic art inspired this enthusiastic comment upon *stchy* and *borsht*:

> There is nothing in the culinary science of any other land known to me to be compared with these two kinds of soup. The *stchy* has for its essential element cabbage, and the *borsht* is based upon beets.

He bought an "authoritative cook book and carefully studied the prescriptions for both these works of art", but he couldn't get "any Western cuisinier or cuisiniere who could make and serve them in a style that would please an international expert".

Even warmer waxed his eloquence over another dish in the Russian menu, which was "always to be found at every railroad restaurant in Russia, as in every palace and every hut, always in transcendant perfection, such as all other peoples are not able to rival. I mean tea. The tea itself is something ecstatic, and you may voyage all around the earth from London to Formosa, and then back to Dover, and never find any tea of such beautiful, inexplicable, delightful, living exquisiteness". Usually this was served in a glass with a slice of lemon, but it could also be had in a cup and even with cream, but always it was "something to enchant an ascetic and to rejuvenate an antediluvian".

In a word, Dana had a real palate, not least among the gifts of the gods, and cultivated it with the same care and understanding that he applied to his other talents, developing finally into that rare thing in America, a gourmet. To dine then with Dana was to enjoy a repast which had to please his critical taste. Lord tells of an occasion when he directed the butler to bring back to the table the sherry and Madeira to illustrate his exposition of the differences between these two wines and the excellencies of each, pointing out how these were influenced by the sun, moisture and temperature during the growth of the grape, as well as by treatment after the juice had been extracted. In the same manner he could analyze the most complicated *plat*, and make clear the delicacy required in the manipulation of its ingredients.

It was often a motley party that sat down at his table. Not every guest came in conventional attire. Himself always immaculate, he did not base his invitations upon understanding of the social refinements. Many a man who never possessed a dress suit was guest of honor at his dinner, while others prominent in the social life of the city were near the foot of the table. As in his professional life, those who counted most were those who could bring to the board the interesting and the unusual. He did not even demand a certificate of character. As always, it was his tremendous appetite for information, for knowledge, that controlled above all things, and he was psychologist enough to know that men unburden themselves more freely after good food and wine than at any other time.

This alone would explain Gerzoni, for instance, at Dana's table. It was in the early 'Eighties that he had come to the *Sun* office with a sheaf of manuscript, the epitome of interesting and informative articles printed in Russian papers. He was a hunchback, with a flat face, cunning dark eyes, a drooping brown mustache, and flat-chested. His long, bony fingers were stained yellow from the cigarettes he was continually rolling and smoking, and so was his mustache. Moreover, he suggested general lack of care for his person; one was sure he was a stranger to the bath. Finally, he was poorly dressed, even to the wearing of a mustard-colored flannel shirt, with marks of perspiration where the rolling collar fell away from his scrawny throat. Not a pleasant-looking object, and the intelligent office boy was justified in barring his entrance when he asked for Mr. Dana. However, his manuscript was conveyed to the chief, and the following Sunday saw a new column in a conspicuous part of the supplement containing the book reviews, under the heading, "Interesting Russian News and Views". It was made up of short paragraphs, some only two or three lines, and was set in agate, but each paragraph was the condensation of a distinctive article. Altogether it gave a comprehensive survey of current everyday life and happenings in the great empire of the Czar, with a bit of sly satire or sarcasm here and there to show the intervention of Gerzoni. It must have taken days of reading and compilation to produce it.

Gerzoni appeared at the office again after the publication of his offering and this time he saw Dana, for the latter had left instructions to admit him. It was always difficult to understand their relations—the elegant, fastidious gentleman and this shabby product of the ghettos of Russia. The column became a standing feature of the Sunday paper, and the author was never refused an audience. In fact, more often than not Dana would come to the gate when apprised of Gerzoni's presence, would welcome him warmly, and usher him into his private office. Then Dana would close the door between his room and that of the editorial writers, otherwise left open, and also that leading to the library. Thus cut off from all communication, he would hold the Russian in conversation sometimes for an hour or more. After a time it became known around the office that Gerzoni made an occasional appearance at Dana's dinners. Possibly he wore a white shirt on those occasions.

Of course, it was all due to the fact that the man was a scholar and a mine of information about Russia, its history, its politics, its peculiar outlook upon life and the rest of the world. Moreover, he had the biting wit of a real pessimist, having been an adventurer over the Seven Seas. Dana must have known something of his career, which was none too savory, for it had been published in the Jewish journals when they discovered that he had been baptized in England and had been a paid missionary among the Jews of London. At another time he had been a rabbi in some small western synagogue, and when the revelation came he was editing a Jewish weekly in a western city. Naturally, that job ended abruptly. A conscienceless rogue, surely enough, but he had much to impart, and the seeker for all kinds of knowledge had a broad and indulgent mind when it came to talents and scholars, as was shown with the writer who padded his bill to the *Sun*.

Gerzoni lived to fool all the papers in New York, including Dana's. That happened when the Hebrew scholar called Chief Rabbi Joseph by the New York press came from Russia. The whole orthodox East Side was in a ferment, for this man had an extraordinary reputation for holiness as well as scholarship, and it was expected that he would remain as the chief rabbi of a federation of East Side synagogues formed for the express purpose of securing his ministrations. So intense was the excitement that the police had to guard him when he appeared in the streets from his over-zealous admirers. Thus he became a subject of general interest and the newspapers all sent reporters to tell about his doings. The great rabbi could not speak or understand a word of English and there were no Hebrew or Yiddish experts among the reporters in those days. Yet interviews must be had and likewise reports of the sermons which the rabbi was scheduled to deliver.

In this emergency the elders consulted anxiously. They had not been in this country long and were worried lest the irreverent reporters should indulge their imaginations and leave with the Christian community false and possibly hurtful impressions. Evidently they must take some action to avoid this, and there was no time to waste. It was then that the ban on Gerzoni, who had been regarded with scorn and horror, was temporarily lifted, and he was employed as the rabbi's press agent. Not openly, of course, but he prepared the answers to the questions of the reporters and he wrote the sermons the rabbi was supposed to have delivered. It was his own suggestion that a mere translation of the rabbi's sermons would not answer, for who among the uninitiated would understand those fine-spun interpretations of the laws and the prophets which were for the appreciative the potent evidence of his genius and learning?

Wonderful were the counterfeit sermons which appeared

in the New York papers, and were copied thereafter throughout the land; models of justice, wisdom and the benign spirit, demonstrating what an excellent vicar of God was lost when the author failed to live up to the potentialities of his talents and eloquence. Rabbi Joseph could not have created such sermons if his soul had been the stake. They contained the ethics, wisdom and philosophy of Socrates, Plato and Aristotle rolled into one; the stern justice of Moses and the Prophets and the exaltation and kindliness of Jesus and Buddha. Even Lao Tzu and Confucius might have claimed bits here and there. Here were the Fatherhood of God and the Brotherhood of Man in many forms, and the whole country applauded. But over on the East Side some who had heard the real sermons and were able also to read English went about dazed and unable to comprehend.

Music was another of the arts to which Dana was devoted, and many of the great musicians of his time were entertained at his home. Paderewski was a frequent visitor. Often these great artists performed and found their host not only an attentive but also an informed listener. There was one night when a young woman pianist had played some Chopin and was about to leave the instrument.

"Can't we have some Beethoven?" Dana asked her. "How about the Apassionata?"

"Who would appreciate it?" she returned, with a side glance at the company, which happened to include more than the usual proportion of the frivolous.

"You and I," he replied.

Charming as was this home with its many treasures of art and beauty, he was even fonder of the little island in the Sound off Great Neck, Long Island, which he purchased and developed into a garden spot and a veritable arboretum. When he traveled he was as much on the alert for a new and strange species of tree as for a rare specimen of porcelain. In Turkey he came upon a dwarf beech tree, with "leaves exceedingly small and lustrous", which the professional dendrologists had overlooked. Invariably such finds were transported to his island, whose forty acres contained trees from all parts of the earth.

It was this intense interest in arboriculture which made him the first champion of the preservation of the forests of the country. At frequent intervals the *Sun* would have an editorial pointing out the waste of our forests and the dire consequences certain to result, together with lucid explanation of the scientific methods used abroad, especially in Germany, to keep the land properly wooded.

Among his greatest joys was to wander about his island with his learned gardener, discussing and planning, or with some appreciative guest, to whom a casual stroll about the grounds became a revelation of curious and interesting information.

XXV. ODD CHARACTERS DEVELOPED FOR THE *Sun's* CIRCUS—SOME REAL FIGURES PICKED OUT OF THE HUMAN MAELSTROM, SOME CREATURES OF ROLLICKING IMAGINATION—THE STAFF HELD TO RIGID STANDARDS.

NOTHING delighted Dana more than the odd and singular in human beings. Some of them were permitted to visit him in his office. "George, the Count Joannes," the George Jones who kept a small cigar shop until something went wrong and he took to issuing proclamations, declaring himself "counselor of the Supreme Court" and announcing new and individual interpretations of Shakespeare, was one of them, and it was intimated that Dana financed his famous appearance as *Hamlet* at the Academy of Music in April, 1876, the most tumultuous performance known to the New York stage until some dozen years later, when an imitator tried the same stunt and was knocked out by a cabbage hurled from the balcony. When he came to the *Sun* office he was received with all the distinction befitting his exalted rank. Sometimes he appeared blazing with wrath against the individuals who claimed to know his real history, threatening death and destruction. It was to mollify him on such occasions that Dana printed occasional items of local intelligence under the heading, "Specially reported for *The Sun* by George the Count Joannes," for which he received the usual space rates.

George Francis Train, the once distinguished engineer, who developed a harmless mania which drove him from the society of adults to that of children, and who was for years a picturesque figure on a bench in Madison Square, surrounded by children of all ages, was another visitor at the *Sun* office. Apparently his dislike for grown-ups did not extend to editors, for he made Mitchell as well as Dana his confidant in revealing that almost any moment he might become the infallible Dictator of the universe, with a life line of at least two hundred years. The *Sun* introduced him to the people of New York and mentioned him frequently, always in kindliness, while Dana humored him personally.

With this example from the fountainhead the men on the staff were ever on the alert to drag from New York's human maelstrom characters which entertained and amused. Cummings was especially apt at this. He too took delight in personal contacts with the queer or the picturesque, and one of the sights of the office was his appearance with his two thirsty intimates, the Poet Geoghan and that temple of wisdom, Bryan G. McSwyney, the one fat and squat, the other slight, with reddish blond hair and mustache. Both were small tradesmen and reveled in the publicity Cummings provided through antics and conversations existing only in his fertile brain.

Julian Ralph invented a German barber with a voluble assistant, but Monsieur Pujol, the French barber, whose philosophy continued to appear for some years, was a real person, and trimmed the locks and beards of many distinguished New Yorkers, including those of the editor of the *Sun*.

John Mahoney's tales of *Fatty Wollosh* and *Jerry Hartigan*, the former warden of the Tombs and father of Blanche Walsh, the actress, and the latter an East Side politician, were as excellent character sketches as could be found in the famous plays of Harrigan and Hart. Not infrequently they appeared in the four-page daily edition, taking valuable space usually reserved for news.

The *Old Settler* was forever having strange and moving adventures in the woods and mountains of Pike County, in which the barrels of rifles would get bent and twisted through peculiar accident, thereby projecting their bullets in such extraordinary flights that even the cunning fox, with all his twists, dodges and turns could not escape them, and Ed Mott's foxes were fiends for strategy. The *Old*

Settler was an expert in hard cider and applejack, and his tales inspired visions of fat round jugs, their sides polished by much contact with embracing arms. On the morning following one of these a little old man appeared at the gate of the city room. He was only a few inches above five feet tall, and his weather-beaten features were buried in white run-around whiskers. In his arms he carried a large paper bag, evidently the envelope of something of weight and substance.

"I wanter see the feller thet wrote thet article 'bout applejack," he called across the room. "He never drunk no real applejack!"

A reporter was sent to interview the visitor. After some conversation it was noticed that the parcel had been transferred to the reporter's welcoming arms, and the stranger departed.

"He says Mott's been drinking raw stuff," the reporter explained, "so he left this to improve his taste. He made it himself forty years ago and took it out of the wood to bring it here." Lifting the cork carefully he applied a nostril to the opening. "Concentrated nectar of the gods!" he exclaimed.

All the qualified judges agreed it would be a sin to subject it to the dangers of transportation to the fastnesses of Pike County, so Mott's education remained unimproved, but their own palates were no doubt benefited. With the reverence due its ripe old age it was handled with the utmost consideration—never more than a small glassful, called a pony in those sinful days, was allowed to any one throat at one time. Consequently it remained to cheer though not inebriate for quite a long time, and with every lifting of the cork there rose a prayer for the health and happiness of that dear old man, a simple soul, but of true understanding. All agreed his vaunting was fully justified. Like cream in substance, with the fragrance of sunlit orchards and the soothing touch of Nirvana. There was quite a ceremony when the last of the jug, not enough to make a decent drink around, was poured over one of the inimitable mince pies at Harry Clifton's chophouse.

John Bogart's "Retired Burglar", another *Sun* creation, went through adventures far more extraordinary than any encountered by Sherlock Holmes, always ending in the discomfiture of the enemy of society through unexpected and mirth-raising incidents. Never was midnight silence broken by such infernal racket as when he stepped into some tin pans forgotten by a careless maid, and burglar and pans rolled together down the uncarpeted wooden stairs. The devil himself must have been in those pans, for they would never stop bouncing and rolling, and always there would be one wherever he placed his foot, to be started by his touch into new gyrations and reverberations.

Edward W. Townsend's "Chimmie Fadden", one of the most popular of the character sketches, was based on a youth in the employ of the *Sun's* business department. There were many minor efforts, some developed from life and others creatures of the imagination—these often convenient pegs to hang quaint or amusing reflections on—and the tradition continued on beyond Dana's day, when some of the best developed.

But the ambitious young men had to be careful. Even though their efforts might be successful in the main, a slip here or an error there was sure to be caught up. Especially in the use of words. Dana took a paternal interest in his reporters, referring to them as *"The Sun's* bright young men". But the Lord help him who erred in choosing the words to express his meaning.

"Mr. Rosebault must be discharged. I like his article but ——" This was what I received from the city editor a few days after I had left on my summer holiday. In the hurry of preparing for departure I had stumbled sadly in a sketch describing the performance of the cook of a visiting Maharajah in the kitchens of the Waldorf-Astoria. I was rather pleased with the job myself—being only twenty— and thought I had made a fairly vivid portrait of the swarthy Hindu, with his snappy black eyes under a huge white turban, fixing one of his numerous dishes of rice for his princely master, while the French chefs looked on with indulgent interest. I even thought I had achieved a master stroke by securing the Hindu's recipe and the secret of getting his rice so that every kernel was swollen to bursting and yet stood alone. Perhaps Dana agreed with that, being so interested in gastronomic perfection, and there was that confession of his approval of the article as a whole, but never could that atone for the unpardonable sin I had committed. I had used the word "balance" in the sense of remainder, a colloquialism which never should have passed the copy-reader. He undoubtedly got what was coming to him, too. To rub it in, that letter told me I had not only been discharged but I ought to realize that the discharge was fully justified.

Dana's keen eyes were not the only ones on guard to keep the *Sun's* English undefiled. "Tommy" Hitchcock likewise possessed an uncanny instinct for detecting the slightest error; only, while Dana in his sternest criticism never departed from his usual dignity and courteous speech, the financial editor would appear before the city editor sputtering with wrath. Discharge the writer, discharge the copy-reader, discharge the compositor! Even a slip in the type or the accidental transposition of letters moved him to fury.

Among the lingering traditions is one of a rebuke administered to the editor who conducted the column in the Sunday edition called, "Answers to Correspondents". A graduate from the ranks of the *Sun's* "bright young men", talented and well-informed, he was inclined to be sniffy and impatient with some of the duller inquirers who appealed to the paper for enlightenment. For instance:

Question: Has the Barbers got a ounion in Brooklyn the same as they has in New Yoark?—Samiel Man.
Answer: Well, Samiel, you ought to be spanked. You say you've taken *The Sun* for twenty years, yet this is the way you spell!

Answer: David, do you never think when you read? Of course, you must think, because you ask questions; but think twice before you ask any more questions like these.

One day came a question which struck the editor as being unpardonably silly. It asked why a cow got up with her hind legs first, while a horse got up with his front legs first. The editorial response reflected upon the inquirer's mentality. The following Sunday this appeared at the top of that column:

The answer to X. Y. Z. in this column last Sunday was neither wise nor courteous.

Then followed the logical explanation that a cow got up with her hind legs first in order to protect her udders, while the greater bulk and weight in the forepart of the horse made it necessary for him to use his front legs in rising, as he would otherwise be unable to maintain his balance.

There was an awful hush as the men gathered around the bulletin board where someone—not Dana—had placed a clipping of the above. Had the offender "been shot at sunrise" the effect would not have been more devastating. Incidentally, there was less acerbity in the answers from that time on.

Once a clergyman who had literary ambitions sent an article to Dana. Imbued with the idea that to appeal to the editor it was necessary to be real devilish, the author did his best to be ultra-worldly. Dana sent it back with this written across the first page in blue pencil:

"This is too damned wicked!"

Sometimes even Dana's criticisms were merciless, unmindful of the conditions under which the fault had been committed. The reporters were on duty for long stretches at times—ten to twelve hours usually and not infrequently fifteen. They suffered physical hardship often. The present habit of using the telephone for interviews would have been thought a rank evasion of duty. The interviewed had to be seen, studied, analyzed, cross-examined. The way a man looks or acts is often more significant than what he says, besides giving the reporter the opportunity to put the color of life into what he writes. His manner may suggest the wisdom of going further a-field to get the truth.

The first lesson drilled into the new reporter for the *Sun* —called a croton bug, meaning a cockroach, by the cynical Clarke, because he was just about as useless as that noxious insect—was to be thorough. There must be no skimping, no glossing over of anything which might open a new door to information. That meant hard thinking, the utmost use of his ingenuity, and tireless effort. He had to be alert and on his toes every minute. Fortunately, the interest in the game kept him indifferent to fatigue until he was hardened and thoroughness became as much a habit as eating or sleeping. In the late hours, when seconds might mean making or missing the time of going to press, reporters wrote out their articles on their knees on the way to the office in bumping street cars, praying meanwhile that these might not jump the tracks, a far from infrequent occurrence in those days of bad pavements and uncertain car rails.

Visualize, for instance, the task of the reporter who was sent out around eleven o'clock one winter's night to investigate a rumor that Grant was dying of cancer. That was all he had to go on—that and Clarke's suggestion that a friend of the General lived on lower Fifth Avenue. Grant himself and his family were believed to be out of the city.

Eleven o'clock in the mid-'Eighties was past most people's bedtime, and it was half past when the reporter had found his man's residence. After repeated ringing of the bell a head was thrust out of the front door. By good fortune it was the man wanted, and he was not cross over this late summons. But he knew nothing about the alleged cancer. He had heard the General was ill—yes, and he seemed to remember that Dr. Fordyce-Barker was his physician.

Away sped the reporter, on the hunt for a drugstore where he might consult a city directory for the address of the physician. It was in one of the 'Forties, and the only way to get there was to dash across to Fourth Avenue and control his nerves while the horse car slowly rolled on up to Forty-second Street and then to Madison Avenue.

Fordyce-Barker, a distinguished physician and a courtly English gentleman, was luckily awake and in his library when the reporter arrived. Moreover, he was Grant's doctor and was ready to confirm the rumor. Only, being a devotee of accuracy himself, he insisted that what the *Sun* proposed to print about this should be the truth, the whole truth, and nothing but the truth. To make sure of this he took his seat at the library table and carefully wrote down the history of Grant's illness, its exact nature and the probability of its duration.

A handsome man, and the embodiment of culture and refinement as he sat in his big leather chair, writing carefully, pausing every now and then to ponder. A room of noble proportions, lined with books in mahogany shelves, so cosily warm and cheerful with the crackling logs, and such a contrast to the bitter cold dark streets from which the reporter had just come. But for the young man with the frost-bitten face it was a torture chamber, its only significant furniture the big Grandfather clock in the corner, ticking away the vital minutes. Already it was after midnight and the *Sun* office miles away. Will the old codger never finish!

Yes, he is done with his writing, he has read it over, but even with the surrender of the precious bit of paper the ordeal is not finished.

"Read it aloud, so that we may be sure you can master my writing," says the physician, smiling amiably. "I write such a wretched hand."

In calmer moments the reporter wondered how he had held back from throttling him. Here was a big news story, a sure beat on all the other papers, and he was being done out of it by this doddering old fossil!

At last! at last! He is out and free again. Little does

he reck of the biting night as he runs like a hound through slush and ice to the nearest station of the Third Avenue elevated road. His one chance is to catch a train within the next few minutes. He can give no heed to the probabilities that he will come a cropper on the slippery pavements. Panting, thoroughly winded, he forces his tired legs to forget their weariness, his sopping feet to skip like a fairy's as he leaps up the steps to the platform. Thank God! virtue is rewarded. He lands on the train just as the guard is closing the gate!

No sooner in his seat, than he has his roll of copy paper on his knee and his numbed fingers are racing the pencil across sheet after sheet. When the train rolls into City Hall station, his article is finished. Again he forces his stiffened body to the courser's pace, bounding up the two flights of stairs to the city room. Is he in time, after all?

The omniscient Clarke is standing at the little dumb waiter which carries the copy to the composing room, his omnipresent pipe tipped at an impertinent angle. He has just sent up a final item.

But there are still a few minutes' grace, and for Clarke emergency only stimulates to action. Without moving from his place he dashes off a heading—the reporters did not write the "heads" in those days—and skims the pages with a glance. It is all over in a jiffy and the manuscript on its way.

"Looks like a beat," he remarks, with just a suggestion of satisfaction.

That is all. Limply the reporter goes down to the street again to stand on a windy corner until his street car shall carry him home, an operation taking the better part of another hour. It is nearly two in the morning when he finally tumbles into bed.

Yet he wakes when the maid deposits his copy of the *Sun* outside his door some five hours later. To leap from bed, open the door just wide enough to grab the paper on the threshold and get back under the covers has become so automatic it is like one operation. For a moment he restrains the eagerness to look, enjoying this evidence of his self-control, but the suspense is not carried beyond a mild delay. The paper is spread out and the front page brought close. Just a glance is sufficient to catch the Grant article. It has a place of honor and occupies the better part of a column. "Ain't it a Grand and Glorious feeling?" had not been invented yet, but the full meaning of it is in the reporter's soul as he drops the paper, snuggles back and resumes his interrupted slumbers.

Yet, suppose in his hurry he had perpetrated an unbalanced "balance"? There would have been ructions and not praise when he reached the office, even though the *Sun* was the only paper in the country to have the news, and its report was quoted far and wide.

I was discharged a second time by Dana after an experience very similar to that described. I had been sent up into the hills of Westchester County to get the facts in an alleged kidnapping of a small boy, had worked hard all day and far into the night with no food but a few sandwiches snatched at the station buffet on my way back, and had turned in six thousand words, most of which appeared on the first page of the next day's paper. When I reached the office the next morning the city editor sang me a paean of praise, before sending me back to get a second day story. Again I put in a hard day—which seemed nothing in the flush of my triumph—and again turned up late with a bunch of copy all written. As I entered I met the night editor, Carr V. Van Anda, later managing editor of the *Times*, who saluted me with enthusiasm and high words of commendation. But he had just come in and was not in the know. Dana had put his thumbs down hard.

This time it was not any particular word. In fact, nobody knew just what had aroused his wrath. The city editor, to whom he had given the command to discharge me, thought it might have been the artist who was the real cause of his ire. Newspaper illustrations in those days were fearful things, and the portrait of the bereaved mother made her an awful hag, totally at variance with my description of a comely young woman.

Of course, I didn't stay discharged then any more than I had the first time. Lord had a way of soothing the chief's ruffled feelings which seemed never to fail; or if it did he would forget the order until time had worked its miracle. Once Erasmus Darwin Beach fell under the ban. He had occupied a seat in the inner editorial room, right under Dana's eyes. Lord transferred him to the city room to a desk near his own. Dana came out one afternoon to speak to Lord and saw Beach working away as usual. For a moment he looked annoyed. Then he said quietly:

"Mr. Lord, I have come to the conclusion that I am the only man on the *Sun* who can't discharge anybody."

His memory must have recalled as he spoke this anecdote of Greeley he told to some college students later on:

> I remember once we had in the *Tribune* a smart young fellow named Henderson. He was afterward a rather conspicuous Republican politician in Michigan. He had written something one day that Mr. Greeley didn't like. Greeley came in and said, "Henderson, did you write that?" "Yes, sir," said he. "Go away from here!" said Greeley. "I don't want you here any more; I discharge you!" The next morning I came down to the office and found Henderson sitting at his desk and working tranquilly away as usual. I said: "How is this? I thought Mr. Greeley discharged you." "Yes, sir, he did," said Henderson, "but I didn't put confidence in all that he said."

Not so very long after the Beach incident Dana took to having his luncheon brought up from the Savarin—the Savarin of Raymond Dorval, not to be confounded with any other restaurant sporting the name of the great French gastronome—and Beach was almost daily his luncheon guest.

Just the same, though we weren't really discharged we

were always keenly alive to the danger of the great man's disapproval, and no one ever dreamed of advancing the excuse of hardship or pressure of time for the lapses Dana frowned upon. Instinctively everybody felt there could be none. Who would be of the Legion must keep its pace!

XXVI. INSPIRATION FOR THE WORKERS—APPRECIATION OF THE UNUSUAL—OSCAR WILDE'S GHOST STORY—STIRRING INCIDENTS IN THE CONDUCT OF A GREAT INSTITUTION.

BUT if one had to live up to the Spartan standard, and the commander-in-chief was sometimes severe in criticism, he was equally ready with praise and repeatedly went out of his way to show appreciation of good work. The *Sun* paid the highest rates of any newspaper in the country in Dana's time, but there were no pecuniary rewards for especial merit or unusual service. Every man was supposed to give his best, and if one man's best happened to be superior to another's, his the greater glory. Of course, all of them should have been geniuses to be entitled to the privilege of being on the staff, but as the supply of geniuses was short, we commoner sort had to be admitted.

Somehow, though he had no direct contact with the workers outside the writers for the editorial page and the more important executives, Dana had a faculty for finding the stars. Let even a paragraph appear in which there was the reflection of an original or brilliant mind and Dana was on a quiet hunt for the author. The man who possessed a spirit of original humor, or facility in coining unusual phrases, was sure to find himself confronted by the chief, come to tell him in no doubtful terms of his appreciation.

One such looked up from his writing to see the chief looking down upon him with that warming smile in his blue eyes which transformed his usually dignified and somewhat aloof expression into one of intimate kindliness. In his hand he held a small clipping, which the reporter had no difficulty in recognizing as his own offspring, a vagrant paragraph but written in the *Sun's* peculiar vein and with a snap all its own.

"Very good, young man, very good," said Dana. "I wish I could write like that!"

It was a ramshackle old building that housed the *Sun* in those days, the favorite abiding place of rats and enormous roaches, and one of the miracles was that it didn't go to pieces like the famous one-horse shay. There was a tradition that its foundations rested on shifting sands and one of the mechanics boasted that he could bring it tumbling down at any time with no other tool than a shovel. It had been condemned repeatedly by the Health Board, had caught fire many times, and yet nothing happened. It held the stamping hordes of Tammany for half a century, and all the machines required to get out the paper from the time Dana took over the *Sun* from Moses Yale Beach until William C. Reick, a successor in control, moved the paper to the building of the American Tract Society, another half century, and succumbed only in the conventional way to wreckers who had to tear it down as though it had all along been a substantial edifice.

Dana must have felt that it would be inappropriate to introduce any luxuries into even his private office, which was as bare a workshop as any in the city. A bare wooden floor, with a single rug, a black walnut table, on which stood a small revolving bookstand surmounted by a stuffed owl, an old leather sofa, a rarely used old-fashioned desk off in a corner, and two ordinary chairs made the entire picture. Dana usually sat at the table, where he could talk to the editorial writers in the adjoining room and could see any one approaching from the library.

The city room, long and bare, contained the desks of the reporters, in two rows down the center, with those of the managing editor, the city editor and the copy readers near the five windows facing City Hall Park. There were several rows of iron pillars supporting an upper floor, and in the timbers remained the hooks and ring bolts once used by a *turn verein* which had rented this room from Tammany Hall. It could not be properly ventilated and it was not

unusual on hot summer nights for the thermometer to record a temperature of more than one hundred degrees. Up
to the mid-'Eighties, when Hitchcock introduced electric
lighting, the only illumination had been from gas jets many
feet above the desks.

Into this room Dana would come frequently with what
Mitchell described as "his characteristic stride, firm as a
sea-captain's on the quarter-deck", sometimes to consult an
editor, sometimes just to chat or make a comment. If the
latter, it was done in the manner of the head of the house
relaxing in the bosom of his family. Naturally it was a
different Dana from the one described by Dyer, and his
portrait varied with the years. Mitchell first saw him in
1875 when "he was well set physically, his generous brown
beard and mustache just beginning to be tinged with gray."
The golden curls had disappeared and the not over-abundant
locks which remained were covered by a cylindrical skull-
cap of embroidered silk. By the time of the first Cleveland
campaign there were no locks and the beard was almost
white, but the cap had been doffed. What struck one particularly was the still masterful tread and the way the head
was tilted back, giving an almost belligerent angle to the
beard.

One of those characteristic entrances occurred on a Monday morning before the work of the day was fairly started.
Proceeding directly to the desk of the city editor he asked
abruptly:

"Mr. Kellogg, did you read Oscar Wilde's story in yesterday's paper?"

"No, I didn't," Kellogg confessed.

"Did anybody here read it?" Dana demanded, turning
to the reporters.

All admitted shamefacedly they had not.

"The best ghost story ever written," he said reproach-
fully, "and not one of you has read it."

He turned to go to his office, but came back again.

"Do you believe in ghosts, Mr. Kellogg?" he asked.

Kellogg, one of the most brilliant men that ever worked for the *Sun*, but sometimes matter-of-fact and decisive in speech, snapped his jaws as he said:

"No, sir, I do not."

"Neither do I," said Dana slowly, the blue eyes half-covered as though searching his soul, "but I have been afraid of them all my life."

One evening, when the city room was humming with the activity which always accompanied the shifting from the day to the night editorial force, he appeared in the doorway between the city room and his own quarters, and stood there surveying the scene. Most of the reporters were at their desks, either writing or waiting for their night assignments. The managing editor was looking over inquiries from correspondents and dictating replies. In the far corner sat Bogart, explaining to Clarke the day's work and his suggestions for the night. Suddenly Dana's voice boomed out:

"Mr. Bogart, who wrote the football story in today's paper?"

Bogart, dazed and struggling out of his concentration, had to pull himself together before he could remember. Then he called back:

"Mr. Fairbanks."

Charles Mason Fairbanks, reporter and copy-reader by turns, as he was needed, was sitting at his desk, not ten feet away from where Dana stood. The latter gave no sign of seeing him, but this was what he said:

"Reads like a page from Homer; another battle of Troy!"

With that he turned and retired to his own quarters. But in that tense atmosphere his words had penetrated to the remotest corner and everybody was staring as though enthralled. Everybody, that is, but Fairbanks. Except for a moment, when a deprecatory smile had appeared upon his lips, there was no indication that he was concerned. With admirable self-control he was still pushing his pen across the paper, his head bent over his work, his brow serene.

A moment later he had to give up this masquerade, for

from all over the room came men to congratulate and to exclaim.

It was incidents like that which made the wonderful spirit of the office and inspired men to outdo themselves. The Staten Island reporter almost cleaned out the office one day through his excess of zeal. He had climbed up the side of an incoming ship before the Quarantine doctor's arrival to discover that some of the passengers had cholera. When the captain refused to let him leave the ship he jumped overboard at the risk of his neck and got away on the tug he had hired to take him there. Of course, it was all wrong, and he was told so, but it went to show how seriously the men took their work.

John R. Spears, just returned to his home in the North Woods after nearly a year of exploring in South America, repacked his grip and rode lickety-split over almost impass- able roads to catch a train for the city. He had hardly had a chance to say a word to his family, but there was the wire from the *Sun* asking him to return, to which there could be but one response.

It was not an order he had received, mind you; just a courteous request. I happened to be with him at the time, and my message was identical with his. It read: *"Please* come to the office as soon as you conveniently can."

All the telegrams from the office began that way. Years later, when the duty devolved upon me as business manager to be on guard against unnecessary expense, that word "Please" came up for consideration. It was being used thousands of times every year. Always at so much per word, according to the distance it traveled. And there were countless other messages ending with "Thank you". Judged by the prevailing standards of business, in newspaper offices as elsewhere, a needless expense. Really the best investment ever made by an editor. It warmed the heart and fastened the devotion of many a correspondent who never saw the *Sun* office and had no other way of knowing its kindly spirit.

It is an oft-repeated tale. Lord has written about it and this was set down by Mitchell in his *Memoirs*:

> So affectionate was this editor's relations with those under him, so entirely absent was the least symptom of jealousy of his subordinates, so slow was he to fasten blame upon the blameworthy, so quick and cordial was his recognition of a good thing done by anybody in *The Sun's* employ from star reporter to office boy, that there grew up around Charles A. Dana a fealty more like that of a patriarchal family, or a club of good friends—all life members—working together, than an organized force for business enterprise.

And every man was treated as an equal. For the average worker, the humbler sort that did not attract attention by the quality of his product, the immediate head was the city editor; the court of last resort the managing editor. The Chief sat remote, like Wotan in the halls of Valhalla. Yet his influence was felt by all. Dimly, perhaps, but unmistakably, everybody realized that Dana was a gentleman, a superior sort of person—an aristocrat. Therefore the *Sun's* bright young men could not resort to acts which would bring the paper into disrepute. The tricks of so-called yellow journalism were not permissible—not even to get that most longed-for prize—a beat on the other papers. Yes, and a man must show his quality in a pinch; he could not afford to sacrifice his self-respect.

Clark Bell afforded a test of this. He was a lawyer, who had discovered a way to gain public attention which would not have come from his achievements in his profession; one of the first to found a society of the kind that draws persons of consequence to its banquets, and secures free newspaper space through what these have to say on questions of public importance. He called it the Medico-Legal Society, a title which suggested more than its performance justified. A fat man, with Dundreary whiskers and a putty face, he was rather suspect in newspaper offices, but he drew sufficiently big names to his dinners to make it necessary to send reporters to look out for a possible expression of public interest. He began to puff up with this success and one night, when he had corralled an unusually large number of big lights, he determined to put the reporters where they belonged.

"Gentlemen," he told them, "we have put up a screen in the dining room, behind which you may sit and listen to the speeches."

The practice at all public banquets had been to have either a special table for the press or to sandwich the reporters in among the guests, and they came dressed for the occasion. Bell's innovation, with its implication that they were considered unfit to mingle with the diners, aroused a general protest.

"That is the best we can do," he declared. "You will be able to see the speakers, while remaining unseen ——"

"I can't see myself sitting behind a screen," the *Sun* reporter broke in, and started for the door, followed by a number of other indignant ones.

It was a daring thing to do. There were two important United States Senators in the list of speakers, and who could foresee what they might have to say? It was also a breach of the rule to get what one was sent for, despite saints or the devil. Finally, it was a personal sacrifice. The article he was expected to write would have been worth at least five dollars and possibly ten. But—could a *Sun* man submit to insult?

The question was answered by the higher powers. Clarke, with one of his cynical grins, seemed to enjoy the situation. Lord asked how many reporters had remained.

"Only one," said the reporter, and gave his name and the paper he represented.

"We'll be beaten," said Clarke.

"Yes," said Lord.

That was all. But curious students of the history of such institutions in the city of New York will find that the Medico-Legal Society did not long survive that night, and that Clark Bell's name ceased quite suddenly to appear in the newspapers.

Dana left no doubt in anybody's mind about his determination to stand back of the men. A powerful Wall Street financier took umbrage at one of the sketches penned by the author of "The Veteran of Wall Street", and word was conveyed to the latter from what appeared to be an authoritative source that there was trouble in store for him. The financier, it was pointed out to the writer, was a friend of Dana and of Hitchcock, and his grievance would not pass unnoticed. The writer only smiled. Bred in the traditions of the office, the suggestion of that kind of interference with honest work was inconceivable to him, even though it came from such good authority. In his next sketch he went even farther along the lines complained of. There were no further intimations. That the financier had gone to headquarters was true, but evidently his reception had not encouraged further efforts to intervene.

Dana's indignation flamed out red-hot after a police outrage of which a *Sun* man was the victim. The latter had gone home late one summer's night and when he opened the door of his home such a hot blast came from within that he had sat down on the stone step at the threshold, hoping to get some relief from the cooler night air. Along came one of the policemen whose belligerency was more feared than the professional criminals of that day and, refusing to listen to explanations, dragged his victim off to the police station. There he was denied the right to communicate with his friends and was locked up in a cell with two drunks. In the police court the next morning he was discharged and the policeman was reprimanded.

Dana himself wrote the editorial denouncing the offender and the system which permitted such as he to be a menace to helpless citizens. It seared and scorched all concerned from the police commissioners to the patrolmen. It excoriated the political higher-ups. It raised such a rumpus that the other newspapers felt impelled to take it up. Almost daily for twelve months the *Sun's* editorial page carried some reference to the outrage.

His personal judgment of his reporters was given in the course of a talk on journalism in these words:

> Accomplished men, men familiar with every branch of study that intellectual young men ordinarily devote themselves to, men who have prepared themselves either by college studies or by practical life in their departments for the peculiar duty they have undertaken; . . . men of extraordinary talent, knowing the world well, able to see through a deception, and sometimes able to set one up.

XXVII.
THE FRUITS OF LOYALTY—MEN FORGOT FATIGUE, BRAVED DANGER, AND DISREGARDED HARDSHIP TO SERVE THEIR IDOL— THE FIRE AT THE HOTEL ROYAL.

IN A BOOK describing his journalistic adventures, Samuel G. Blythe, an able newspaperman before he became one of the pillars of *The Saturday Evening Post*, had this to say of the esprit de corps in an average newspaper office:

> Another trouble with the newspaper game is the jealousy of the men in it. A gathering of newspapermen is like a gathering of soubrettes—few people can see anything but themselves. If any man sticks his head above the universal level of the grass in which they are all travelling they all take a clout at that head. Almost all praise is given grudgingly!

The men on Dana's staff would have rubbed their eyes if they had seen that. At all events, they knew nothing of it from personal experience. Dana's spirit had permeated through the ranks down to the humblest recruit, so that it was indeed a "happy family". Not only was there loyalty to the chief, but likewise genuine affection among the men. The beginner found the editors with whom he came in contact patient as well as wise guides, tolerant of human weakness and exhibiting at all times confidence in the rectitude of his intentions. The older reporters would take him in tow and make him feel that he belonged.

Although the bright young men were competitors one never would have known it from their relations either in or out of the office. Pride in the paper made every one agree that the pickings should go to those best able to make the most of them, and the only time there was dissatisfaction was when chance put opportunity for fine work in the hands of one not equipped to do it.

Every day as the men came to the office could be witnessed the spectacle of a group gathered around the one who had turned out the best-handled piece in that day's paper. Rarely was there any question as to which that was. Those boys knew. Their judgment of workmanship was as infallible as their knowledge of the conditions under which it had been carried on was certain. And invariably their judgment was sustained by the editors. Usually also by the reporters on the rival papers.

Why these did not hate the *Sun* men is almost incomprehensible. The latter were almost snobs in the way they lorded it over the others, always taking it for granted that the superiority of the *Sun* was beyond discussion.

"Did you read Blank's story in today's paper?" the *Sun* man would ask the first man from another paper he happened to meet. The implication, of course, was that Blank's version was so much better than all the others that it must call forth the admiration of anybody who assumed to know anything about reporting.

Was it always so? Hardly. There were some excellent writers on all the big papers. But it was beyond dispute that usually the *Sun* yarn did seem to be the best. Otherwise the paper would not have won the reputation it had in newspaper offices throughout the country for being the best-written paper extant. It may have been one of Clarke's inimitable heads, or the little touches peculiar to the paper, or the mere placing of it, but a really good piece of work stood out and commanded attention as it did nowhere else. Nor is it unlikely that on the average the *Sun* had the best-written articles. It paid the best rates, trained its men from the ground up, and maintained a definite standard which had to be met or the man could not remain. That and the spirit of the office could not fail to bring exceptional results. "This comradeship of effort under autocratic rule", as Mitchell termed it—meaning by autocratic rule that Dana was after all the unquestionable and unquestioned commander—won for the *Sun* the approval of the profession.

In and out of the office everybody was everybody else's friend. Dana had quite a few at his Sunday night dinners, but every night a lot went out to the same restaurant, as many crowding around a single table as it would hold. Snobbery was unknown, and editors and even young reporters put their legs under the same mahogany and were on a par in the badinage and arguments that followed.

Mouquin's, on Fulton Street, was the favorite resort downtown. French cuisine, French wines and French waiters; the type of restaurant which the French call *un marchand du vin*, where one gets good food well cooked, but with no fancy trimmings in style or service. One could get through with half a dollar, while a dollar provided food, wine and a ten-cent cigar. A pint of Swiss or French *vin ordinaire* cost only twenty cents, while thirty paid for a wine that need not offend a susceptible palate. A succulent and filling *navarin* cost only twenty cents, a small sirloin thirty, and poultry and game from fifty up, all with vegetables and as much good French bread and butter as anyone wanted. The cover charge had not yet been imported.

Sometimes there would be parties uptown, visiting the best of the little French, German or Italian restaurants— Martin's, then an unpretentious French hotel unknown to millionaires or drummers; Plavano's, on Third Avenue— supplying the best spaghetti New York ever ate; the Manhattan Café, on Second Avenue, occupying a famous old mansion with fine mantels and lovely cornices, where the corners were occupied by parties buried in the concentrated silence of chess, and big tables were covered with files of German and Austrian newspapers and magazines, including, of course, *Die Fliegende Blatter*; the Widow's, on South Washington Square, genuine replica of a thousand little restaurants in France, where the phrase home cooking is not a byword but means what it boasts; Schwarz's, in Little Hungary, as yet unspoiled by the slummers; or, if in search of plain yet filling food, the Clifton or Tony Eschbach's chop-houses. Not a few of these, as a matter of fact, were discoveries of the *Sun's* gourmets, who were forever scouring the by-ways in search of further gastronomic revelations.

But the locale made little difference. Everything tasted good to these merry, jesting fellows, rattling off quip and story, making the most of this interlude in a hard, trying day, talking shop freely and careless in gossip, knowing full well nothing would be carried back to the office to offend, no matter who was present or how indiscreet the utterance was.

Perhaps the greatest joy came with the close of the working day. Sometimes after midnight this, sometimes two or three in the morning. Tired in body and mind, but still buoyant with the spirit of young manhood, and fired with the irrepressible feeling that school was out.

A common gathering place was Hudnut's drug store— later Perry's—where, in a little space behind the screen marked "Prescriptions", liquid refreshments of a kind not served at the soda fountain could be obtained by friends of the shop. Other newspapermen came there, too, and it would be a rare occasion when some old-timer, rich with anecdote of men and happenings of an earlier period, failed to be there to pour out his tales to eager listening ears.

But, whether the first stop was here or with William-by-the-Bridge, to discuss with that prince of barkeeps his latest invention in palate-ticklers, the final glorification was always along the Bowery. Here was the great adventure of each twenty-four hours. Idle to attempt to explain to the citizen of the Twentieth Century what was the lure of this street of marvels to him of the Nineteenth, especially if he happened to be one of the *Sun's* bright young men, always in the know of significant events, aware of all the little currents in the great dark river along which flowed the seamy side of metropolitan night life, of the beginnings of strange haunts of strange creatures, of the meanings of lights behind drawn shades and the interest of the police in places apparently asleep behind a veil of darkness.

Knowing all these, the Bowery could not fail to be of perennial concern. Never did they proceed northward through Chatham Square without an instinctive quickening of the pulse, without the conviction that before they reached Cooper Union, the terminus of the magic thoroughfare, something extraordinary was sure to happen—some new phase of life exposed, a new chapter begun in the Knickerbocker History of Strange and Moving Events.

Under the roaring, rattling trains of the elevated, the shadows were long and heavy, and anything might happen. Always without warning. The laws of the town did not run there after nightfall, and all its habitués were in conspiracy to flout them, no matter what their own internecine wars might be. The criminal was abroad from sunset to sunrise, but what distinguished this haunt of the underworld from all others was that comedy strode so often on the heels of tragedy.

A cry from the darkness, a crowd sprung suddenly from an apparent void to stare at the victim, but when the police arrived assailant and prowlers generally would have disappeared—swallowed up in the blackness of yawning doorways, or vanished down equally murky side streets. Suddenly there would be another cry. One of the curious, usually a Rube drawn there by the marvelous tales appearing in the New York correspondence of his home newspaper, had discovered that his purse was missing. Haws-haws from the crowd—there would not be much sympathy for the victim; too many small-town church deacons were in the habit of roaming this haunt of the Devil and his works when they came to the big city.

Even in the midst of their sport the *Sun* men were ever on the alert for good copy. Keenly observant, with eyes trained to select the picturesque from the merely drab and vulgar, many a good yarn was picked up in these nightly wanderings through riffraff and curious idlers. In any event they were always jolly affairs, cementing a little closer the bonds of good will and companionship, and rarely failing to bring out something new in the ways and habits of the motley crowd.

Now and then something happened that cut short the fun and plunged them all back into hard work, and their readiness to take this on for the honor and glory of the paper when only the excitement and good time were making them forget their weariness, is perhaps the best evidence of all of the extent to which their affections centred upon it.

One such occasion, which passed into the history of the *Sun*, followed a sudden decision to visit the *Sun's* bureau at Police Headquarters, just a few steps from the Bowery on Mulberry Street. Arrived there, someone proposed a game of poker and soon they were seated around a table at which the play was being constantly interrupted by stories and effervescent talk.

It was getting along towards three o'clock when a fire alarm came in. Automatically, the game stopped, and the players listened. It must be a big fire, for the alarm called for all the engines in the city. One of them got up and consulted the chart showing the locality designated by the number being rung out.

"Sixth Avenue and Fortieth Street," he called out.

It was like an electric shock to the lot of them. Cards were thrown down, the coins lying on the table were not thought of, though even silver was not indifferent to any of them, and the next instant they were dashing down the stairs and chasing like mad to the station of the Sixth Avenue elevated road at Houston Street. By a lucky chance they caught a train—otherwise there would have been a delay of twenty minutes—and arrived upon the scene in time to be eye-witnesses of one of the greatest fire tragedies New York has experienced.

A disreputable hotel, called the Hotel Royal, really an assignation house and a perfect fire trap, was a roaring mass of flame as the reporters came up. It was at once a thrilling and a horrible sight. Men and women clung desperately to window sills until the flames came and they had to let go, dropping to the pavement. Then out fell the wall, carrying the last of them into the roadway, a dreadful mess of bricks, mortar and broken bodies.

A terrifying experience for most of the onlookers, but these professionals were regarding it with other eyes. It was because they had foreseen the possibilities with the first location of the fire that they had made such a wild rush for it, and when they saw from the car platform that their fears were justified they laid their plans before the train drew into the station.

Not a moment was wasted. One was selected to rush to the nearest police station to note down the identifications of the bodies which would be brought there. He was also to communicate with the office, where there would still be an editor and a reporter, waiting for just such emergencies, and ask that the mechanical force be held to get out an Extra. The man to have general supervision and write the introduction, the one to visit the hospitals, the one to seek the hotel register, if it still existed, and get as many names of guests as possible, in any event, the one to keep in touch with the police and fire authorities on the spot—all these details were arranged before they had touched foot to the street. Consequently, when New York turned out as usual some four to five hours later there was waiting on the news-stands one paper with a thrilling story of the tragedy, the result of hard, grinding work, plus invincible loyalty—and, undoubtedly, favoring fortune.

Men went out from the *Sun* to enter other walks of life, or to become members of other newspaper staffs throughout the country. Having served under Dana proved an open sesame everywhere. Eugene Field wrote another poem, "The Man Who Worked With Dana On The New York Sun", which bore incontrovertible testimony to this. As for these and all the other veterans it can be safely said that no decoration of the courts of Europe was more highly prized than the title of *Sun* alumnus. Whatever their own stature may have been they once walked with the giants, those who were by common consent the aristocrats of the profession.

Perhaps it will not be regarded as the least of Dana's achievements that he made and led this organization of men who were like brothers, gloried in each other's success and cherished to their last days the golden memories of their association.

XXVIII. LAFFAN, A NEW FIGURE IN THE *Sun* OFFICE—A BRILLIANT WRITER, CONNOISSEUR OF ART AND FINE LIVING, HAVING IN HIS TRAIN MULTIMILLIONAIRES AND CAPTAINS OF INDUSTRY.

IN THE 'EIGHTIES it was not unusual for the reporters to look up from their work around midnight and see a strange figure standing in the doorway leading to the inner editorial rooms. A man of slightly less than medium height, stout, with a large head, brown hair, short Vandyke beard and a stare through heavy spectacles in which insolence struggled with vacuity. Perhaps it was the emptiness in expression which gave the suggestion of impertinence, for it was manifestly a deliberate pose. No man not an idiot or a paralytic could hold himself so expressionless except through force of will. After a survey of perhaps five minutes' duration he would retire to the library.

This apparition made quite an impression. Some of the boys swore out loud. Some grinned. All resented that stare. No less so because the fellow had the further impertinence to appear invariably in dress clothes—claw-hammer and white tie. In those days dress clothes in a newspaper office meant only one thing. The wearer had been to some formal function, like a banquet or a ball. As this man wore his nightly he must be putting on swank.

When it became known he was the new dramatic critic, the resentment did not disappear. It was pure affectation for a critic of the 'Eighties to appear nightly at the theatre in dress clothes. One could make allowance for dudishness in a man like Hazeltine, who had attended an English university, and was one of the sights of Printing House Square when his tall figure, top-hatted and swathed in frock coat and broad-striped trousers over white spats and patent leather shoes, aroused the loungers on the City Hall Park benches; or Arthur Brisbane, just then a youngster fresh from Paris, and naive in his pride in the suit made for him by Bell of Fifth avenue at the unheard-of price of one hundred dollars; or, later on, the handsome and distinguished David Graham Phillips, starting off to report a strike of miners in the Tennessee mountains clad in white duck and wearing in his coat lapel the largest chrysanthemum to be procured in New York. None of these had gone as far as nightly dress clothes.

However, feeling died down after a time. For one thing the fellow could write. His criticisms, rarely more than three inches long, and sometimes only a few lines, demonstrated that behind that vacuous expression resided an unusual brain, wit and scholarship. A mordant wit, sometimes irremediably cruel. At the close of a review would appear some such comment as this:

"Tottie Twinkletoes also appeared, and achieved an unostentatious failure."

It was in this way the rank and file came first to know one who was destined to have a momentous influence upon the *Sun* and all the men identified with it, including even Charles A. Dana.

William Mackay Laffan—always written W. M. Laffan —was one of the most remarkable of the many extraordinary men who entered intimately into Dana's life. At one time his influence was thought to be quite as sinister as that of the elder Bartlett. Certainly it was as expensive.

His own story of his connection with the paper was that he had suggested to Dana at their first meeting that he would like to write some articles on art for the *Sun*, to which Dana had replied he had little faith in writings on art, for the reason that those who could write understood little of art and those who understood art had little talent for writing.

One must take this anecdote with some reservation. Laffan was one of the many talents who do not hesitate to supply what their tale may lack to make a desired effect. He went on to say that the very next day he sent to Dana a comment upon some art matters which caused the editor to revise his opinion and invite him to become a member of the staff. Be this as it may, it was as dramatic and not as art critic that he served the paper at the time mentioned.

A man of many accomplishments, he had thus far failed to record any marked success. Some years later, when he had obtained authority in another department, a protegé of his, a long, lank Irishman, in a moment of relaxation thrust his feet into the interior of his roll-top desk, puffed hard at his long cigar, and exclaimed aloud between yawns:

"This is the fifth time I've followed Bill Laffan into a new venture and they've all gone up the spout. I wonder how long this one will last!"

Laffan had started in Dublin, his native town, making sketches of different parts of the human body for the Pathological Society—he had himself studied medicine. This probably required more accuracy than artistry, though it was the beginning of a lifelong interest in art. Naturally such work could not hold a man of his mental gifts and ambition. He drifted to San Francisco, became a reporter on the *Bulletin*, rose to be managing editor, and from there went to Baltimore, where he ran a paper of his own with the same title. It was a failure, but it was also the foundation of his future success.

For he had made the acquaintance of the first of the multimillionaires who were thenceforward to be his supporters whenever he needed them. Henry Walters was the name of this one, and through him he came to know Dana. Walters and his son Henry remained among the staunchest and most valuable of his friends to the end of his career.

It was Laffan's understanding of the luxuries and refinements of life that made his success with such men. That and his ability to make himself useful as well as entertaining. Why should not a Walters or a Morgan appreciate the man who was a stimulating companion and at the same

Charles Anderson Dana.
From the Bronze Plaque by August Saint-Gaudens.
(*Courtesy of the New York Sun.*)

time almost an expert in the matters to which they were giving much of their time and attention? Laffan was a gourmet—his terrapin sauce was the equal of any obtainable at the Union Club, the Manhattan or the Lotus. His knowledge of wines, especially Burgundies, was equally sound. He had a mind that closed around desired information as a steel trap snaps on the intruder, and a tongue which could give it out with exhilarating eloquence. As for the many abilities needed to make one proficient as a collector of antiquities of the kind his rich friends wished to assemble, he certainly had more than they—probably more than the average dealer. Among the canny top-notchers, those remarkable professionals who have acquired fame and enormous fortunes, he was of course an amateur, but who wasn't? At least, they respected his power if not his judgment.

Many were the tales told of his extraordinary influence with Walters, and later with J. P. Morgan, the elder. One day he walked into the New York office of Duveen and offered a million for a small but choice collection belonging to the latter. And be it remembered millions were not as plentiful in private possession, even among millionaires, as they became later. In Rome he bought the collection of a Cardinal for Walters, paying not much less than a million. It was not a bargain price, for when his agent made out the invoice at considerably less—the duty on antiques had not yet been abrogated—the United States Consul General remarked that the invoiced price was the fairest he had ever known, for the collection had been offered to him at exactly that sum. Of course, the agent, a dealer of high reputation in New York as well as Paris, did not repeat this to Laffan.

There was another occasion when his judgment proved not impeccable, and this time he was the victim. One of the Paris dealers, having decided to open a branch in New York, thought it wise to pay his respects to Laffan and called on him at his home in Lexington avenue. A junior partner, who knew Laffan well, accompanied him. In the course of an inspection of Laffan's *objets d'art* the stranger—let us call him Monsieur Blanc—paused before an example of the bronze worker's art of the Eighteenth Century.

"La-la-la!" he exclaimed. "Where, if I may ask, Mr. Laffan, did you obtain this?"

Laffan looked sharply at his questioner, then at his companion, after which, following an old habit, he adjusted his big-lensed spectacles and said quietly:

"I bought it several years ago in Paris."

Collectors sometimes prefer to be indefinite, and Monsieur Blanc understood this. For some moments he was engrossed in a careful examination of the bronze, then he turned to Laffan, and said impressively:

"Mr. Laffan, allow me to offer you my congratulations. You have there a genuine Jacques Caffieri."

Is it necessary to add that even Laffan's wonderful self-control was momentarily shaken? Although he had purchased this bronze because he liked the workmanship, and was convinced it was a genuine product of Eighteenth Century art, it had always been regarded as a minor object in his collection. To be told it had been made by the great Caffieri, first among the *fondeurs ciseleurs* employed by Louis XVth, and so highly esteemed by that monarch that he and his son Philippe were lodged in the palace at Versailles, was equivalent to Jones, Smith or Robinson hearing that the indifferent etching picked up for a dollar was one of the rarest masterpieces of Rembrandt. A new cordiality showed itself in Laffan's manner towards his guest, and there was unwonted enthusiasm in his voice when he bade him farewell.

The door closed behind them, Monsieur Blanc turned to his associate, and said musingly:

"I wonder who palmed off that rotten bronze on him?"

"If you thought it rotten why did you tell him it was a Caffieri?" retorted his partner, rather sourly.

"Did it hurt me to tell him that?" demanded Blanc, with

a joyous little laugh, and added deliciously, "It certainly made him feel good."

At an exceptionally early hour the next morning Laffan called at the office of the junior partner, who had been conducting a business of his own in New York for some time before his association with Monsieur Blanc. Adjusting his spectacles with meticulous care and holding the dealer under his owl-like stare, Laffan asked:

"Do you remember the bronze I bought from you last year?"

Experience had taught the dealer to be wary with his customer, so he confined his reply to the simple monosyllable:

"Yes."

"What did I pay you for it?"

"You paid me four thousand francs, Mr. Laffan."

"That is about eight hundred dollars."

"Quite right, Mr. Laffan."

Laffan readjusted his spectacles, using both hands.

"Yesterday afternoon," he went on, speaking very slowly, "Mr. E. J. Berwind called on me, and when I told him that Monsieur Blanc, the greatest expert on French art living today, had pronounced that bronze the work of Jacques Caffieri, he offered me thirty-five thousand dollars for it."

Although staggered, the dealer controlled himself sufficiently to say:

"I congratulate you, Mr. Laffan."

After a pause for another manipulation of his glasses, Laffan inquired, with just a ghost of a smile:

"Are you not sorry that you sold me for eight hundred dollars what I can sell for thirty-five thousand?"

"No, Mr. Laffan. I did not think it worth more, and I made a reasonable profit. Such things happen now and then. I am only glad it turned out such a bargain for you. Of course, you accepted Mr. Berwind's offer?"

"What! After Monsieur Blanc, the greatest expert of our time, has declared it a genuine Caffieri?"

"The difference between thirty-five thousand and eight

hundred dollars will buy many rare and beautiful objects," observed the dealer.

Laffan moved towards the door.

"If it is worth thirty-five thousand dollars to Mr. Berwind," he said, "it is worth thirty-five thousand to me."

Monsieur Blanc found little difficulty in establishing himself in New York. He was besieged with invitations to visit the collections of the multimillionaires. He was an honored guest at the Metropolitan Museum, of which Laffan was now a trustee, and his business flourished from the opening of the doors of his shop on Fifth Avenue. But, at the sale of the Laffan collection after Laffan's death, at the American Art Galleries, the bronze brought just one thousand dollars.

But all this is anticipating. Although, thanks to the letters of introduction from Walters, Laffan made his valuable connections with wealth and aristocracy even while he was only the dramatic critic, it was with the death of Isaac W. England, the publisher of the *Sun*, and his promotion to that profitable office, that the path to success really opened for him. Unfortunately, that did not carry with it promotion of the fortunes of the *Sun*, or, consequently, those of Dana.

The paper had been prosperous as well as famous, even though it had suffered some severe reverses through Dana's wilfulness. From now on it was at the mercy of one far more obstinate and capricious than Dana ever had been. But here again, as in the case of Bartlett, having once given his confidence, Dana would listen to no criticism and always stood behind his lieutenant. And Laffan was not the one to hold back in exercising his authority. It soon became known among the powerful in finance and in politics that W. M. Laffan had to be considered in any matter calling for the cooperation of the *Sun*.

"My God!" exclaimed James Huneker, after his first interview with Laffan, "only a Balzac could do justice to that man. That face! And his hat!"

The beard had disappeared by then and the face was more like a wooden idol's than ever. It turned out that one of his blue eyes was glass, which may have emphasized the stare. The big spectacles, worn long before these became a commonplace, but with metal frames, and his manipulation of them, helped. But almost uncanny was his habit of sitting in brooding silence with never a change of expression. For some years I sat on the opposite side of the big desk which almost filled his private office and have seen him sit thus, never stirring, his eyes as fixed as his body, remote, a study in abstraction, for hours at a time.

Often one suspected him of acting. Huneker's mention of the hat was not without significance. It was a Derby hat unlike any other to be found across the Seven Seas; impossible to describe, except that it was small, round in crown and different. His daytime garb was also distinctive. Conventional and yet giving the distinct impression that it was designed specially for W. M. Laffan.

In speech he was continually springing surprises. After listening for some time to Kellogg's rather laudatory remarks about a mutual acquaintance of whom he, too, was supposed to approve, he said softly:

"Ah, yis, the dur-r-ty dahg!"

He had a habit of breaking into brogue at times, though ordinarily there was not a trace of it.

A merchant named Flannigan came to protest against the position in the *Sun* allotted to his advertising.

"Mr. Laf-*fan*," said he, "Oim a mimber av th' fir-rm ev Adams ahnd Compiny, ahnd Oi wahnt ye to know Oi don't loike th' way ye're tratin' us ——"

"Misther A-*dams*," Laffan broke in, "Oi don't care a dom about yer loikes or disloikes ——"

"Pity you weren't here," he remarked afterwards, "you could have picked up the brogue with a shovel."

After he had been warned about a certain individual who was flattering him to his face and maligning him behind his back, he sat silent for some moments as though pondering the situation, then said solemnly:

"I can't understand it. I don't remember ever having done that man a favor."

I had left the *Sun* to engage in other work and one day Laffan came to my office to discuss my return, this time as business manager. As he was about to leave, with his hand on the knob of the door, he turned half-way around, and said:

"Don't say anything about this and one of these days it will come to something." He pulled the door partly open and added: "I am an Ishmaelite—my hand against every man and every man's against me." With that he was gone.

Doubtless he amused Dana, as he did the multimillionaires. And the former would not be indifferent to his understanding of art and his apparent standing with the great dealers, who were continually coming to his office to pay their respects. Besides, the man had real scholarship and could write as few others.

But his performance as a publisher will ever remain a mystery. Being born a Roman Catholic there is a bare possibility that he carried the explanation to the confessional, but it is not likely. In religion, as in about everything else, he had become a thoroughgoing cynic years before.

XXIX. UNDER THE NEW INFLUENCE THE *Sun* BECOMES THE CHAMPION OF GREAT ENTERPRISE—A BULL IN THE CHINA SHOP, SMASHING TRADITIONS AND, INCIDENTALLY, COURTING DISASTER.

UP TO THE TIME of Laffan's becoming the publisher Dana had still maintained his fondness for the underdog, even though it was not as pronounced as it had been. With Laffan's ascendancy it diminished to the vanishing point. Laffan's second home was the Union Club. Almost daily he went to the office of J. P. Morgan & Co. The United States Steel Company was in the process of formation. Other great mergers were under way. It was the time of the trusts, of the launching of the theory of the Higher Law and the rise of the Captains of Industry. Presently the *Sun* was their outstanding champion.

No question about Laffan being now the strongest influence upon Dana. Those luncheons from the Savarin were served in Laffan's office. He walked in to Dana's at any time, which no one had dreamed of doing before him. He did not hesitate to give orders in other departments than the one he was supposed to be occupied with and to which his predecessor had held himself strictly. Finally he caused a complete upset in the news service of the paper.

Undoubtedly Pulitzer's advent, and his success in attracting part of the circulation lost by the *Sun* when it opposed Cleveland, had something to do with Dana's quarrel with the Associated Press, in which he had been a prominent figure, but it is equally certain that the break was forced by Laffan. It was he who advanced propositions which it was a foregone conclusion the other members would not accept; he who had ready a plan for the *Sun* to gather its own news and sell it to newspapers in other cities, which only a Laffan or a Don Quixote could have proposed.

Lord has told how Dana came to him and asked how much it would cost, and how he figured it out and added a thousand dollars a week to cover unanticipated contingencies, whereupon Dana replied promptly:

"Oh, that is much less than I had supposed you could do it for."

"We will be beaten out of our boots every day in the week," Lord warned him.

"I suppose we shall be beaten occasionally on the news," Dana admitted cheerfully, "but you can make an interesting paper, can you not, even though you do not get every little scrap of news?"

Lord opined that he could. He was not enthusiastic about it, naturally. It meant a vast lot of effort and work as well as added responsibility. A shrewd person himself, he knew well enough that failures would be laid on his shoulders even though he was not to blame. Laffan would see to that.

But Laffan carried the day. The *Sun* threw away its Associated Press franchise, which was valued at half a million within a decade and cannot be purchased today at any price, and Lord was informed one afternoon that he was expected to secure the news for the next day's paper through his own efforts.

Only a practical newspaperman can appreciate the absurdity of this proposal. While the *Sun*, like every important newspaper, had its own correspondents in important centers, like Washington, London, Paris, Berlin, the routine news even there came through the press associations, which also conveyed the news from all the rest of the world. Suddenly the managing editor was summoned to find a substitute for the long-established, carefully-planned and ably-executed operations of these associations, with their myriads of correspondents and existing connections with the channels through which news must be obtained! It was preposterous to the extreme, and only a cool-headed, well-balanced man could have stood up under the strain.

Laffan organized a press bureau of his own, called it by

his name, and set out to secure the news from abroad and to make sales thereof to certain papers outside of New York. It proved an expensive undertaking. Lord, being a methodical person, had amassed through the years a lot of names of newspapermen throughout the country upon whom he had called at various times for special work, and these proved an excellent nucleus for the building up of a staff of special correspondents in this emergency. Even though the rivalry with the Associated Press developed into a bitter fight, and the *Sun's* correspondents were under a ban in many newspaper offices, the paper managed to get by without missing anything of real importance.

In Europe the paper was equally fortunate in having as its chief correspondent Henry R. Chamberlain, an excellent organizer as well as a brilliant journalist, who had established good connections in all the principal cities of Europe. Then the difference in time worked in his favor, the London papers being obtainable in plenty of time to secure from them any items overlooked by his correspondents. Altogether the paper made a very creditable showing and occasionally its special correspondents turned in something worth while which the press associations had not. But it cost a lot of money, it took a lot of time the managing editor and his assistants might have employed profitably in other channels, and it accomplished nothing. It would be no exaggeration to say it cost the stockholders a million.

But that was only the beginning of Laffan's strange performance. As is usually the case in a newspaper office, the advertiser had always been *persona non grata* in the *Sun* office. Not content with being allowed to use its valuable space—for a *quid pro quo*, of course—he had the impudence to believe that this entitled him to consideration otherwise. The *Sun* was very chary about write-ups, even of the briefest and most conventional kind, but it was annoying even to consider them. Now and then some big merchant would ask to be interviewed, imagining that his expenditures with the paper entitled him to air his views on politics or what-not. Or another, who was a patron of art, would think the art critic had nothing better to do than look at his pictures. It is only proper to say that these received only slight consideration. It even happened that the pictures were so thoroughly roasted their owner withdrew his advertising for a considerable period.

Dana, as has been shown, was fundamentally opposed to advertising, though he personally was gracious with the advertisers as with everybody else. Almost from the start it had been his ambition to clear it all out of the *Sun* and rely entirely upon the sales of the paper for its income. Unfortunately, the tendency was towards ever increasing size in newspapers, and also increasing costs, and what would have been possibly feasible with a four-page *Sun*— before the break with the Associated Press, of course—was but an idle dream later on.

Laffan, however, solved the problem in his own way. In a comparatively short space of time he managed to get rid of most of the advertisers, more particularly of those sought by the *Sun's* rivals. One of these, a large department store of Brooklyn, actually had its advertising copy thrown back at its messenger, nor was there ever any explanation. It was as though the paper had adopted a new motto for its relations with the advertisers—"Spite 'em!" Many of the big advertisers withdrew, not to return for years, and their example was followed by the small fry that always follow them. It would be understating the truth to say that a million of income went with them.

The fight forced with the typographical union came after Dana's time, when his son Paul had succeeded him, but it was along the same lines. Men who had served the *Sun* a lifetime, and who had as great pride in their service as any editor, wept as they were forced out. Their relations with Dana had been cordial and, in some instances, affectionate. They could not comprehend the new order of things. It was a hard fight and ended in a compromise. It too was mighty costly.

With these various assaults upon its treasury the fortunes of the paper dwindled fast. Dana did not live to see the day when a mortgage had to be put upon the building and the dividends ceased, but the symptoms were strong enough in his time. So strong, in fact, that members of the staff were asking themselves what it all meant, and was Laffan deliberately setting about ruining the *Sun* with the thought of buying it cheaply when it was forced upon the market?

Laffan did buy it later—or, rather, one of his multimillionaire friends bought it and let him appear as the owner—but there is no reason to believe he deliberately played Mephisto to Dana. It was the latter's misfortune in his later days to have introduced a bull in his china shop. The bull did not undergo any metamorphosis when the shop was all its own. Only when the financial horizon became so threatening that even a bull might lose its sportive humor did it lose its appetite for rampages, and even then one could not be safe against lapses. An influential advertiser, induced to come back by a new advertising manager, found himself pilloried on the front page of the *Evening Sun*, where a scandal in which he had become involved was published *in extenso*. It required no Sherlock Holmes to discover the reason for this exceptional emphasis. Out went the indignant advertiser, whose account meant many thousands a year.

One evening the cashier came to me with a batch of telegrams all ready to be sent out as night letters. They were addressed to some of the biggest advertising agents in the country and notified them that unless they remitted for the full amounts of their unpaid balances by the first mail suit would be started against them at once. When I explained to Laffan the next morning that only by my intervention had he been saved from insulting the agents from whom we were receiving the greater part of our advertising, and that their accounts were not overdue, he was not at all disturbed.

It is quite probable he enjoyed his role during Dana's lifetime as much as when he had himself the control. His ambition seemed to be rather to be the power behind the throne than the actual wearer of the crown, not that he cared a whit about accepting responsibility for his acts, but he had an inherent dislike for being in the public eye. To be off-stage and direct the play afforded him as much pleasure as a page write-up would bring to the average. Art, finance, politics were the three strings to his bow, which meant that the stronger he grew the more attention he gave to them—and the less to the *Sun*—except as this served to support his purposes.

He had his man Friday in the art world, a Frenchman with a real gift for detecting the genuine in that extraordinary game which was going on between the sellers and buyers of old masters and old masterpieces. He had been an officer in the French army, but for some reason had drifted to New York and into the business side of art. As cynical as Laffan himself, well-informed, a past master in the psychology required to hold the good will of the million-aire collectors, he was at Laffan's beck and call, and kept him informed about all the gossip of the art world; occasionally serving to distribute some of Laffan's creation.

In politics the *Sun's* able reporter not only supplied the information but made suggestions and carried them to the right parties. Franklin Bartlett, who was naive in some respects, came to Laffan's office one day and remarked casually:

"They say Eddy Riggs is no longer a reporter, but that he has become a director of politics."

Laffan glowered, and the purple glow—product of rare old Burgundies—which appeared when he was thoroughly angry, came into his cheeks. He could not tolerate references to the games he was playing under cover.

"Roosevelt is very much worked up over the way Platt is treating him," Riggs told him, just after Roosevelt's nomination for Governor of the State of New York.

"Ah, is that so?" Laffan returned. "Tell Teddy I'd like to see him."

That same day Roosevelt appeared. Laffan greeted him cordially, for all was well between them at that date.

"Riggs tells me you're having some trouble with Tom Platt."

"He doesn't want me to make any speeches," Roosevelt complained.

"Ah, he doesn't!" exclaimed Laffan, his one eye aglow. "Well, you're going to talk all you want to. Go back now, and tell him I said so."

That message was sufficient for the Boss of the Republican party of the State of New York.

His part in the financial history of his time was probably slight. It was a subject he did not discuss even with intimate friends.

"When Mr. Dana knows of a good thing he tells his friends," Franklin Bartlett said once, "but I never got anything out of Laffan."

It would have been strange had it been otherwise. The man who made a daily pilgrimage to the office of his friend, John Pierrepont Morgan, and who consorted nightly with multimillionaires at their club, had to keep a close mouth. And for the first time since Dana had taken possession the *Sun* had friends as well as enemies to consider.

XXX. DANA TALKS ABOUT THE EDUCATION AND TRAINING OF NEWSPAPER MEN, AND THE ETHICS OF JOURNALISM—DOUBTFUL ABOUT SCHOOLS OF JOURNALISM—THE *Sun's* NOTICE OF HIS DEATH.

AT THE DEATH of George Ripley, from whom he had been estranged because of the *Sun's* campaign against Grant, Dana wrote a tribute to the idealism of those engaged in the Brook Farm adventure, concluding with:

"The faith of democracy, the faith of humanity, the faith of mankind, are steadily growing towards a society not of antagonisms, but of concord; not of artificial distinctions, but of spiritual development towards a society commanding the forces of external nature and converting the earth into an abode of peace and beauty, excelling the mythical Eden of old; this we say still lives among men."

That was in 1880. A year later he warned that "a great struggle between the power of the multitude and the power of the individual, wielded through corporate forms, is at hand". Individuals like Vanderbilt and Gould were exercising an influence which made them the balance of power in the country. Compared with editorial expression in the *Sun* after Laffan's influence became apparent the foregoing reads strangely.

Yet it was perhaps only normal evolution in the history of a newspaper. Almost all editors begin by being radical and devoted to the common people. With success and the acquisition of wealth and power they develop conservatism. It is based on one of the oldest and commonest of human phenomena. Perhaps Laffan only hastened it.

It was in this later period that Dana was much in demand as an adviser to young people who were contemplating entry into journalism. He spoke at various colleges and public dinners and, though he lacked the voice of eloquence, what he had to say attracted wide attention and was quoted and made the subject of comment in the press all over the country. As was to be expected, some of his remarks provoked opposition, and none more than this:

> There is a great disposition in some quarters to say that the newspapers ought to limit the amount of news that they print; that certain kinds of news ought not to be published. I do not know how that is. I am not prepared to maintain any abstract proposition in that line; but I have always felt that whatever the Divine Providence permitted to occur I was not too proud to print.

Here again he was at his old habit of "stirring up the animals". There were always some things which he was too fastidious to give publicity and others that were too dull and uninteresting, but already there had come into view that theory of suppression which was expressed later in the motto adopted by Adolph S. Ochs for the *New York Times*, "All the News That's Fit to Print".

That would never have been accepted by Dana. "The Sun Shines For All" was mounted on his banner and, within the limits of reasonable propriety, that was what he meant it to do. He loathed vulgarity, in type or in word, but—what was fit to print? The standards of judgment would certainly vary. Such a motto for the *Sun* might have been ruinous. It could easily put a damper on humor, and humor to Dana was almost equal to accuracy.

After conducting the *Sun* for a score of years without ever establishing a rule or promulgating a single maxim, Dana announced the following as a guide for newspaper men:

> I—Get the news, get all the news, and nothing but the news.
>
> II—Copy nothing from another publication without perfect credit.

III—Never print an interview without the knowledge and consent of the party interviewed.

IV—Never print a paid advertisement as news matter. Let every advertisement appear as an advertisement; no sailing under false colors.

V—Never attack the weak or the defenseless, either by argument, by invective, or by ridicule, unless there is some absolute public necessity for so doing.

VI—Fight for your opinions, but do not believe that they contain the whole truth or the only truth.

VII—Support your party, if you have one. But do not think all the good men are in it and all the bad ones outside of it.

VIII—Above all, know and believe that humanity is advancing; that there is progress in human life and human affairs; and that, as sure as God lives, the future will be greater and better than the present or the past.

Later he added these:

Stand by the Stars and Stripes. Above all, stand for liberty, whatever happens.

A word that is not spoken never does any mischief.

All the goodness of a good egg cannot make up for the badness of a bad one.

If you find you have been wrong, don't fear to say so.

Mostly he talked about the reporter, whose importance in giving character and individuality to the newspaper he emphasized at every opportunity; but the reporter he had in mind was not of the Grub-street variety. At various times he had this to say about him:

The qualifications of the reporter you cannot estimate too highly. In the first place he must know the truth when he hears it and sees it. There are a great many men who are born without that faculty, unfortunately.

He must be qualified to discuss the questions which

the clergyman has to discuss. He must be qualified to judge of the science of the physician, and he must even be able to rise to those sublime intellectual complications which make a great lawyer.

How was the young man to prepare himself for such severe tests of mentality and knowledge? Dana quoted Greeley frequently, almost always with an *arrière pensée*. There must have been a smile lurking behind the gray beard when he said:

"I have known very distinguished authorities who doubted whether high education was of any great use to a journalist. Horace Greeley told me several times that the real newspaper man was the boy who had slept on newspapers and ate ink. Although I served him for years, and we were very near in our personal relations, I think he always had a little grudge against me because I came up through a college."

When Dana had started with the *Tribune* not many of the educated youth of the country were seeking careers in journalism. The older professions, the church, the law and medicine were drawing the college graduates. Society disesteemed the newspaper man, holding him on a par with the actor. Conditions had not changed when Dana took over the *Sun*. Many regarded the newspaper as the refuge of the failures, the uncertain and the drifters. The best they could say of it was that it might be the bridge on which one crossed to more practical, respectable and reliable vocations. Worthy fathers and nice mothers dissembled their humiliation when Son John became a reporter, and told their friends he was getting a little experience of the world before settling down.

Even newspaper men were apt to speak of their vocation as a blind alley. Pay was small and the prizes few. How many arrived at the end of their tether with anything like a competence, no matter how economical they had been? In any other occupation ——

One evening early in my own experience I was halted

one night on the inner stairs of the *Sun* office by S. S. Carvalho, one of the star reporters.

"Get out of this business before you get stuck in it," he cautioned. "It leads nowhere. Look at me. I am making three thousand a year. If I go on I may become a city editor and earn seven thousand. Compare that with what I could do with the same effort as a lawyer. Don't wait until it's too late!"

He meant well, but I was in no mood to hearken to croaking ravens. I had had two spread-head stories on the front page within a week, and the file of the *Sun*, towards which I was hastening, had more lure than all the mines of Golconda.

Yet no doubt he was right at the time. There were quite a few terrible examples right in the office—broken-down reporters with empty pockets whose miserable end it required no seer to foretell. And if they were themselves responsible for their miserable plight, there were others who worked hard, did not get drunk, and yet had little to show for their labor. Still, a recent survey of the legal profession of New York had shown an average income of seven hundred and fifty dollars a year, while the doctors had fallen below that. Possibly the prizes attainable by the talented were fewer in journalism, but there were some and who could tell who would win them? Incidentally, Carvalho stayed in it and became the general manager of all the Hearst publications, amassing a fortune which even lawyers might envy.

"If I could have my way," said Dana, "every young man who is going to be a newspaper man, and who is not absolutely rebellious against it, should learn Greek and Latin after the good old fashion. I had rather take a young fellow who knows the Ajax of Sophocles, and who has read Tacitus, and can scan every ode of Horace—I would rather take him to report a prize fight or a spelling match, for instance, than to take one who has never had those advantages."

Repeatedly he asserted his belief in college training and in the higher education, but he was flatly against the school of journalism. Give the young man a first-class general education—and there was no kind of knowledge which was without usefulness—but when he began "to practice the profession of a newspaper man that was the time to learn it. The newspaper office is the best postgraduate college that the newspaper profession can have."

> How [he asked] is a professor who teaches journalism, and who sits up in his chair and delivers generalities on the subject, going to help forward the ambitious young man who is anxious to lay hold of one of the great prizes—for there are great prizes—that are to be drawn in this intellectual lottery? I do not see how a college instruction in journalism can be of any adequate practical use. The school which takes the young minister and carries him through a course of theology, church history, homiletics, dialectics, philosophy, and metaphysics, instructs him in the essentials of his profession, all after his college course is completed. So it is in the case of a physician. He studies anatomy, physiology, and chemistry, and fits himself in that way for the professional work that he is to perform. But it is impossible, in my judgment, that there should be any special school which will take a young man intending to pursue the profession of journalism, after he has finished his college studies, and give him much valuable instruction in the duties and labors of his future professional life, and in that general experience in business which I recommend as most indispensable.

Schools of journalism were only in their infancy then. Whether they were able to invent ways to usefulness not in Dana's contemplation is an open question. They have multiplied in the land until now there are conventions of professors of journalism, and certainly some editors make use of their graduates. Joseph Pulitzer, one of the greatest editors of modern times, believed in schools of journalism or he would not have left a fortune to found one.

But there was a lot of wisdom in those lectures. There was Dana's old insistence on the value of languages. Besides the indispensable Greek and Latin there was the old Teutonic—"the man who has not that knowledge does not really know the English language, and does not command its wonderful resources, all the subtleties and abilities of expression which are in it."

Of course, there were exceptions—there always would be exceptions where talent came into play. One of the best reporters he ever knew "was a man who could not spell four words correctly to save his life, and his verb did not always agree with the subject in person and number; but he always got the fact so exactly, and he saw the picturesque, the interesting, and important aspect of it so vividly, that it was worth another man's while, who possessed the knowledge of grammar and spelling, to go over the report and write it out".

Picturesque, interesting, important—there were the three fundamentals after accuracy. "The invariable law of the newspaper," he declared, "is to be interesting. Suppose you tell all the truths of science in a way that bores the reader; what is the good? The truths don't stay in the mind, and nobody thinks any better of you because you have told him the truth tediously." If the reporter can state his facts "with a little degree of life, a little approach to eloquence, or a little humor in his style, why, his report will be perfect". And to do that, even when he has the ability, he must himself be interested in it, "must give his story in such a way that you know he feels its qualities and events".

What did he mean by style? It was the subtle something "which distinguishes one writer from another. This style is something of such an evanescent, intangible nature that it is difficult to tell in what it consists. I suppose it is the combination of imagination and humor, with the entire command of the word resources of the language, all applied together in the construction of sentences. I suppose that is what makes style. It is a very precious gift, but it is not a gift that can always be acquired by practice or by study".

There were certain books with which the young man should make himself familiar, and among these the Bible came first, not as a book of revelation but because of the force and eloquence of its writing. Then Shakespeare and Milton. And he must train his interests in certain directions. Politics, for instance. He used to watch any new man who came to him with special recommendation. If he saw him turn to the political part of the news, he considered that promising; but if he took up a magazine instead, and busied himself with a love story, that showed he had not the material to make a good newspaper man. He might, of course, make a good writer of love stories, which was all very well in its way, but he would never "play any important part upon the stage of public affairs, and that is the sphere of activity to which the generous-hearted and courageous youth looks forward".

The reporter was the eye of his paper, it was for him to decide which was the vital fact in a story, to produce it, tell it, write it out.

What did the reporters think of Dana? At a memorable dinner of a lot of them in the mid-'Nineties, he came up for discussion. Very likely the disciples of Plato talked in much the same way of their great master. Never a word of criticism, and one summed up the thoughts of all when he said:

"I'd rather be Charles A. Dana than President of the United States. He means a lot more."

Dana died in 1897. The obituary notice printed on the October 17 editorial page of the *Sun* was of his own suggestion, and it carried out the prediction he had made to John Swinton, an assistant editor, when the latter asked him how much space the *Sun* would give to him when he died.

"For you, John," said Dana, "two sticks." Turning to Mitchell, then his chief editorial aid, he added: "For me, two lines."

They ran as follows:

Charles Anderson Dana, editor of the *Sun*, died yesterday afternoon.

THE END